"If you truly want to prove your mettle in the gaming arena, then getting your name in the Guinness World Reco...s Edition is the only way to go about it."
PC World

...care about gaming, something ...re is going to fascinate you"
Popular Science

...re a gamer, you need this on your shelf"
PSW Magazine

...hensive that no gamer should ...t it. It is the gamer's bible"
Daily Echo

...ull of goals to shoot for..."

networkworld.com

Yeah! If you're a serious, ...o this book, it's really cool."

...ct.com

GUINNESS WORLD RECORDS 2009

GUINNESS WORLD RECORDS™

GAMER'S EDITION

⏵ FACTS

British Library Cataloguing-in-Publication Data: a catalogue record for this book is available from the British Library

ISBN
10: 1-904994-45-8
13: 978-1-904994-45-9

Check the official GWR: Gamer's Edition website

www.guinnessworld records.com/gamers
regularly for record-breaking gaming news as it happens, plus exclusive interviews and competitions.

Sustainability
Guinness World Records: Gamer's Edition is printed on paper certified in accordance with the guidelines of the Forest Stewardship Council for responsible forestry management. SGS-COC-1425 (valid until 22 June 2013)

FSC
Mixed Sources
Product group from well-managed forests and other controlled sources
Cert no. SGS-COC-1425
www.fsc.org
© 1996 Forest Stewardship Council

Owing to the innovative use of a combined gas and steam turbine power plant, our printer, Mohn Media, emits 52% less CO^2 in comparison to the average energy mix in Germany.

THE JIM PATTISON GROUP

© 2009 Guinness World Records Ltd, a Jim Pattison Group company

EDITOR-IN-CHIEF
Craig Glenday

GAMER'S EDITOR
Keith Pullin

MANAGING EDITORS
Matt Boulton
Ben Way

CONTENT EDITOR
Robert Cave

EDITORIAL TEAM
Harry Boteler, Joel Meadows

CONSULTANT EDITOR
Barry Hitchings

DIRECTOR OF PRODUCTION
Patricia Magill

PRODUCTION MANAGER
Jane Boatfield

PRODUCTION ASSISTANT
Erica Holmes-Attivor

PRODUCTION CONSULTANT
Roger Hawkins

PRINTING & BINDING
Mohn Media Mohndruck GmbH,
Gütersloh, Germany

INDEX
Chris Bernstein

PICTURE EDITOR
Michael Whitty

DEPUTY PICTURE EDITOR
Laura Jackson

PICTURE RESEARCHER
Anna Wilkins

ORIGINAL PHOTOGRAPHY
Paul Michael Hughes, Joe McGorty,
Andy Paradise

CONCEPT CREATION & LAYOUT
Itonic Design Ltd, Brighton, UK

COLOUR ORIGINATION
Colour Systems, London, UK

GAMER'S CONSULTANTS

Pro-Gaming: Philip Wride
Best Of: Ellie Gibson
War Games: Richie Shoemaker
Point 'n' Click Games:
David Crookes
Superhero Games:
Dan Whitehead
Space Games, Movies & Games: Martin Korda
Wheels & Thrills: Simon Parkin
Genre Busters: David McCarthy
Fantasy & Sci-Fi Games:
Dave Hawksett
Gadgets & Gizmos:
Gaz Deaves
Top 50 Console Games, At A Glance:
Martyn Carroll

RECORDS MANAGEMENT

Director of Records Management
Marco Frigatti (Italy)
Adjudications Manager
Andrea Bánfi (Hungary)
Records Management Team
Gaz Deaves (UK)
Laura Farmer (UK)
Ralph Hannah (UK)
Kaoru Ishikawa (Japan)
Danny Girton (USA)
Tzeni Karampoiki (Taiwan)
Mariamarta Ruano-Graham (Guatemala)
Carlos Martínez (Spain)
Chris Sheedy (Australia)
Lucia Sinigagliesi (Italy)
Amanda Sprague (UK)
Kristian Teufel (Germany)
Wu Xiaohong (China)

SALES AND MARKETING

SVP Sales & Marketing:
Samantha Fay
UK Marketing Director:
Paul Kenny
US Marketing Director:
Laura Plunkett
English Language Sales Director:
Nadine Causey
International Sales Director:
Frank Chambers
National Accounts Manager:
John Pilley
PR Manager:
Amarilis Espinoza
US Marketing Manager:
Doug Parsons
UK Licensing Manager:
Beatriz Fernandez
US Licensing Manager:
Jennifer Osbourne
International Marketing Executive:
Justine Bourdariat
PR Executive:
Karolina Thelin
Marketing & PR Assistant:
Damien Field
US Marketing Assistant:
Jamie Panas

GUINNESS WORLD RECORDS

Managing Director:
Alistair Richards
VP Finance: Alison Ozanne
Finance Manager: Neelish Dawett
Asst Finance Manager:
Jack Brockbank
Director of IT: Katie Forde
Webmaster:
Aadil Ahmed

Director of HR: Kelly Garrett
Legal: Raymond Marshall
Contracts Administrator:
Lisa Gibbs
Business Development:
Stuart Claxton (USA)
Director of Television:
Rob Molloy
Digital Content Manager:
Denise Anlander

GUINNESS WORLD RECORDS 2009

GAMER'S EDITION

Amazing scenes from classic games jump out from every page

All the gaming records you could imagine at your fingertips

The greatest record-breaking games of all time discussed in detail by award-winning writers

Influential figures are profiled and interviewed

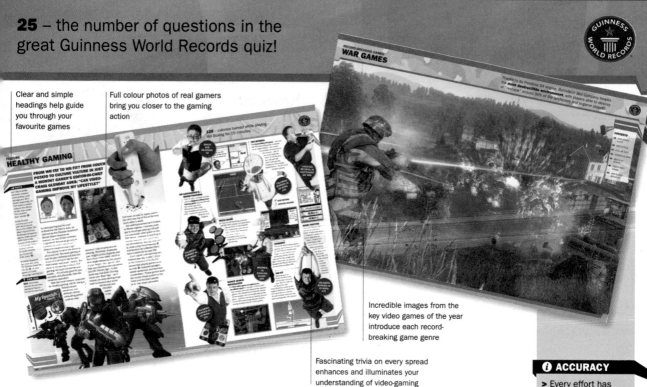

Clear and simple headings help guide you through your favourite games

Full colour photos of real gamers bring you closer to the gaming action

Incredible images from the key video games of the year introduce each record-breaking game genre

Fascinating trivia on every spread enhances and illuminates your understanding of video-gaming

ℹ **ACCURACY**

> Every effort has been made to bring to you the most accurate and up-to-date records. If, however, you believe that you know of a more impressive achievement or a higher score, please let us know. We rely on your help to keep our books as fresh and as accurate as possible. Visit www.guinnessworldrecords.com/gamers to find out how you can contribute...

> Text in **bold type** refers to an official Guinness World Record.

HOW TO BE A RECORD BREAKER

ANYBODY CAN BECOME A GUINNESS WORLD RECORD HOLDER: ALL YOU NEED IS PRACTICE, DEDICATION AND A GAME YOU REALLY, REALLY LOVE TO PLAY.

▪▪▷ FACTS

> The technical term for dressing as a character from TV, movies, anime or video games is "cosplay"; people who indulge in this hobby are called "cosplayers".

> Guinness World Records adjudicators attend events all around the world to ensure that all record attempts are carried out according to a standard set of rules and guidelines. They can also offer PR support and instant certification. Should the record attempt they are attending prove successful, our adjudicators are able to announce the new world record immediately and present an official certificate to verify the achievement.

★ RECORD

> The ▼ **longest video-game marathon on a first-person shooter** is 24 hr 4 min by the Fragdolls ②, playing *Rainbow Six Vegas 2* ①.

Welcome to the second *Guinness World Records: Gamer's Edition*, a book we've compiled during another incredible year for video games, with new releases that included *Grand Theft Auto IV*, *Metal Gear Solid 4* and *Wii Fit*. All generated a frenzy of record attempts, but the most hotly contested has been the ▼ **highest score for a single track on *Guitar Hero III***. A global battle has raged between Luke Albiges (UK), Danny Johnson (USA) and Chris Chike (USA). Turn to page 154 to discover who was the ultimate guitar hero.

Our mission for 2008 was to showcase as many different types of record holders as possible. We got off to a great start with the *Gamer's Edition* launch party on 31 January 2008, where the UK's finest pro-gamers descended upon the Old Blue Last pub, in London, UK, and duly set a raft of records. Michael "Bazza" Barrett and Samantha "Ricochet" Whale (both UK) ④ scored 2,048 points, the ▼ **highest campaign score in *Halo 3* in five minutes by a team** and David Kelly (UK) ⑥ set the ▼ **fastest lap time for "Old City Loop" on *Project Gotham Racing 4*** with 47.53 sec.

We've also travelled the globe to track down key figures in the games industry. It was a huge honour to award Ralph Baer (USA) the Guinness World Record for the ▼ **first home video games console**, the "Brown Box" at the San Francisco Game Developers Conference in February.

Another highlight was surprising legendary game producer Hideo Kojima (Japan) with certificates for the **first ever stealth video game** for *Metal Gear* on the MSX2 and the **best-selling stealth game** for *Metal Gear Solid 2: Sons of Liberty* on the PS2 ⑤.

At the Leipzig Games Convention in Germany, we recognized more gaming achievements, including **fastest-selling guitar-based**

> At GWR, we believe gamers and gaming achievements deserve the same recognition as all other kinds of Guinness World Record.
>
> **Keith Pullin, Editor**
> **Guinness World Records:**
> **Gamer's Edition**

▼ **NEW RECORD**   ▽ **UPDATED RECORD**

game for *Guitar Hero III* ⑨, **most games in an action-adventure series** for *Castlevania*, ▼**best-selling simulation series** for *The Sims* and **most successful fighting game series** for *Mortal Kombat* ⑧.

At GWR, we believe gamers and gaming achievements deserve the same recognition as all other kinds of Guinness World Records, from the **most consecutive games of *Wii Tennis* won**, 21 by Stas Kostrzewski ⑦, to the ▼**fastest completion of *Sonic the Hedgehog 3***, at 49 min 17 sec,

set by James Richards (UK) on 9 August 2008.

For some records you won't even need a joypad. On 18 March 2008, 80 people in full, glorious costume gathered on the Millennium Bridge, London, UK, for the ▼**largest gathering of people dressed as video-game characters** ③. The social aspect of gaming was also evident at the ▼**largest mass-participation LAN party**, where 203 gamers "partied" for 36 hours at NVISION 2008, San Jose, California, USA.

So, there you have it. We'd like to think that everybody has a chance to be a record breaker. The big question is: can you be? Check out the right-hand column to find out more. Good luck!

EXPERT

To Break a Record...

1. Decide what record you're going to break.

2. Do your research. There are some world record attempts we don't recognize. For more information, visit: www.guinnessworldrecords.com/gamers

3. Register online at the website and we'll send you an agreement to sign that sets out how we approve records.

4. Send back the signed agreement (fax or email attachment is fine). Once that's done, we'll get in touch to let you know the guidelines for the attempt.

5. Carry out your record attempt. For us to consider an attempt as valid, you'll need to convince us that your claim is genuine. Generally speaking, GWR requires video footage, photos or screenshots and witness statements.

6. Leave the rest to us, but remember: our word is final. In most cases, we'll approve your record based on the evidence you send us, but sometimes we may ask for more info.

7. We send you a certificate celebrating your achievement.

BEAT US AT OUR OWN GAME

↻ OVERVIEW

GUINNESS WORLD RECORDS THE VIDEOGAME

> This is your chance to set a record – on a global scale, at a country level or even just in your circle of family and friends. In *Guinness World Records: The Videogame* you can travel the world and attempt 36 of the most fun Guinness World Records challenges, such as tightrope walking, cow pat tossing, washing machine throwing and landspeed record-breaking – all without leaving your home!

> On the DS version, players must blow into the device's microphone for challenges such as blowing the biggest bubblegum balloon.

> For more infomation about *Guinness World Records: The Videogame* please visit www.guinnessworldrecords.com/gamers, www.warnerbros.com and www.ttgames.com

WANNA BE A RECORD BREAKER WITHOUT GETTING OFF THE SOFA? THEN GET YOUR HANDS ON GUINNESS WORLD RECORDS: THE VIDEOGAME – WITHIN MINUTES YOU CAN BE PLUCKING TURKEYS, EATING AIRPLANES AND SMASHING MELONS!

▮ NEW RECORD   ▽ UPDATED RECORD

As we go to press, the finishing touches are being made to the first-ever *Guinness World Records* video game for the Nintendo Wii ① and DS ⑨, co-published by Warner Bros. Interactive Entertainment and TT Games.

The development of our game, cunningly titled *Guinness World Records: The Videogame*, has been entrusted to TT Games, the fine folks who brought you the best-selling *LEGO® Star Wars* games, which also boast the records for **most playable characters in an action-adventure game**.

With 45 million games sold over its 18-year history, TT Games are the ideal choice to bring Guinness World Records to life.

What makes this game different is that, after each successful world record attempt, your scores and times are sent to Guinness World Records for official ratification. You might even find your name listed in this very book, like Florian Mack (Germany) ⑤ who claimed the record for the ▶ **most melons smashed with the head in one minute challenge** ⑦, with 60 smashed melons; Max Schoenemann (Germany) ④, who set the record of 13.71 sec in the ▶ **fastest time to shear five sheep challenge** ⑧; and Christian Kurka (Germany) ②, who took just 10.48 sec in the ▶ **fastest time to pop 100 balloons challenge** ⑥. All these feats were achieved on the Nintendo Wii at the game's grand unveiling at the Leipzig Games Convention 2008 ③. Can you do better?

In addition to the challenges themselves, the game is also chock full of information about other Guinness World Records. Ultimately, we wanted to create a game that brought the spirit of record-breaking on to a games console. We've spent nearly two years working with TT Games to plan every element of its look and feel – which records work best on the Nintendo Wii and DS, what award mechanisms we could include and how the game should perform.

So, you've got the book, now play the game! We're very pleased with the end result and hope you will be too!

◗◗ FOLLOW IN THE FOOTSTEPS OF GWR LEGENDS...

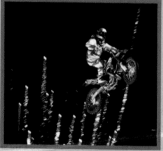

FASTEST TURKEY PLUCKER
Vincent Pilkington (Ireland) plucked a turkey in 1 min 30 sec on Dublin's RTÉ television in 1980.

MOTORCYCLE RAMP JUMP
The longest motorcycle ramp jump is 106.98 m (351 ft) by Robbie Maddison (Australia) in Melbourne, Australia, on 29 March 2008.

STRANGEST DIET Mr Mangetout – a.k.a. Michel Lotito (France) – chopped a plane into small pieces and ate it over a two-year period. Thanks to the power of the Wii and DS, you can do it in seconds!

LONGEST NAILS Lee Redmond (USA), who last cut her nails in 1979, has grown and carefully manicured them to reach a total length of 8.65 m (28 ft 4.5 in)!

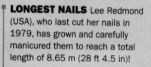

PLANE PULL David Huxley (Australia) pulled a Boeing 747-400, weighing 187 tonnes (412,264 lb), 91 m (298 ft 6 in) in 1 min 27.7 sec on 15 October 1997.

◗◗ FACTS

> Using the Wii Remote as an intuitive control system is key to the fun of the Wii version. Some challenges contain two phases requiring different interactions. With the fastest time to eat a plane challenge you first need to smash the plane up using the Wii Remote as a virtual hammer then eat the debris, using cartoon dentures as the cursor!

GAMING AWARDS ROUND-UP 2008

EACH AND EVERY YEAR, MAGAZINES, WEBSITES AND GAMING ORGANIZATIONS AROUND THE WORLD CELEBRATE THE BEST GAMES IN LAVISH AWARDS CEROMONIES. WE GATECRASHED A FEW OF THE MAJOR EVENTS TO LOOK AT THE KEY AWARDS OF THE LAST YEAR.

III▶ FACTS

>The Golden Joystick Awards ceremonies have a long history of celebrity hosts dating back to the first awards in 1982, hosted by notable BBC Radio 1 DJ Dave Lee Travis (known affectionately as "the hairy cornflake"). The most recent host was comedian David Mitchell, famous among the gaming community for playing the part of the PC in Apple's TV advertising campaign in the UK.

> Will Wright was the first video-game creator to be inducted into the prestigious British Academy of Film and Television Arts (BAFTA) Hall of Fame. Wright created worldwide phenomena *The Sims* and his most recent creation is the eagerly-awaited game *Spore* from Electronic Arts.

> Celebrities spotted attending the Spike Awards in 2007 included Samuel L. Jackson, comics godfather Stan Lee, skateboarder Tony Hawk, boxing promoter Don King and *The Simpsons* creator Matt Groening.

> Musical acts Foo Fighters and Kid Rock provided the live entertainment at the 2007 Spike Awards.

GAME CRITICS AWARDS: BEST OF E3 2008

Judges on the esteemed Game Critics Awards panel include representatives from *Electronic Gaming Monthly*, Gamepro and GameRadar as well as mainstream publications such as the *Los Angeles Times*, *Hollywood Reporter* and *TIME Magazine*.

AWARD	GAME (DEVELOPER/PUBLISHER)	FORMAT
Best of Show	*Fallout 3* (Bethesda Softworks)	PC, PS3, Xbox 360
Best Original Game	*Mirror's Edge* ① (DICE/EA)	PC, PS3, Xbox 360
Best Console Game	*LittleBIGPlanet* (Media Molecule/Sony)	PS3
Best PC Game	*Spore* (Maxis/EA)	
Best Handheld Game	*Resistance: Retribution* (Bend Studio/Sony)	PSP
Best Hardware/ Peripheral	*Rock Band 2* Ion "Drum Rocker" Set (ION Audio/MTV Games)	Xbox 360
Best Action Game	*Gears of War 2* (Epic/Microsoft)	Xbox 360
Best Action/ Adventure Game	*Dead Space* (EA Redwood Shores/EA)	PC, PS3, Xbox 360
Best RPG	*Fallout 3* (Bethesda Softworks)	PC, PS3, Xbox 360
Best Racing Game	*Pure* (Black Rock/ Disney Interactive Studios)	PC, PS3, Xbox 360
Best Sports Game	*Madden NFL 09* (Tiburon/EA)	All Formats
Best Fighting Game	*Street Fighter IV* (Capcom)	Arcade
Best Strategy Game	*Tom Clancy's EndWar* (Ubisoft Shanghai/Ubisoft)	PS3, Xbox 360
Best Social/ Casual/Puzzle Game	*LittleBIGPlanet* (Media Molecule/Sony)	PS3
Best Online Multiplayer Game	*Left 4 Dead* (Valve/EAP)	PC, Xbox 360

SPIKE AWARDS 2007

The Spike TV Video Game Awards ③ were inaugurated in 2004 and celebrate the best games of the year. Votes are cast by the predominantly male audience of the US cable channel, Spike TV.

AWARD	GAME (DEVELOPER/PUBLISHER)	FORMAT
Game of the Year	*Bioshock* (2K Boston/2K Australia/2K Games)	Xbox 360
Studio of the Year	Harmonix	
Best Graphics	*Crysis* (Crytek/EA)	PC
Best Original Score	*Bioshock* (2K Boston/2K Australia/2K Games)	Xbox 360
Most Addictive Video Game	*Halo 3* (Bungie/Microsoft)	Xbox 360
Best Shooter	*Call of Duty 4: Modern Warfare* (Infinity Ward/Activision)	Xbox 360, PS3, PC
Best RPG	*Mass Effect* (BioWare/Microsoft)	Xbox 360
Best Military Game	*Call of Duty 4: Modern Warfare* (Infinity Ward/Activision)	Xbox 360, PS3, PC
Best Handheld Game	*The Legend of Zelda: Phantom Hourglass* (Nintendo)	Nintendo DS
Best Game Based on a Movie or TV Show	*The Simpsons Game* ② (Rebellion/EA Redwood Shores/EA)	Multi-Format
Best Driving Game	*Colin McRae: DiRT* (Codemasters)	Xbox 360, PS3, PC
Best Action Game	*Super Mario Galaxy* (Nintendo)	Wii
Best Team Sports Game	*Madden NFL 08* (EA Tiburon/EA)	Multi-Format
Breakthrough Technology	*The Orange Box/Portal* (Valve/EA)	Xbox 360, PS3, PC
Best Xbox 360 Game	*BioShock* (2K Boston/2K Australia/2K Games)	Xbox 360
Best Wii Game	*Super Mario Galaxy* (Nintendo)	Wii
Best PS3 Game	*Ratchet & Clank Future: Tools of Destruction* (Insomniac Games/Sony)	
Best PC Game	*The Orange Box* (Valve/EA)	
Best Multiplayer Game	*Halo 3* (Bungie Studios/Microsoft)	Xbox 360

2007 GOLDEN JOYSTICK AWARDS

▼ NEW RECORD ▽ UPDATED RECORD

First awarded in 1982, the Golden Joysticks are the ▼ **longest-running gaming awards** in the world. They are highly prized, as they are voted for by gamers.

AWARD	GAME (DEVELOPER/PUBLISHER)	FORMAT
Ultimate Game of the Year	*Gears of War* ▲ (Epic/Microsoft)	Xbox 360
Xbox Game of the Year	*Gears of War* (Epic/Microsoft)	Xbox 360
PC Game of the Year	*LOTR: Shadows of Angmar* (Turbine/Codemasters)	
PlayStation Game of the Year	*God of War II* (SCE Santa Monica/Sony)	PS2
Nintendo Game of the Year	*The Legend of Zelda: Twilight Princess* (Nintendo)	Wii
The Editor's Choice Award	*Gears of War* (Epic/Microsoft)	Xbox 360
The Publisher of the Year	*Nintendo*	
UK Developer of the Year	*Codemasters*	
Online Game of the Year	*World Of Warcraft: The Burning Crusade* (Blizzard/Vivendi)	PC
Family Game of the Year	*Wii Sports* (Nintendo)	Wii
The *Bliss* Girls' Choice Game of the Year	*Guitar Hero II* (RedOctane/Activision)	PS2, Xbox 360

BAFTA VIDEO GAMES AWARDS 2007

The British Academy Video Games Awards focus on creativity and innovation as opposed to commercial success alone. They first took place on 25 February 2004.

AWARD	GAME (DEVELOPER/PUBLISHER)	FORMAT
Action and Adventure	*Crackdown* (Realtime Worlds/Microsoft)	Xbox 360
Artistic Achievement	*Okami* (Atsushi Inaba – Clover/Capcom)	PS2
Best Game	*Bioshock* (2K Boston/2K Australia/ 2K Games)	Xbox 360
Casual	*Wii Sports* (Nintendo)	Wii
Gameplay	*Wii Sports* (Nintendo)	Wii
Innovation	*Wii Sports* ▲ (Nintendo)	Wii
Multiplayer	*Wii Sports* (Nintendo)	Wii
Original Score	*Okami* (Atsushi Inaba – Clover/Capcom)	PS2
Sports	*Wii Sports* (Nintendo)	Wii
Strategy and Simulation	*Wii Sports* (Nintendo)	Wii
Story and Character	*God of War 2* (Cory Barlog, David Jaffe, Marianne Krawczyk – SCE Santa Monica/Sony)	PS2
Technical Achievement	*God of War 2* (Tim Moss, Christer Ericson – SCE Santa Monica/Sony)	PS2
Use of Audio	*Crackdown* (Realtime Worlds/Microsoft)	Xbox 360
Academy Fellowship	Will Wright (USA)	

G-PHORIA 2008

The G-Phoria awards are voted for by viewers of G4tv.com, one of the premier web-based gaming portals.

AWARD	GAME
Game of the Year	*Halo 3*
Best Graphics	*MGS 4: Guns of the Patriots*
Best New Character	Niko Bellic – *GTA IV*
Best Party Game	*Rock Band*
Best Strategy Game	*Sid Meier's Civilization Revolution*
Best Sports Game	*skate*
Best Action Game	*GTA IV*
Best Shooter	*Call of Duty 4: Modern Warfare*
Best Racing Game	*Mario Kart Wii*
Best RPG	*Mass Effect*
Most Original Game	*Portal*
Best Online Multiplayer Game	*Call of Duty 4: Modern Warfare*
Best D'load Content	*Rock Band*
Best Handheld Game	*God of War: Chains of Olympus*
Best Voice Acting	*MGS 4: Guns of the Patriots*
Best Soundtrack	*Rock Band*
Most Deserving an Uwe Boll Movie	*Turok*

ℹ TRIVIA

> *The Elder Scrolls IV: Oblivion* cleaned up at the Spike Video Game Awards back in 2006, winning five awards.

> The organizers of the G-Phoria awards felt that German film director Uwe Boll was so notorious for making spectacular gung-ho movies out of heroic action games that they made a joke category to suggest what game he might like to make into a movie next.

❓ GWR QUIZ

Q1. How many awards did *Bioshock* win at the Spike Awards 2007?

PROFESSIONAL GAMING

PROFESSIONAL GAMERS WANT TO BE THE BEST AND TAKE THEIR ENJOYMENT OF PLAYING A STEP FURTHER BY PRACTICING HARD AND COMPETING IN TOURNAMENTS ACROSS THE GLOBE FOR LARGE CASH PRIZES.

The current generation of pro-gamers regularly pinpoint one single event that triggered the birth of "eSports". Back in 1997, John Carmack, creator of *Quake*, offered his Ferrari 328 as the main prize in the "Red Annihilation" *Quake* tournament. US gamer Dennis "Thresh" Fong won the final and claimed Carmack's car.

In truth, pro-gaming actually started years before that landmark event. In 1983, Twin Galaxies' Walter Day set up the US National Video Games Team, who travelled the globe showing off their skills. Pro-gaming has come along way since then, with millions of dollars of prize money being offered each year across multiple tournaments **3** for a variety of games. The

▸ **longest-running professional tournament organizer** was the CPL (CyberAthlete Professional League). It was founded in 1997 but ceased operations in March 2008. The CPL was also the ▸ **first tournament organizer to sign high-profile players** to compete in its events. Other major American and European tournament organizers still in operation include Quakecon, Electronic Sports League, World Cyber Games, Major League Gaming, Esports World Cup and the Championship Gaming Series.

In 2005, CPL offered a prize fund of $1 million (£540,000) for a *Painkiller* **5** tournament, in which Johnathan "Fatal1ty" Wendel (USA) **4** walked away with the ▸ **largest cash prize won in a professional**

video game tournament – a first prize of $150,000 (£81,000).

So what makes a pro-gamer? Like most professional sports, it takes dedication and drive to get to the top. Many hours are spent honing skills and practicing to become the best, with some top gamers spending more than six hours a day practicing. Teamwork also play a big part in pro-gaming, with players signed to teams in return for salaries and financial support to attend events **1**.

The ▸ **longest-running team** is Ocrana. Conceived in 1996, these veteran German sharpshooters cut their teeth on *Quake*. Since then, they have played a variety of other games including *Counter-strike* **6**.

The ▸ **most successful western gamer** is "Fatal1ty".

CHOOSING THE RIGHT GAME

The newest pro-gaming league, the Championship Gaming Series, uses Forza Motorsport 2 in events for its in-car camera angles or "spectator modes".

Viewers must be able to tell the difference between competitors' cars instantly.

Re-skinned cars depicting the competing teams' unique livery allow viewers to spot their favourite gamer more easily.

Open tracks are used to allow for the best possible camera views.

A range of camera angles are perfect for televised professional gaming. The idea is to make the viewer feel as if they are watching from the stands.

① TRIVIA

> Following a two year gap from his previous major title (Quakecon 2004, USA), Paul "czm" Nelson (USA) won the *Quake 3* event at CPL Winter 2006.

> Manuel "Grubby" Schenkhuizen (Netherlands) is the first *Warcraft 3* player to have won titles from the World Cyber Games Gold Medal, Samsung Euro Challenge, Esports World Cup, Blizzcon and the World Series of Video Games.

▶ FIRST ROYALS IN MAJOR LEAGUE GAMING

Khalid and Abdulaziz Althani, both members of the Qatari Royal family, competed in the 2008 Major League Gaming *World of Warcraft* tournament in Orlando, Florida, USA, becoming the first Royals to enter such an event. The pair were joined by Justin Dalton (USA) in a three-man team.

including the Championship Gaming Series, are continuing to establish new leagues and competitions all the time.

The natural end result, some pro-gamers argue, is the establishment of eSports as an Olympic discipline. Discussions were had to bring competitive gaming to Beijing in 2008 but nothing materialized, although two *World of Warcraft* players – XiaoFeng "Sky" Li and Jae ho "Moon" Jang – carried the Olympic torch through China on its

▐▐▶ FACT

As of December 2007, the greatest earning *Counter-Strike* teams were fnatic and CGS Franchise Chicago Chimera with career prize winnings of $134,694 (£68,000) and $287,500 (£145,000) respectively.

▐ NEW RECORD   ▽ UPDATED RECORD

He has won the **most World Championships on different games** (five titles). Meanwhile the Schellhase brothers ❷ from Germany claim the title of the family with the **most gold medals won at the World Cyber Games** with two wins each on *FIFA*, totalling four Gold Medals (2003, 2005, 2006 and 2007).

With eSports continuing to develop at a rapid pace, a number of developers and publishers are now tailoring their products for competition. Many publishers have created spectator modes so matches can be replayed and enjoyed by gamers across the world. Some game types, such as first-person shooters and racing games, are being retooled to suit competitive play. New companies,

way to Beijing as part of a sponsorship deal with the peripherals manufacturer Razer. It's a step in the right direction – for China and the rest of the gaming world – so can we expect London 2012 to host the first eSports Olympics? Let's wait and see...

PRO-GAMING: ASIA

PRO-GAMING IS SERIOUS BUSINESS IN ASIA, WITH MILLIONS OF FANS FOLLOWING THE FORTUNES OF THEIR FAVOURITE PROS ACROSS A VARIETY OF LEAGUES, TV CHANNELS AND EVENTS.

For many years, Asia has been the home of some of the greatest real time strategy (RTS) players and competitions in the world. *Starcraft* and *Warcraft 3*, both from the renowned developer Blizzard, have proven particularly popular among Asian video game enthusiasts, with South Korea widely regarded as the centre of Asia's pro-gaming scene.

South Korea even boasts two 24-hour subscription TV channels dedicated to competitive gaming: ongamenet and MBC Game. However, despite South Korea's traditional dominance, China's pro-gaming community is rapidly catching up and may soon overshadow its more established gaming neighbour.

China is home to one of the greatest *Warcraft 3* players, Xiao Feng Li **4**, more commonly known as "Sky", who plays as the Human race. He was the ▸ **first player to win two consecutive Warcraft 3 Gold Medals at the World Cyber Games**, with titles in 2005 and 2006.

GAMING STAR

South Korea's Lim Yo-Hwan **3**, variously known as "SlayerS_BoxeR", "The Emperor" and the "Godfather of *Starcraft* in Korea", has won the greatest number of televised matches, with a total of 500. Yo-Hwan is the only *Starcraft* gamer to win two consecutive Gold Medals at the World Cyber Games (2001, 2002). Following his successes in pro-gaming, Lim has become something of a celebrity. He has already written a highly popular autobiography and regularly appears in commercials on South Korean TV. His name has been used to endorse everything from chocolate bars to backpacks.

One of Sky's bitterest rivals is Jang "Moon" JaeHo, a South Korean gamer who plays as the Night Elf race **1** in *Warcraft 3*. Moon is the most decorated player in Korean competitions but has struggled to match his wins on home soil with major overseas success. Despite this, Moon was also the highest-earning *Warcraft 3* player in 2007,

with total prize winnings of $168,000 (£84,862).

On the stats front, it is Moon's fellow gamer in the MeetYourMakers team Jung-Ki Oh, a.k.a. "Susiria", who leads the rest of his Asian pro-gaming compatriots. In the Electronic Sports League (ESL) *Warcraft 3* official compilation of player stats for Seasons 1–12, he has played 158 matches, the ▸ **most league matches for any South Korean player**, amassing a total of 119 wins and 39 losses.

The Samsung KHAN team won the 2008 trophy in South Korea's prestigious ShinHan Bank ProLeague pro-gaming competition, after narrowly missing out on the top spot in the 2007 season.

Since 2000, all South Korean pro-gamers have been required to register with the Korean eSports Pro-gamer Association (KeSPA). As of May 2008, there was a total of 432 KeSPA registered gamers playing one of 23 official games.

520,906 – the number of members in South Korean pro-gaming superstar SlayerS_BoxeR's official fanclub.

> **GAMER'S BYTE**
> *There are a total of 12 professional gaming teams in South Korea's Shinhan Bank Proleague.*

NEW RECORD **UPDATED RECORD**

Competitive first-person shooter tournaments featuring games such as *Counter-Strike* or *Quake* have also been growing in popularity on the Asian pro-gaming scene in recent years, with many Chinese and South Korean *Counter-Strike* teams entering GotFrag's (www.gotfrag.com) world ranking for the first time in 2005.

wNv-Gaming (China) was the first Asian team to reach the No.1 spot in the GotFrag rankings in May 2006. They went on to become the **first Asian team to win a World eSport Games (WEG) Masters title** in 2006.

On the Deathmatch singles circuit, China has outshone its neighbours with two players of particular note. Following victory against Jonathan "Fatal1ty" Wendel (USA) in the Great Wall Shootout, held in China in 2004, Meng "Rocketboy" Yang (China) went on to secure a sponsorship deal with Great Wall Shootout host, computer components manufacturer ABIT. He has also competed in a range of pro-gaming events both within China and around the world.

Yang's fellow countryman, Fan "Jibo" Zhibo, has a growing reputation and first proved his skills when he won the CPL Nordic *Quake 3* tournament in Sweden in 2006, before being narrowly beaten at the CPL Winter event in Dallas, USA, in 2006.

WARCRAFT 3: ASIA LEADERBOARD

NAME	GAMER NAME	PLAYED	WON	LOST
Jung-Ki Oh (KR)	Susiria	158	119	39
Jae Wook Noh (KR)	Lucifer	140	99	41
Dae Hui Cho (KR)	FoV	89	67	22
Kim Dong Moon (KR)	GoStop	87	62	25
Kim Sung Sik (KR)	ReMinD	82	57	25
Lee Sung Duk (KR)	Soju	75	49	26
Jang JaeHo (KR)	Moon	69	47	22
Tae Min Hwang (KR)	Zacard	61	39	22
Chun Jung Hee (KR)	Sweet	53	34	19
June Park (KR)	Lyn	63	37	26
Xiao Feng Li (CN)	Sky	34	25	9
Lee Hyung Joo (KR)	Check	37	18	19
Wei Liang Lu (CN)	Fly100%	27	13	14
Zhuo Zeng (CN)	TeD	25	12	13

FIRST MILITARY PRO-GAMING TEAM

In August 2006, South Korean pro-gaming legend Lim Yo-Hwan was called up to perform his compulsory military service. Like a number of other pro-gamers before him, Lim was assigned to the Air Force's Intelligence unit. In 2007, the Air Force formed Air Force Challenge eSports (ACE) 8, its own pro-gaming team, to compete against civilian teams in the professional leagues. However, despite an impressive line-up of pro-gamers, ACE only managed 11th place in the Shinhan Bank Proleague 2008 final standings.

TRIVIA

> Lee Yun-Yeol 2 (South Korea) – more commonly known as "NaDa" – is the only player to win three Ongamenet *Starcraft* League (OSL) titles (2003, 2005 and 2006). He was also the first player to win three consecutive MBCGame Star-league (MSL) titles.

> Traditionally, pro-gamers and fans alike await events such as South Korea's G-star expo 7 for their first chance to see the next generation of games they will be playing or watching.

> KeSPA was established in 2000 with the approval of the South Korean Ministry of Culture, Sports and Tourism to help oversee such events as the World Cyber Games 6, held in South Korea in 2001.

? GWR QUIZ

Q2. Which year did South Korean *Starcraft* legend, SlayerS_BoxeR, begin his national service?

HARDWARE

In May 2008, Xbox 360 became the **first next-generation console to break through the 10-million-unit sales barrier in the US**.

CONTENTS

HISTORY OF GAMING: 1889–1979

COMPUTER GAMES HAVE EXISTED FOR ALMOST A CENTURY. THE FOLLOWING PAGES CHART THE RISE OF THE VIDEO-GAMING PHENOMENON AND OUTLINE THE KEY EVENTS THAT TURNED IT INTO A MULTI-BILLION DOLLAR INDUSTRY.

TRIVIA

> Nintendo Koppai's *hanafuda* ("flower card") deck contained 48 cards, and Fusajiro Yamauchi's employees made each one by hand using bark from mulberry or *mitsu-mata* trees. Fusajiro sold the cards in two shops, one in Kyoto and the other in Osaka.

> In 1947, Akio Morita and Masaru Ibuka formed the Tokyo Telecommunications Engineering Co. Their first consumer product was a commercially unsuccessful rice cooker. In 1952, the name was changed to Sony, from the Latin *sonus*, or "sound".

> Nolan Bushnell and Ted Dabney established a company called Syzygy Engineering in 1972. "Syzygy" was already a registered company name, so Bushnell decided to call the company Atari after a strategy used in the Japanese game *Go*.

1889

> Japan's Fusajiro Yamauchi forms Nintendo Koppai to make *hanafuda* playing cards **2**. (Nintendo means "leave luck to Heaven".) Later renamed the Nintendo Co., Ltd.

1912

> Leonardo Torres y Quevedo builds *El Ajedrecista* **3** ("The Chess Player"), a mechanical computer that plays a chess end game.

1947

> Thomas Goldsmith Jr and Estle Mann file a patent for a simple missile firing game based on a cathode-ray tube device.

1948

> Alan Mathison Turing writes a computer program to play chess but no computer is capable of running it. Turing, considered by many to be the father of modern computer science, commits suicide six years later in Cheshire, UK, aged 41.

1952

> Alexander S. Douglas programs the game *OXO* to play tic-tac-toe. It plays a perfect game and is unbeatable.

1951

> Ferranti build the Nimrod computer to play the game *nim* **1** for the Festival of Britain. Christopher Strachey writes the first known computer game of draughts on a Manchester Mark I computer.

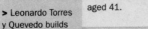

1958

> William Higginbotham creates the **first visual computer game for public play**; *Tennis for Two* is a simple two-player tennis game played on an oscilloscope.

1961

> Steven Russell and friends write *Spacewar!* for the DEC PDP-1 computer. Within a year, the two-player shoot-off in space is included with each PDP unit released.

1967

> Ralph Baer provides the first TV presentation of a simple chase game where two spots chase one another on a TV screen. His invention, the "Brown Box", the **first home video-game console**, enters production two years later.

1971

> Bill Pitts and Hugh Tuck create the **first two-player coin-operated arcade game** based on *Spacewar!* called *Galaxy Game* **7**. It is installed in the Coffee House at Tresidder Union, Stanford University, California, USA, and costs 10 cents per game.

> Nolan Bushnell **4** and Ted Dabney engineer *Computer Space* **5**, the **first commercial dedicated video arcade game**.

1972

> Magnavox Odyssey **9**, the world's **first commercially available games console**, is launched. It plays 12 games and requires at least two people to play them.

> Al Alcorn creates *Pong* **6** for Atari.

> Rick Rashid and Gene Ball write the **first networked multiplayer space battle game** called *Alto Trek*, based on *Star Trek*.

1973

> The **first first-person perspective game** is born after Steve Colley writes a simple 3D maze game called *Maze War*, in which two players hunt each other down inside a basic 3D labyrinth.

1974

Brad Fortner creates *Airfight*, the **first networked combat flight simulator**. Some of those involved with the game would eventually go on to work on the *Microsoft Flight Simulation* series in the mid-80s.

1975

> *Pong* home version launched by Atari. US retailer Sears place a large order for the machine, which was sold as the Sears Telegames Pong unit.

> John Haefeli writes a multi-player tank battle game called *Panther*. It is the **first 3D wireframe** and **first deathmatch game**.

> William Crowther writes a text-based adventure game called *ADVENT* (a.k.a. *Adventure*). It would be massively improved over the years and eventually became known as *Colossal Cave Adventure*.

1976

> Fairchild Channel F **8** launched as the **first cartridge-based console** and the **first console to use a processor**. It was also helped along by six co-processors and 64 bytes of RAM. The cartridge format is so successful that it becomes the standard method of loading games into consoles for the next 25 years until the switch to CD-based media led by PlayStation in 1994.

1977

> Atari launch the Atari Video Computer System (VCS) **10**. It is also known as the Atari 2600. Sales are reasonable but it isn't until *Space Invaders* became available for the console in 1980 that sales really rocket.

> Mattel release the **first handheld electronic game** called *Auto Race*. This simple LED racing game would start a trend for companies to make small, cheap electronic games.

1978

> Speak and Spell **11**, the electronic spelling game by Texas Instruments, is the **first game to use speech**.

WRONG. TRY AGAIN. WELCOME.

1979

> Milton Bradley Company releases the **first cartridge-based handheld** called Microvision. It features a 16 x 16 LCD black block display and fairly simple games.

HISTORY OF GAMING: 1980–1993

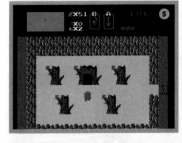

1980

> *PAC-MAN* becomes one of the biggest games of all time and one of the first games to appeal to female gamers.

> *Game and Watch* handheld game *Ball* is the **first LCD game to use drawn characters** rather then basic shapes or boxes.

1981

> *Donkey Kong* ① arcade game is released, initiating Jumpman's (hastily renamed to Mario) long career in video games.

> IBM launch the 5150 PC – the **first PC**; it has text-based graphics and a beeper for sound.

1982

> Sinclair ZX Spectrum ② and Commodore 64 ④ hit the shops, kick-starting the home-computer boom and instigating "geek" culture, with many people learning programming and making games in their own bedrooms.

1983

> Nintendo Famicom is launched with 16 games in the first year. It becomes one of the most successful consoles in Japan and is released in Europe in 1986 as the Nintendo Entertainment System (NES).

> The MSX is launched as a home-computer standard that manufacturers can license and make. Sony becomes a successful manufacturer of MSX-based machines.

1984

> *Elite*, the **first open-ended game**, is released. The classic space trading game for the Acorn BBC Micro gives players a sense of freedom spanning multiple galaxies.

1985

> *Tetris* launched; it would go on to become the **best-selling puzzle game ever** with over 70 million versions of the game sold worldwide.

> *Super Mario Bros.* launched. Around 23 years later, it is verified as the **best-selling video game of all time** with over 40 million copies sold.

> *Little Computer People* ③ is one of the first life-simulation games where you control a simulated person in his house.

1986

> *The Legend Of Zelda* ⑤ is the launch title of the Famicom Disc System.

> *Metal Gear* ⑥ inadvertently starts the stealth genre (although it is not classed as that until years later). The game actually originates from the MSX home computer.

> *Dragon Quest* (a.k.a. *Dragon Warrior*), the first title of the *Dragon Quest* series, is released. The series goes on to sell well over 40 million units worldwide.

1987

> Cash-strapped Square release *Final Fantasy* and good sales save the company.

> Appearing on the US GEnie service, *Air Warrior* is the **first massively mutliplayer online game to have graphics** rather than text-based output.

> NEC PC Engine is released in Japan; it is the **smallest commercial games console ever made** at 14 x 14 x 3.8 cm (5.5 x 5.5 x 1.5 in). PC Engine proves to be very popular and soon begins to out-sell Nintendo's Famicom.

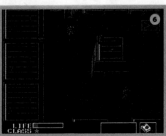

⑧

FACT

> The eight special zone levels in *Super Mario World* (1990) were called Gnarly, Tubular, Way Cool, Awesome, Mondo, Groovy, Outrageous and Funky.

1988	1989	1990	1991	1992	1993

> Sega Mega Drive ⑦ (a.k.a. Sega Genesis in the USA) eventually becomes **Sega's best-selling games console** with over 29 million units sold worldwide.

> **The first CD-ROM unit for a console** is released for the PC Engine as an add-on.

> Electronic Arts release *John Madden Football*, marking the beginning of the successful Madden franchise.

> Game Boy hits stores around the world and ends up selling just under 119 million units to date...

> Originally designed by the games company Epyx and code-named Handy, Atari bring the Atari Lynx to the market as the **first colour handheld games console**.

> Will Wright creates *Sim City* ⑩.

> Peter Molyneux makes an impact on the video-games industry with the seminal God game *Populous*.

> Nintendo Super Famicom hits Japan. Eventually launches in the west in 1992 as the Super Nintendo (SNES) ⑪. It would go on to sell just under 50 million units worldwide, making it the second best-selling Nintendo console ever.

> Sega's *Sonic the Hedgehog* ⑧ takes on Mario.

> *Street Fighter 2* kicks serious butt on the Super Nintendo with reports of some people buying import copies from Japan for hundreds of dollars.

> *Mortal Kombat's* violent digitized graphics puts games in the spotlight in a negative way. Many versions of the game had to be doctored to change the colour of the blood and to remove gory finishing moves.

> Sega releases the *Virtua Racing* arcade game, one of the first 3D polygonal racing games.

> *Myst* is one of the first CD-ROM-only games, making use of the medium by having lots of pre-rendered, high-res graphics.

> Landmark first-person shooter *Doom* is released for the PC. It is originally distributed as shareware so people could play the first episode for free.

> *Virtua Fighter* ⑨ turns heads in arcades; it is the **first fighting game to use hardware 3D polygons** as well as using real-world fighting techniques.

> The 3DO console standard is introduced ⑫.

⑨

TRIVIA

> Is a game truly a game if there is no way to win? This is the question that has been plaguing Will Wright's *Sim City* (1989) ever since the release of this sandbox game with no ending.

> *Street Fighter 2* (1991) was the first fighting game to introduce combos, although this was a completely unintentional side effect of the gameplay that cropped up during development.

⑩

⑪

⑫

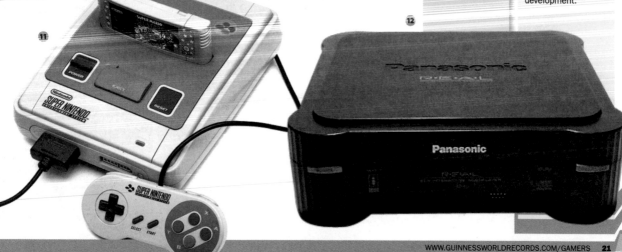

HISTORY OF GAMING: 1994–2008

1_23 FIGURES

> Turnover in the US video games industry shot up an astonishing 43% in 2007, with chart-busting performances in every product category. The industry brought in $17.9 billion (£9 billion) compared to $12.5 billion (£6.3 billion) in 2006, which is the **biggest year-on-year increase in the gaming industry**.

> According to a Reuters report, the number of Internet users in China reached 221 million at the end of February 2008.

> Sales of Nintendo Wii consoles hit the 20-million mark worldwide in May 2008 – a significant milestone that the Wii reached far faster than PS2.

1994

> PlayStation ④ arrives in a blaze of glory. Its award-winning advertising ① helps it become the **first console to sell 100 million** worldwide.

1995

> Satoshi Tajiri's *PokéMon* (or Pocket Monsters, as it is called in Japan) is born and rapidly becomes popular with both boys and girls.

1996

> Nintendo 64 is delayed until *Super Mario 64* is finished. Upon release, *Super Mario 64* becomes one of the most successful launch titles ever, grossing over $200 mllion (£100 million) worldwide.

> Lara Croft ③ stars in 3D action-adventure game *Tomb Raider* and soon becomes the **most recognized female game character**.

1997

> Tamagotchi ⑤, the handheld digital pet, is the must-have toy of the year in Japan. Tales of distraught, starving electronic animals are common and it's not long before the rest of the world is hit by the electronic epidemic.

> *Mario Kart 64* is released by Nintendo in the USA and Europe, having been released in Japan in December of the previous year.

1998

> *Gran Turismo* blows people's minds with its graphics and realistic gameplay. It becomes the **best-selling PlayStation game ever**.

> *Dance Dance Revolution* kicks off a rhythm-game revolution. There are now 50 different versions available.

> Academy of Interactive Arts & Sciences hosts the 1st Annual Interactive Achievement Awards; inducts Shigeru Miyamoto of Nintendo to the AIAS Hall of Fame.

1999

> Dreamcast ② is Sega's final games console. It is also the **first console to have a built-in modem** for online gaming.

> After 10 years of the Nintendo Game Boy dominating the handheld market, the Game Boy Color arrives and is the **first reflective LCD colour screen handheld console**.

2000

> When launched, PlayStation 2 ⑥ is the cheapest DVD player on the market, which fuels massive sales in Japan.

> Strategic life-simulation game *The Sims*, designed by Will Wright, becomes the **best-selling PC game** as well as one of the most popular PC games franchises.

10 million – the number of *World of Warcraft* subscribers worldwide as of January 2008.

2001

> Only two years after the release of the Game Boy Color, Nintendo introduces Game Boy Advance, the **first 32-bit handheld games console** to the market. It goes on to sell over 80 million units.

> Microsoft Xbox arrives with a fanfare. It is the **first console to have built-in Ethernet** as well as a hard drive for games storage.

> The GameCube is the first Nintendo machine to use optical media. In terms of sales, it is Nintendo's least popular video games console.

> *Halo*  becomes Xbox's "killer-app". Three years later, *Halo 2* becomes the **best-selling Xbox game**.

> *Grand Theft Auto III* becomes one of the best-selling PlayStation 2 games.

2002

> Xbox Live is launched. It is the **first** and **largest successful online console gaming service**.

2003

> *Trackmania* becomes one of the most successful online racing games of the year.

2004

> *World of Warcraft* changes online gaming forever. It is currently the **most successful Massively Multiplayer Online Role-Playing Game** with 10 million subscribers as of the start of 2008.

> Looking at ways to make portable gaming more accessible, Nintendo come up with the Nintendo DS 10, which is launched in this year.

> Sony challenge Nintendo with the release of their own portable gaming system in the shape of the PlayStation Portable 7.

2005

> Nintendo work with Dr Ryuta Kawashima 8 to create *Brain Age*, a game that can improve players' mental abilities. The game sells well, especially to a new, more mature gaming audience.

> Xbox 360 launches in the USA.

> *GTA: San Andreas* launches and soon becomes the best-selling *GTA* game to that date.

2006

> Nintendo Wii launches worldwide 12.

> Sony PlayStation 3 launches in Japan.

2007

> *Halo 3* shoots into the record books with the **fastest-selling game launch**.

> Game *Call of Duty 4: Modern Combat* becomes the **best-selling game of 2007** with over 9 million units sold worldwide.

> *Devil May Cry 4* becomes the first instalment in the action series to reach the top spot in the UK All-Formats Top 40.

> Gary Gygax, inventor of pen and paper role-playing game *Dungeons & Dragons*, dies.

2008

> *Grand Theft Auto IV* 9 becomes the **most successful entertainment launch in history**.

> Recent years have seen an increasing number of gaming documentaries focusing on record-breaking gamers. *King of Kong* and *Chasing Ghosts: Beyond the Arcade* (both USA, 2007) followed the stories of old-time gamers such as Billy Mitchell and Steve Wiebe; another currently unnamed documentary

following the life of Lil Poison, the world's **youngest professional gamer** is in the pipeline.

> In 2007, *Manhunt 2* became the first ever game to be refused certification by UK games rating board, the BBFC.

ⓘ TRIVIA

? GWR QUIZ

Q3. What was the first games console to sell 100 million units globally?

BEST OF XBOX 360

MICROSOFT'S THREE-YEAR-OLD MACHINE IS STILL GROWING IN POPULARITY THANKS TO ITS ONLINE SERVICES, SUCH AS XBOX LIVE ARCADE AND VIDEO STORE, AND DIFFERENT HARDWARE OPTIONS.

HARDWARE CHANGES

In February 2008, the next-gen HD format war came to an end. Toshiba announced the discontinuation of HD-DVD ②, leaving the Sony-backed Blu-ray format to dominate the market. Just days later, Microsoft announced it would no longer manufacture the separately available HD-DVD player for Xbox 360. Instead, Microsoft shifted its focus more fully on to digital distribution, adding new films and television shows to the Xbox Live Video Store ① and signing new distribution deals with movie companies. In June 2008, Microsoft executive Robbie Bach confirmed the company was already thinking about how to develop its next console – and had been doing so since before the launch of Xbox 360.

> GAMER'S BYTE
By May 2008, more than 12 million users had signed up for the Xbox Live Arcade service.

LOST ODYSSEY
Publisher: Microsoft

⊪▶ This platform-exclusive role-playing game was produced by Hironobu Sakaguchi, the creator of the *Final Fantasy* series. *Lost Odyssey* ④ tells the story of Kaim, an immortal who has lived for a thousand years and has lost his memory. It's a traditional role-playing game in the Japanese style and is unlikely to appeal to those who aren't already fans of the genre but it has a cult following in Japan, a territory where western consoles have often struggled to find sales.

BURNOUT PARADISE
Publisher: Electronic Arts

⊪▶ The introduction of an open-world environment in *Burnout Paradise* ③ was met with scepticism before the game's release and proved unpopular with some die-hard fans of the series. However, the opportunity to explore freely, combined with *Burnout*'s trademark gameplay and spectacular crash animations, helped to make the game a huge hit. Developer Criterion has continued to build on its success by introducing new features via downloadable content, such as the option to add motorbikes to the game's roster of vehicles.

XBOX 360 ARCADE

CPU: IBM PowerPC Custom Core
HDD Size: None
(includes a 256 MB memory unit)
Memory: 512 MB GDDR3 RAM
Xbox compatibility: No
Colour: White
USB 2.0 ports: 3
Wi-Fi: No (add-on available separately)

XBOX 360

CPU: IBM PowerPC Custom Core
HDD Size: 60 GB
Memory: 512 MB GDDR3 RAM
Xbox compatibility: Yes, for over 300 titles
Colour: White
USB 2.0 ports: 3
Wi-Fi: No (add-on available separately)

XBOX 360 ELITE

CPU: IBM PowerPC Custom Core
HDD Size: 120 GB
Memory: 512 MB GDDR3 RAM
Xbox compatibility: Yes, for over 300 titles
Colour: Black
USB 2.0 ports: 3
Wi-Fi: No (add-on available separately)
Headset included: Yes
HDMI cable included: Yes
Network cable included: Yes

i TRIVIA

> The best-selling Xbox 360 game is *Halo 3*. It sold 8.1 million copies worldwide between its release in 2007 and the beginning of 2008.

ROCK BAND

Publisher: Electronic Arts

➡ Harmonix, the creators of *Guitar Hero*, followed up their musical hit with a game that gives players more options than just lead or bass guitar. *Rock Band* ⑤ also works with microphone and drum peripherals, so up to four players can make music together. It's expensive to buy the full kit, but with a huge catalogue of downloadable songs on offer, along with a multiplayer gaming experience like no other, *Rock Band* fans would say that it's pricey, but it's well worth the investment.

BATTLEFIELD

Publisher: Electronic Arts

➡ The *Battlefield* ⑥ series first became an established hit on PC and was best known for its intense multiplayer battles. But with *Battlefield: Bad Company*, developer DICE presented console gamers with a strong single-player campaign. The game was also praised for its destructible cover system, detailed visuals and free-roaming environments.

BEST OF PLAYSTATION 3

BY THE END OF 2008, THREE DIFFERENT VERSIONS OF PS3 HARDWARE WERE ON SALE AROUND THE WORLD. IT WAS ALSO A VINTAGE YEAR FOR PS3 GAMES.

LITTLEBIGPLANET
Publisher: Sony

▶ LittleBIGPlanet ① is hard to categorize but one thing's for sure – it's one of the most original titles the world has ever seen. The intuitive level editor allows all gamers, old and new, to create physically accurate playgrounds that are so immersive you'll never want to leave.

GRAN TURISMO 5: PROLOGUE
Publisher: Sony

▶ Some would argue that charging the consumer for a demo is a little unfair. Still, it didn't stop an avalanche of digital purchases and subsequent critical praise that announced GT5: Prologue ③ as a technical masterpiece and left the two million who downloaded it salivating as they waited for the release of the full game due in 2009.

SPEC A – PAL (UK)

CPU: Cell Broadband Engine
HDD Size: 80 GB, 160 GB
Memory: 256 MB XDR
PS2 compatibility: No
Colours: Black, White, Silver
USB 2.0 ports: 2
Wi-Fi: Yes
Flash Card Reader: No
Chrome Trim: Yes
SACD Support: No

SPEC B – NTSC (USA/JAP)

CPU: Cell Broadband Engine
HDD Size: 40 GB (Japan only), 80 GB, 160 GB
Memory: 256Mb XDR
PS2 compatibility: Yes
Colours: Black
USB 2.0 ports: 4
Wi-Fi: Yes
Flash Card Reader: Yes
Chrome Trim: Yes
SACD Support: Yes

HARDWARE

PlayStation 3 hardware changes occur as components become cheaper and manufacturing costs are reduced. Another factor is where in the world you live – machines will often be tailored to suit the differing requirements of the consumers in different territories.

METAL GEAR SOLID 4: GUNS OF THE PATRIOTS
Publisher: Konami

At last, all questions answered and time for series producer Hideo Kojima to move on. The fourth instalment of the classic stealth series follows the same style of gameplay and is beautifully presented. It is also one of the best war-based narratives ever written for a game.

CALL OF DUTY 4: MODERN WARFARE
Publisher: Activision

Call of Duty 4: Modern Warfare **2** is anything but just another FPS. Epic set-pieces and incredibly evocative dialogue blend with explosive gameplay to keep the trigger fingers happy. By Christmas 2008, this was the biggest-selling next-generation FPS to date.

FALLOUT 3
Publisher: Bethesda Softworks

After a 10-year break, many will not be familiar with the previous two *Fallout* titles. That doesn't matter. *Fallout 3* **4** developer Bethesda know what they're doing when it comes to epic RPGs and this is everything sci-fi fans could have hoped for. This is an apocalyptic adventure you will never forget and a must-have game.

GRAND THEFT AUTO IV
Publisher: Take 2/Rockstar Games

For some this is the greatest game of all time; for others it's more of the same violent gameplay but with better graphics. One thing's for sure – GTA IV has smashed sales records all over the world and shows no sign of abating.

WARHAWK
Publisher: Sony

This Sixaxis controller-enabled, multi-vehicular action game remained at the top of the PS3 download charts for 12 weeks. Extra content continues to be released for this ever-popular exclusive PS3 online shooter.

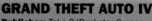

FACTS

> The prototype for the PlayStation 3 controller was more reminiscent of Batman's "Batarang" when first revealed in 2005 and was not well received by fans. The classic Dualshock shape used for both PlayStation and PlayStation 2 was reinstated soon after.

> The PS3 sold twice as many units around the world in the early part of summer 2008 than during the same period the previous year. Between April and June 2008, 1.56 million were sold – over double the 700,000 figure from 2007.

> PlayStation 3 console sales in Europe hit 5.8 million units in May 2008, overtaking sales of Xbox 360, which launched 16 months earlier than Sony's machine.

BEST OF NINTENDO Wii

NINTENDO CONTINUES TO BRING GAMING TO A WIDER AUDIENCE WITH THE Wii, A CONSOLE THAT IS CHANGING HOW PEOPLE PLAY GAMES THANKS TO ITS INNOVATIVE REMOTE CONTROLLER.

PRO-EVOLUTION SOCCER 2008
Publisher: Konami

▥▶ This game was highly praised by critics for offering a new approach to the football games genre. *Pro Evolution Soccer 2008* ① for Wii uses a "point and drag" system that allows players to guide their team with the Wii Remote and Nunchuk. It's a highly intuitive, fluid control method and offers a whole new gaming experience.

SUPER SMASH BROS. BRAWL
Publisher: Nintendo

▥▶ A superb single-player adventure, offering multiplayer fun for up to four players, online battles and customizable arenas. Is it any wonder fighting game *Super Smash Bros. Brawl* ② became the fastest-selling Nintendo game in the US when it was released on 9 March 2008, with 874,000 copies sold on day one? Other highlights include the introduction of a host of new characters such as Sonic the Hedgehog and even *Metal Gear*'s Solid Snake.

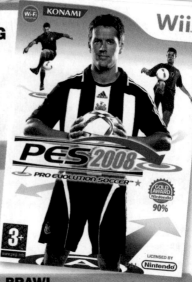

Wii FIT
Publisher: Nintendo

▥▶ *Wii Fit* is an inventive game that comes bundled with the Wii Balance Board ④, a device that can measure weight and detect shifts in a player's balance ⑤. It includes more than 40 training activities aimed at improving the fitness levels of gamers. There is even a calendar feature, enabling players to track their progress.

BOOM BLOX
Publisher: Electronic Arts

▥▶ In this game developed by Steven Spielberg in collaboration with EA, *Boom Blox* ⑥ players use the Wii Remote and a number of in-game objects to protect or destroy structures made from various blocks. The Havok physics engine used in *Boom Blox* is highly sophisticated, yet the gameplay is instantly accessible – and incredibly addictive.

MARIO KART Wii
Publisher: Nintendo

▸ The first Wii instalment in Nintendo's classic racing series doesn't disappoint. Motorbikes have been added to the vehicle line-up, but the big news was the Wii Wheel that comes bundled with the game and turns the Wii Remote into a steering wheel. With an online mode, new circuits and the brilliant gameplay fans have come to expect, *Mario Kart Wii* ⑦ is an essential purchase.

ℹ TRIVIA

> The first WiiWare games were released in Japan in March 2008, with Europe and the US following in May. The most popular launch titles included *Final Fantasy Crystal Chronicles: My Life As A King* and *Lost Winds*, which was praised for its unique control system.

> In the UK, Wii sales hit the 1 million mark just 38 weeks after launch in December 2006, beating the PS2 and the Xbox 360 to the same target.

HARDWARE CHANGES

There is still only one version of the Wii console available, but Nintendo has continued to introduce new peripherals to enhance gameplay. The biggest news of the year was the launch of WiiWare ⑧. Like the Virtual Console shop, this service allows users to purchase and download games paid for in Wii Points. While games on the virtual console have been adapted for the Wii, WiiWare games are all new and specially designed for the console.

NINTENDO Wii

CPU: PowerPC-based "Broadway" processor
Flash Ram Size: 512 MB
Memory: 64 MB GDDR3 RAM
GameCube compatibility: Yes
Colour: White
USB 2.0 ports: 2
Wi-Fi: Yes
Ethernet: No (available separately)

PSP SALES CONTINUED TO RISE IN 2008, THANKS LARGELY TO THE WIDE AVAILABILITY OF SOME GREAT GAMES. IN SOME COUNTRIES, IT EVEN BEAT LONG-TIME RIVAL, THE NINTENDO DS...

FACTS

> New PSPs launched in 2008 included the PSP-1000 MB (Metallic Blue) and the PSP-2000 DR (Deep Red) in the US, while the PSP-2000 MG (Mint Green) was a big hit in Japan **2**. In the UK, a special Ice Silver PSP – yes, the PSP-2000 IS – came bundled with copies of *Crisis Core – Final Fantasy VII.*

HARDWARE CHANGES

The new PSP 3000 was introduced in October 2008 featuring a microphone and improved screen technology making it easier to use when outside. This was the first PSP hardware change since the Slim and Lite model **1** was introduced in September 2007. However, Sony continued to release firmware updates for the handheld throughout 2008 enabling users to perform tasks such as Google searches and accessing Internet radio stations. The PSP is also now Skype compatible meaning it can also operate as a mobile phone.

PATAPON
Publisher: Sony

The comparisons with previous PSP hit *LocoRoco* are inevitable, but while both games feature quirky 2D visuals and a funky soundtrack, the gameplay in *Patapon* **3** is more complex. You use drumbeats to command your army of brave Patapons and develop different strategies for each mission, which usually involves giant monsters, marauding armies and environmental challenges such as volcanoes. The overall result is a game that is both unique and charming and is also great fun to play.

GOD OF WAR: CHAINS OF OLYMPUS
Publisher: Sony

Kratos made his debut on PSP for the first time with this game, which like its PS2 predecessors is inspired by Greek mythology. The action is just as fast-paced and violent as ever, and there's an excellent balance between combat and puzzle solving. Great visuals and a slick control system help to make *God of War: Chains of Olympus* one of the best games available for PSP **4**.

¹₂₃ FIGURES

> In 2008, the PSP finally surpassed the DS as the **most popular handheld console in Japan**. During the first half of the year, Sony sold 1.97 million handhelds, while the figure for the DS stood at 1.59 million.

> PSP sales were boosted in Japan by the release of key titles such as *Monster Hunter Portable*. Over 2.3 million copies of the game were sold in six months.

CRISIS CORE – FINAL FANTASY VII
Publisher: Square Enix

A prequel to *Final Fantasy VII* – the second-best-selling PlayStation game of all time – *Crisis Core* **5** follows the adventures of a young soldier, called Zack, who uncovers a mysterious conspiracy. Highlights include the stunning graphics and CG cut-scenes, plus an enhanced battle system and more than 300 side missions to complete.

77.5 million – the number of DS units sold worldwide up to June 2008 since its launch in November 2004.

FOUR YEARS FROM LAUNCH, THE DS IS STILL GOING STRONG. IN 2008, A RANGE OF NEW COLOURS WAS LAUNCHED WITH PLENTY OF NEW TITLES.

HARDWARE CHANGES

➠ The DS specs have not changed since the Lite model was introduced in 2006. However, Nintendo regularly issues different coloured units in different regions.

In 2008, new Cobalt/Black and Metallic Rose handhelds were launched in the USA. Australian gamers were able to choose from Blue/Black and Red/Black combinations for the first time.

In Europe, to celebrate the launch of *Cooking Guide: Can't decide what to eat?* ⑦, Nintendo produced red, green ⑥ and turquoise DS units.

ADVANCE WARS: DARK CONFLICT
Publisher: Activision

➠ The latest instalment in this hit strategy series featured a much darker storyline and less-cartoony graphics than its predecessor. Yet, the gameplay remained just as addictive and new units, such as the motorbike and flare, added depth. *Dark Conflict* was the first game to let players battle online using Wi-Fi, a feature that had been highly anticipated.

▼ NEW RECORD
▽ UPDATED RECORD

GUITAR HERO: ON TOUR
Publisher: Activision

➠ This game launched with a special peripheral, the "Guitar Hero Grip" ⑧, which slots into the bottom of the DS. Players use one hand to press the fret buttons and the other hand to strum notes on the second screen using a special plectrum-shaped stylus. Some critics argue that this control system is flawed, while others complain about the sound quality. But this hasn't stopped *Guitar Hero: On Tour* riding high in the charts.

POKÉMON MYSTERY DUNGEON: EXPLORERS OF TIME/DARKNESS
Publisher: Sony

➠ The Pokémon phenomenon continued to grow in 2008 with the release of two more *Mystery Dungeon* games ⑨. New features include the option to trade items wirelessly and send SOS mails to PCs and mobile phones via Wi-Fi. More than 490 Pokémon appear in the two games, including all of those from *Pokémon Diamond* and *Pearl*.

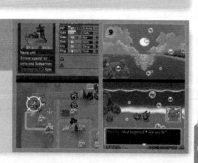

➠ **FACTS**

> The DS Lite has backwards compatibility with the Game Boy Advance and its entire back catalogue of games, giving players access to hundreds of titles.

¹²₃ **FIGURES**

> It took the DS 22 months to reach the **10 million** sales mark in Europe after its launch in March 2005. By the start of 2008 that figure had risen to **20 million**, making it the ▽**fastest-selling handheld console in Europe**.

> By April 2008, the number of DS games shipped around the world had topped **406 million**. On average, each DS owner has five games for their handheld.

FACTS

> Benjamin J. Heckendorm (USA) is a prolific console modder with a collection of nearly 100 pieces. Machines he has succesfully modified include: Atari 2600, Atari 800 Computer, Colecovision, Commodore 64, NES, Sega Genesis, Super Nintendo, Atari Jaguar, PlayStation, PlayStation 2, Nintendo 64, Xbox and Xbox 360. His Xbox 360 laptop mod 6 is perfect for gaming on the move.

> Neo Geo is a popular platform among collectors, with both the home console and arcade versions of the games system having their own active fanbases.

NEW RECORD
UPDATED RECORD

THE WORLD OF VIDEO GAMES OFFERS A WONDERFUL VARIETY OF COLLECTABLES. HERE WE REVEAL SOME OF THE MOST DEDICATED ENTHUSIASTS.

Largest PlayStation collection

Jason Dvorak (USA) 1 owns a 1,500-piece collection consisting of hardware, games and guides. His most cherished game is *Elemental Gearbolt: Assassin's Case*, a copy of which sold on eBay for $1,400. He has been collecting PlayStation items since 2002.

Most technically advanced gaming set-up

Jeremy R. Kipnis (USA) owns the largest, loudest and most expensive gaming set-up 2. It has taken more than 38 years of professional experience as an audio-visual engineer to collect the equipment and create an acoustically and optically ideal gaming room. At its loudest, the audio levels reach 132 decibels at one metre from each of the 8.8 surround-sound channel arrays; the current screen is a 5.4 x 3 m (18 x 10 ft) Stewart Snowmatte Unity Gain Laboratory Grade Motion Picture Screen.

Largest collection of Pokémon memorabilia

The largest collection of *Pokémon* memorabilia belongs to Belle Starenchak (USA), a.k.a. "PikaBelleChu", who has been collecting for over 10 years and owns 5,456 different items as of 1 April 2008 3. As well as a vast assortment of general *Pokémon* merchandise, she also owns a Volkswagen Beetle car kitted out to look like a Pikachumobile.

Largest collection of gaming merchandise

Brett Martin (USA) 4 has been collecting gaming merchandise for 15 years. His collection now consists of at least 467 different gaming items, ranging from cuddly Kirbys to prototype *Star Fox* figures.

> *Video games should be looked upon as fine art rather than a simple form of entertainment for children.*
> **Richard Lecce, owner of the largest collection of game systems**

Largest collection of screenshots from a video-game series

Screen-grab fanatic Rikardo Granda (Colombia) has amassed an impressive collection of over 17,000 digital images from games published in the *Castlevania* franchise. Boasting a selection of screenshots covering the entire 22 years of *Castlevania* history – together with a vast collection of in-game art, including backgrounds, sprites and placeables – Rikardo's status as a *Castlevania* superfan is almost impossible to dispute.

5,456 – the number of *Pokémon*-related items that Belle Starenchak has in her collection.

TRIVIA

> The *Nintendo Powerfest '94* cartridge for SNES was an oversized cartridge featuring levels from several games. It was made especially for a competition to crown the top video-game player in the USA. Only 32 copies of the cartridge were manufactured and it is believed that only one, recently sold to a private collector for $10,000, remains in existence.

> The *1990 Nintendo World Championships: Gold Edition* cartridge for the NES is probably the holy grail of collectible NES games as only around 26 were ever produced.

? GWR QUIZ

Q5. How many pieces are there in the world's largest collection of playable video-gaming systems owned by Richard Lecce?

INTERVIEW WITH... COLLECTOR RICHARD LECCE

In the last decade, 33-year-old **Richard Lecce** (USA) ⑤ has amassed the ⬛largest collection of playable video-gaming systems. The 483 pieces include 73 *Game & Watches*, 260 cartridge or CD-based systems and another 126 miscellaneous handheld games. Lecce also owns the ⬛largest collection of Nintendo Game Boys, numbering 39 systems of different shapes and colours. In addition to this intimidating haul, he also has one of the most comprehensive game collections, with full sets of every game ever released for 12 different systems, including the NES, SEGA Master System and Atari 5200. Finally, Richard has a strong appreciation for video-game artwork and is the proud owner of over 100 original pieces of box art, which include the hand-painted cover from *Ecco the Dolphin* and the box art for the SNES release of *Street Fighter II*.

What is your most expensive piece worth?
I have an original *Computer Space*, the first video arcade game ever – it has only been played 150 times and is probably the finest in existence. I was offered $10,000 and passed. I also have an original Atari 2700 RC. The "RC" stands for Remote Control and there are only about 10 left as far as I know. Atari paid $250,000 to design this system.

What is your favourite piece?
Probably my *Computer Space* because it was the first arcade video game.

Do you have any other collections?
I also collect coins and art. I am a professional numismatist so I have a nice collection of coins put away.

What drives you to keep collecting?
I like searching for and finding that one elusive piece. I take pride in my collection and think of it as a way of keeping the history of video games alive. I feel like a custodian of these things for future generations. I look at all aspects of video games as art, from the design of the box to the characters, gameplay and programming. I really believe that video games are the most undervalued and under-appreciated art form. Video games should be looked upon as fine art rather than a simple form of entertainment for children.

FATHER OF VIDEO GAMING

Now 87 years old, Ralph Baer ⑤ was recently awarded a special certificate by Guinness World Records ① acknowledging his outstanding contribution to the video games industry. It was the latest in a long line of accolades celebrating Mr Baer's inventions and innovations. In 2006, Ralph was awarded the National Medal of Technology by US President George W. Bush ⑦ in recognition of his groundbreaking and pioneering creation, development and commercialization of interactive video games. Further proof, if any was needed, that Ralph Baer truly is the father of gaming.

FACTS

> Ralph Baer's inventiveness is not confined to video games. He has applied his engineering expertise in many different areas, from espionage equipment to computerized toys. One of his most popular inventions is SIMON ②, a fiendishly addictive single-chip microprocessor game that involves memorizing a sequence of notes emitted through coloured buttons on the device. This simple yet remarkable game still sells well more than a quarter of a century after its introduction in 1978.

RALPH H. BAER INVENTED THE HOME VIDEO GAME CONSOLE WAY BACK IN 1967. WE CAUGHT UP WITH HIM RECENTLY AND ASKED HIM ABOUT HIS PIONEERING WORK IN GAMING.

You first had the idea of a television-based gaming device in 1951 but the idea was rejected by your employers of the time. Do you feel frustrated that it could have been possible to build the "Brown Box" 15 years earlier? Or do you believe that every invention has a right time and that the right time for the Brown Box was achieved?

Even the most primitive attachment would have had to be vacuum-tube-based in 1951 and therefore quite large and expensive.

My Chief Engineer at Loral probably made the right decision from a product point of view: one might be able to jump ahead of the curve a bit, but not often and not too far.

You have around 150 patents attributed to you already. However, if there was an invention you wish you had invented, what would it have been?

That's easy: The wheel of course. However, I may be old but I am not *that* old!

A lot of people don't realize that as well as inventing the game console you also invented peripherals such as the light gun. When you look at gadgets like VR headsets, dance mats, guitars, etc., are you surprised at the diversity or do you think there's even more to come?

I'm in the process of developing two accessory items right now. The success of the Wii ③ showed that I was on target in the early 1990s when I showed physically interactive accessory devices similar to those that the Wii finally introduced 15 years later. I showed many of these concepts to Konami and others and couldn't find any takers then, so I'm glad to see it happen now that much more sophisticated solutions are practical.

By the way: Brown Box was accompanied by a joystick with a golf ball at the end of it which you could actually hit with a real putter!

BIOGRAPHY

1922
Born in Germany.

1938: Left Germany for US with parents and sister.

1940
Graduated from National Radio Institute (NRI) as a radio service technician.

1943
Served in US Army in Europe during WWII. Assigned to Military Intelligence in France ⑧. Became expert on military small arms.

1949
Graduated from American Television Institute of Technology (ATIT) as a television engineer.

1956
Joined Sanders Associates, Inc., in Nashua, New Hampshire, USA. Built snooping equipment to monitor Soviet transmissions in Germany.

1967
Built the home video-game system known as "Brown Box", which led to the Magnavox Odyssey system ④ being mass-produced in 1972.

1966 – the year Ralph Baer wrote his original concept for playing games using a home television set. His 1968 "Brown Box" prototype became the commercially produced Magnavox Odyssey ④ in 1972.

Some people believe that video game consoles will eventually be something that can be built into or added straight into the human brain. Is this something you can see happening or do you think it will be the other way round and humans will step into simulation-type computers to live virtual experiences?

There's no question that the process of embedding small electronic devices directly into brain tissue is an ongoing developmental process in medical research. However, that's all a bit too Orwellian for my taste!

What is the most important aspect of gaming?
To me, the answer always was fun – the same kind you derive from board games or card games – but it has clearly moved vastly beyond these limiting applications. Besides, one person's fun is another person's horror story. So, I must conclude that many game players look not so much for fun as for something else, like immersion into an artificial world – and there is nothing wrong with that.

What's your favourite video game of all time?
Believe it or not, I am not a game player. I like to create electronic games because that's how my head works but I don't play them much anymore, especially not now at this benign age!

1975	1978	1985	1994	2004	2005	2006
Began work on a line of video games for Coleco – creators of the Telstar video game console – while still working at Sanders.	Invented and developed single-chip, micro-processor-controlled handheld games, including the best-selling SIMON ②.	Invented interactive VCR game system, including Smarty Bear ⑥, a Teddy bear who "talks" to his cartoon friends on-screen.	Invented a recordable talking doormat. **1996:** Invented "Bike-Max", the talking speedometer.	Produced replicas of experimental video game models built in the 1960s and donated them to the Museum of the Moving Image in New York, USA.	Donated all original video game units to the Smithsonian Institution. For more information visit http://invention.smithsonian.org/baer/	 Presented with a National Medal of Technology by President George W. Bush ⑦ for pioneering development and commercialization of interactive video games.

RECORD-BREAKING GAMES

On the first day of its release, *Grand Theft Auto IV* generated $310 million (£159 million) worth of sales worldwide, making it the **highest grossing video game over 24 hours**.

CONTENTS

NEW CATEGORIES!

The keen-eyed among you will notice that we have brand new categories for this, the *Guinness World Records 2009 Gamer's Edition*. This is so we can pack in more new records covering both classic record-breaking games and 2008's hottest new releases. But on top of all this, we have still found room to cram in all the facts, records and trivia that no gamer's edition should be without – such as **the best-selling video game of all time** (see p.190). In short, the next 170 pages are a celebration of the world's greatest gaming achievements. We hope you enjoy them.

WAR GAMES

Thanks to its Frostbite DX engine, *Battlefield: Bad Company* boasts the **most destructible environment**, with players able to destroy or "reshape" around 90% of the landscape and in-game objects.

CONTENTS

WAR GAMES

WAR... HUH... YEAH...WHAT IS IT GOOD FOR? WELL, VIDEO GAMING, FOR ONE THING! OUR AGELESS OBSESSION WITH BLOWING THINGS UP FINDS PERFECT EXPRESSION IN THE WAR GAME.

👤 **EXPERT**

Richie Shoemaker is the editor of *EON* magazine and author of *The Art of EVE*. He's a regular contributor to *PCZone* magazine and has written for *PC Format*, *Retro Gamer*, *PC Gamer* (US), as well as official Xbox and Dreamcast magazines. When he was nine, he was sick inside a British Army helicopter.

⟳ OVERVIEW

War games were traditionally concerned solely with high-level strategy, but as graphical realism has evolved, military-themed games have hit the frontlines. They offer a combination of fast-paced shooting action, squad tactics

and the command or direct control of individual units, be they soldiers, tanks, aircraft or even battleships.

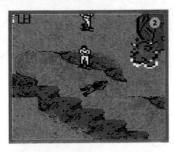

It is all too tempting when trying to define a "war game" – in the context of video gaming, at least – to scatter the net too widely and include far too many titles. Was *SpaceWar!*, the **first shooting game** dating back to 1961, a war game? What about *Space Invaders* – we were surely at war with the aliens, weren't we?

For the purposes of this chapter, the answer to these questions is "no". What we're looking for here are games explicitly associated with dirty, blood 'n' guts, Earth-bound warfare.

As to what the very first game was in the relatively youthful genre of war games, *Sea Wolf*, the classic 1976 arcade game that simulated a submarine naval battle, is a strong contender. Another notable early war game was *Beach Head* ①. Released for the Commodore 64 and 8-bit Atari in 1983, the game required you to navigate a fleet of ships across dangerous waters, shooting down a host of attacking aircraft, avoiding incoming salvos and then

▼ **NEW RECORD** ▽ **UPDATED RECORD**

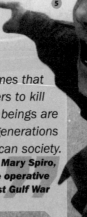

> *Video games that allow players to kill real human beings are desensitizing generations of American society.*
>
> **Mary Spiro, ex-US Air Force operative in the first Gulf War**

TIMELINE

1983

MGM release the movie *WarGames* and ColecoVision issue their tie-in video game. (A much improved version would be released for PS and the PC in 1998.)

Beach Head is released in Europe and sells almost 250,000 copies in the UK.

1986: SNK release *Ikari Warriors* ⑦.

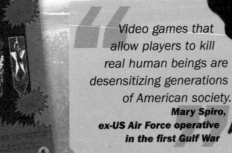

1987

Microprose release *Airborne Ranger*.

1988

Infogrames issue *Hostages* on 11 platforms.

Cascade release *19 Part 1: Boot Camp*, a Vietnam War game inspired by Paul Hardcastle and his song *19*.

10,000 km² – gaming area available in the US military's *Combined Arms Tactical Trainer*, the world's **most advanced battlefield simulator**. It can train 850 personnel at once in an integrated, realistic combat scenario.

TRIVIA

> In common with the games they would inspire almost 25 years later, *Commando* **6**, *Ikari Warriors*, *Raid Over Moscow* **8** and *Beach Head* were the source of much controversy in their day. These titles were the first video games to be put on restricted sale in Europe, having been placed on the infamous index of "youth-endangering publications" in West Germany in the 1980s.

> In one of several instances of the military using a commercial game to aid the training of ground troops, the US Marine Corps adapted Id Software's *Doom II*, switching out monsters for enemy soldiers and plasma guns for M16s in a modification called *Marine Doom*. The following year, in 1997, *Marine Expeditionary Unit 2000* was created – a serious military training tool made as a direct collaboration with a commercial games developer.

> *Urban Resolve*, developed by the US Department of Defense, can model a siege involving 3,000 personnel in a city of 65,000 buildings.

guiding a convoy of tanks to destroy a vast bunker.

Although *Beach Head* lacked bloody infantry assaults, it was the closest gamers had ever got to recreating the thrill of D-Day on their TV screens without resorting to video cassettes.

As processing power increased through the 1980s, military action games evolved beyond the constraints of being mere arcade shooters in tin hats, as elements from role-playing, strategy gaming and simulation were incorporated.

It is from this early period of hybridization that we can start to define the roots of the genre: mission briefings steeped in historical references, detailed weapons info, threaded mission objectives and equipment selection as well as reliance on tactics.

We may have been some years away from realistic bullet wounds, but if any one game set the template for the modern military-themed action game it was 1987's *Airborne Ranger* **2**, a hit that, like

most games from Microprose, was as memorable for the exhaustive manual as for the actual game. Microprose went on to refine their ideas in a series of games – such as *Gunship!* **3** and *M1 Tank Platoon* **4** – that went beyond the controlling of military hardware and did as much to make military simulations popular as they did refine the genre.

A steady trickle of games followed, few of them best-sellers, but all contributing to a reserve of inspiration waiting to break out from the shadows; from the obscurely ahead-of-its-time anti-terror game *Hostages* **10**, Microprose's *Special Forces* **11**, all the way to EA's small-arms squad simulation *SEAL Team* **12**. By this point, first-person shooters such as *Doom* and *Duke Nukem 3D* had taken the gaming world by storm. The second wave – more realistic and backed up with tanks, and teamwork – wasn't too far behind.

The 2000s have parachuted us squarely into the middle of battle.

We're no longer controlling the action from the comfort of our war room, pushing toy soldiers across a table with a rake – we're there in the theatre of war, dodging shrapnel and up to our necks in mud, gore and fallen comrades.

Physics engines – such as *Company of Heroes'* Havok 3 engine – take us closer to the action than we'd ever want to be in real life. Even the real military are getting in on the act: *Urban Resolve* is a combat sim that can model a million different entities involved in a city siege. It seems that the line between gaming and reality are becoming dangerously blurred.

1991	1996		1999	2003	2005	2007
Microprose release *Special Forces* and *Gunship 2000*. **1993:** EA releases *Seal Team*.	US Marine Corps adapt Id Software's *Doom II* to create *Marine Doom*. **1998:** Red Storm release *Rainbow Six*.		The first public beta of *Counter-Strike* is released. EA release *Medal of Honor*.	Activision release *Call of Duty*. Take 2 release *Vietcong*.	Ubisoft release *Brothers in Arms: Road to Hill 30* **5**. EA release *Battlefield 2* **9** and win numerous "Game of the Year" awards.	Activision release *Call of Duty 4: Modern Warfare*.

AMERICA'S ARMY

PLATFORMS

SPEC

Developer:
US Army
Publisher:
US Army
Initial release:
America's Army: Recon
(2002), PC

GAMEPLAY

Created primarily as a recruitment tool by and for the US Army, America's Army was designed to offer a purely multiplayer experience similar to Counter-Strike. The game promotes teamwork by rewarding players who adhere to the "rules of engagement", while punishing those who do not.

Most hours spent playing a free online shooter
According to the US Army, as of August 2008, gamers have spent 230,918,365 hours playing the PC version of *America's Army* ④. Players from over 60 countries have fired more than 4,090,901,016 rounds since it was launched in 2002 ⑤. The PC version of the game also boasts more than 9,349,031 registered users.

Largest travelling game simulator
The *Virtual Army Experience (VAE)* is a highly modified version of *America's Army* that includes six life-size Humvees ② surrounded by multiple flat screens, with room for up to 50 participants. Mounted in the vehicles are modified light-gun weapons. The team inside each vehicle, which shakes in reaction to nearby explosions, are tasked to drive supplies to a beleaguered group of aid workers in dangerous territory. The *VAE* ③ takes up 1,811 m² (19,500 ft²).

Most downloaded war game
According to official estimates, *America's Army*, in all its various iterations, has been downloaded 42,611,601 times. It is also the most downloaded game from Fileplanet.com, itself one of the most popular gaming download sites on the internet. The most recent version of the gaming client software has been downloaded almost 2.4 million times between January and July 2008.

Largest virtual army
In January 2007, *America's Army* recruited its 8 millionth registered user; at the same time, the actual American Army comprised just 519,472 soldiers. This makes the virtual US army 15 times larger than the real thing!

First military website to support a video game
The website americasarmy.com is the first military website to support a video game series. *America's Army* is also the ▼**first multi-platform game to receive a government-licensed trademark**.

▼ **NEW RECORD** ▽ **UPDATED RECORD**

$5.7 million – the cost per year to create and deploy the game of *America's Army*, all of which is paid for by US taxpayers.

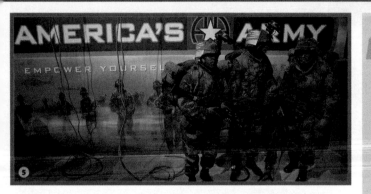

AMERICA'S ★ ARMY

EMPOWER YOURSELF

5

> *America's Army... has had an incredible impact around the world, placing soldiering front and center within popular culture and showcasing the high-tech, team-oriented and values-driven nature of the Army.*
>
> **Colonel Casey Wardynski** 7, **originator of America's Army**

AMERICA'S ARMY: MOUT SHOOTHOUSE

M4A1 Carbine scores – Source: Americasarmy.com/community/scoreboards.php

RANK	USER NAME	FRIEND/FOE	TIME	SCORE
1	.Zarno	0/48	1 min 28 sec	22,970
2	.shrewd	0/49	1 min 41 sec	22,859
3	GaTaMaX	0/49	1 min 16 sec	22,770
4	2cleric2	0/49	1 min 41 sec	22,659
5	[-SnuF-Stuart]	0/49	1 min 42 sec	22,659
6	[Dev]Bishop	0/49	1 min 49 sec	22,549
7	Hacker-Kilia	0/46	48 sec	22,390
8	={falcon}=	0/49	1 min 21 sec	22,370
9	crazy5g	0/48	1 min 34 sec	22,359
10	-(XFG)-KWK	0/48	1 min 25 sec	22,270

7

ℹ TRIVIA

> According to a US Army survey, 60% of new recruits have played a version of *America's Army*, while 4% joined as a direct consequence of playing the game.

> *America's Army: True Soldiers* 1 features five playable character classes: Rifleman, Grenadier, Sniper, Automatic Rifleman and Squad Leader.

> In September 2007, a group known as Iraq Veterans Against the War wore T-shirts with the tagline "War is not a game" and marched through St Louis, Missouri, USA.

❓ GWR QUIZ

Q6. How much does the game *America's Army* cost the US tax payer each year?

▐▐▶ FACT

The *America's Army* brand is growing – not only is it a video game that presents players with scenarios a soldier might face, but it also now boasts a series of action figures. Each was modelled on winners of Silver and Bronze Star honours, such as Sergeant First Class Gerald Wolford 9. As well as appearing in plastic miniature form, Afghanistan veteran Major Jason Amerine 8 served as an expert for *America's Army: Rise of a Soldier* 6, bringing his experience as a serviceman to the game.

8

9

Record Brief for MAJ Jason Amerine 6

MAJ Jason Amerine

Ribbons
(Jason Amerine)

ARMY

VSER

INGS

PPORT

CREDITS

SIGNOUT

U.S.ARMY

BATTLEFIELD

PLATFORMS

SPEC

Developer:
Digital Illusions
Publisher:
Electronic Arts (EA)
Initial release:
Battlefield 1942
(2002), PC

GAMEPLAY

As *Doom* had been for action shooters almost a decade before, *Battlefield 1942* was a watershed PC game for fans of military-themed combat. Focusing on multiplayer online battles, the game was the first to successfully blend infantry and vehicular combat in the same setting, doing away with any kind of narrative almost completely.

Largest controllable vehicle in a war shooter
Battlefield 2142's massive Titans ① are the largest controllable vehicles ever to appear in a shooter game. Not only can Titans be directed across a map by a team commander, they can be assaulted and defended by infantry units once their shields have been neutralized.

First to reach highest rank in Battlefield 2142
The first person to rank as Supreme Commander – the highest position attainable among *Battlefield 2142*'s 44 ranks – was player "Noobish-noob". There can only be one Supreme Commander at any one time.

Most popular Battlefield 1942 mod
One of the first modifications released for *Battlefield 1942* ② was *Desert Combat*, a fan-created add-on that turned the World War II game into one based in and around the first Gulf War. Winner of awards for best mod in 2002, 2003 and 2004, the developers so impressed the creators of *Battlefield* that they were made a subsidiary studio.

Most critically acclaimed war game of 2002
In the wake of its release, *Battlefield 1942* won an unprecedented number of awards: from being IGN.com's game of the year for 2002, to winning four Academy of Interactive Arts & Sciences awards, including Overall

Game of the Year for the same period. The game also won a BAFTA for its multiplayer features, making it the most critically acclaimed game of the year.

First digital-only expansion pack
The final of four *Battlefield* expansions, *Battlefield 2: Special Forces* ⑥, was the first to be made available for sale via EA's digital distribution service. Three

BATTLE WINNERS

Battlefield 2 was one of the first games played as part of the Championship Gaming Invitational, which took place in July 2006 at Treasure Island, San Francisco, California, USA. The event heralded the inaugural season of gaming's first professional North American sports-style pro-gaming league – the Championship Gaming Series. The winners of the *Battlefield 2* invitational were 20id ④, a professional team of *Battlefield* players who won $40,000 (£21,800).

1.5 million – the number of Xbox 360 players who downloaded the *Battlefield: Bad Company* demo within the first two weeks of release.

▶ FACT

Battlefield 1942 was the inspiration for the development of *Star Wars: Battlefront*, a team-based multiplayer game developed by Pandemic Studios that replaced Allied and Axis forces with those from the Rebellion and The Empire, with sets from the *Stars Wars* movies in place of World War II battlefields. *Battlefront* is the **best-selling *Stars Wars* game**.

◣ **NEW RECORD**   ◺ **UPDATED RECORD**

> *This is a pick-up-and-play action extravaganza, a comic book version of WWII.*
> **Review of Battlefield 1942 on gaming website uk.gamespot.com**

BATTLEFIELD SERVER STATS

	BATTLEFIELD 2	BATTLEFIELD 2142
Online Players	14,908,985	N/A
Total badges awarded	37,819,916	14,241,202
Total time played	35,297 years	10,519 years
Total shots fired	142,728,982,440	58,482,040,217
Total deaths	7,626,513,079	2,309,811,345
Total kills	6,300,846,374	2,305,637,424

ℹ TRIVIA

> The precursor to *Battlefield 1942* was 1999's *Codename Eagle* ③, an action game set in an alternate reality World War I. The team behind *Codename Eagle* was eventually bought by Digital Illusions.

Battlefield "Booster Packs" have been released since, all of them available only through EA's Download Manager. Although all three were packaged for retail release, the boxes contained only a code used to download the game.

◣ **Largest online cash prize**
To celebrate the 2005 release of *Battlefield: Modern Combat* ⑤ on PlayStation 2 and Xbox, EA announced a competition for teams to win $250,000 (£145,000) – the largest cash prize offered for playing a game to date. Out of more than 200 teams who entered the competition, the eventual winners were Team Legends, whose members won $25,000 (£14,500) each.

CALL OF DUTY

PLATFORMS

SPEC

Developer:
Infinity Ward/Treyarch
Publisher:
Activision
Initial release:
Call of Duty *(2003)* 3, *PC*

GAMEPLAY

The Call of Duty *games are known for being story-driven and action-packed, allowing you to play as a number of allied characters, often as part of a close-knit team of computer-controlled squad-mates. Aside from* Call of Duty 4: Modern Warfare*, all the games have been based during World War II. Among hardcore gamers, it's currently considered to be the best war-based FPS available for next-generation consoles.*

Best-selling game of 2007

Despite only being released in November 2007, *Call of Duty 4: Modern Warfare* 4 managed to become the biggest-selling game in the world for that year, with the games publisher Activision announcing it had sold 7 million copies for PlayStation 3, PC and Xbox 360 within two months of release, a figure that had risen to 9 million copies by April 2008.

Most-played online game

Since 21 January 2008, according to unique user statistics, *Call of Duty 4* has been the most-played Xbox 360 Live game, consistently beating *Halo 3* into second place. Every day, more than 1.3 million people play *Call of Duty 4* on Xbox 360 alone. High online figures are also reported for the PlayStation 3 edition of the game, while through PC matching service Xfire, which has over 8 million users, in excess of 15 million minutes are played daily of *Call of Duty 2* and *4* combined, making it more popular than *World of Warcraft*.

First Xbox 360 million-seller

Launch title *Call of Duty 2* 1 was the first Xbox 360 game to sell a million copies in the USA (1.4 million currently). With *Call of Duty 3* selling 3 million copies and *Call of Duty 4: Modern Warfare* 3.2 million, together the games constitute the biggest-selling series on the Microsoft console.

Most paid downloads

In just nine days, there were over 1 million downloads of the *Variety Map Pack* 2, a collection of extras for *Call of Duty 4: Modern Warfare*. Released in April 2008, the expansion is the **fastest-** and **biggest-selling item ever via Xbox Live Marketplace.**

NEW RECORD UPDATED RECORD

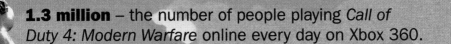

1.3 million – the number of people playing *Call of Duty 4: Modern Warfare* online every day on Xbox 360.

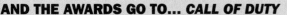

⫸ FACT

Call of Duty 2 was the first retail game to support TN Games' 3rd Space FPS Gaming Vest ⑤, a force-feedback device that you wear and that looks like a bullet-proof vest. Using patented technology, the game can trigger air pockets to simulate anything from passing bullets to nearby explosions. The game supports the HXT Helmet ⑥ also from TN Games, which uses similar technology to simulate the effect of "head shots".

▨ First officially licensed card game to be based on an FPS

Call of Duty: Real-Time Card Game ⑦ is a collectable strategy card game based on the video game series. Set in World War II, it is the first officially licensed card game to be based on a first-person shooter.

▨ First person to reach the highest experience level in Call of Duty 4

Game player Nox Ryan 2 took just a week to reach the highest experience level of *Call of Duty 4: Modern Warfare*; the player cycled through "Prestige mode" ten times to become the first player to complete 605 levels of experience.

▨ Most controversial war game action figure

In 2004, Plan B Toys withdrew from sale a controversial figure based on a Nazi "Totenkopf" soldier featured in the *Call of Duty* game, which had attracted much criticism. Plan B's website now carries the following statement: "Plan B Toys in NO WAY, SHAPE, OR FORM actively promotes ideologies, beliefs or political views that may be associated with the nature of its product."

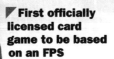

AND THE AWARDS GO TO... *CALL OF DUTY*

The *Call of Duty* series is the only video-game series to have won two Game of the Year awards from the Academy of Interactive Arts & Sciences (AIAS): first in 2004 for the original PC release, then again in 2008 for *Call of Duty 4: Modern Warfare* (Grant Collier ⑧ pictured celebrating the achievement). *Call of Duty 4* was also the biggest winner of the 2008 ceremony, taking Action Game of the Year, Console Game of the Year and the award for Outstanding Achievement in Online Game Play. With *Call of Duty 2* winning an award for Character/Story Development in 2006 and *Call of Duty 3* winning Sound Design in 2007, the series is also the only game series in AIAS history to win successive awards for each main release.

In the UK, the first ever BAFTA Video Game Award for Year's Best Release went to the original *Call of Duty* game (also picking up the award for Best PC Game). The first console release in the series, *Call of Duty: Finest Hour*, won two BAFTAs the following year.

11th annual interactive achievement

MEDAL OF HONOR

⚑ Most exclusive endorsement

Just prior to release of the original *Medal of Honor* ⑥, the Congressional Medal of Honor Society, the organization that guards the integrity of the USA's highest military award and whose members consist of all the surviving recipients of the medal, gave their full endorsement to the Spielberg-inspired game.

⚑ Best-selling WWII series

To date, more than 31 million copies of *Medal of Honor* have been sold since the first game was released in 1999, making the series the most successful to be based exclusively on World War II. It is also among the most successful shooter franchises with the first PC release, *Allied Assault* ⑧, being the second best-selling PC game for 2002.

MEDAL OF HONOR

⚙ PLATFORMS

✂ SPEC

Developer:
Dreamworks Interactive/EALA
Publisher: *EA*
Initial release:
Medal of Honor
(1999), PlayStation

⚒ GAMEPLAY

Released at a time when PC shooters held dominion over those on consoles, the first Medal of Honor *not only challenged the notion that a console shooter could offer a dramatic and fun experience, but that it could also offer a realistic one. The series has since expanded across all platforms and has chronicled many major actions of WWII, casting the player as a hero in the central role.*

①

⚑ NEW RECORD ⚐ UPDATED RECORD

> " *We're choosing a specific group of men who made the difference between victory and defeat, and we're going very deep into their experiences.*
> **Patrick Gilmore, Executive Producer**

②

⚑ Most open environments

Medal of Honor: Airborne ② was the first game of its type to allow players to begin a level wherever they chose, since it was possible to guide the player's character as he descended from the sky. This feature necessitated an AI system where enemy soldiers could make more dynamic use of their surroundings than had been previously possible.

⚑ First use of game music in an election campaign

Music from *Medal of Honor: European Assault* was used in a TV campaign to support Republican John McCain's bid to become US president in June 2008. The piece of music, called "Casualties of War", was used without the consent of composer Christopher Lennertz, who also contributed music for 2003's *Medal of Honor: Rising Sun.*

450 – the number of distinct character movements in the Artificial Intelligence (AI) of the original *Medal of Honor*, released in 1999.

MAKER OF HONOR

The original idea for *Medal of Honor* was conceived by Hollywood's most successful film-maker Steven Spielberg **3** as he was working on *Saving Private Ryan* (USA, 1998). Several games in the series, including *Medal of Honor: Frontline* **5**, feature levels recreating the Normandy landings, echoing scenes from the Academy Award-winning movie. In a further link between the games and the film, ex-US Marine Captain Dale Dye **4**, who appeared in *Saving Private Ryan* and the TV series *Band of Brothers* (itself an inspiration for *Medal of Honor: Airborne*), was recruited as the military advisor on the massively popular series of games. Dye went on to voice characters in a number of the games in the series.

▸ Most instalments in a WWII shooter series

With 12 titles across a total of 13 platforms, the *Medal of Honor* series boasts the record for the most instalments of a shooter series set entirely within World War II. Other franchises have encompassed more recent conflicts, but the *Medal of Honor* games have remained focused on the exploits of forces under US command during World War II.

▸ First Wii game to feature 32-player online play

Medal of Honor: Heroes 2 **1** was the first Wii game to feature online multiplayer game modes capable of hosting 32 players at one time. Released in November 2007, *Heroes 2* was also announced by Nintendo as the first third-party game to support the Wii Zapper, a hardware accessory that transforms the Wii Remote and Nunchuk into a lightgun.

▸ Largest Medal of Honor fansite

Since January 2002, Planet Medal of Honor is the most popular fansite for the *Medal of Honor* series, ranking close to the official EA site in terms of visitors, with between 1 million and 1.5 million US hits per month. In January 2007, it registered more monthly visitors than EA's site.

👍 IF YOU LIKE THIS...

... then try *Call of Duty: World at War*, which sees the long-running series return to its World War II roots.

ℹ TRIVIA

▸ Although 464 Medals of Honor **9** were awarded to World War II combatants, none of the game's characters are named after real medal recipients. In fact, only the second game in the series, *Medal of Honor: Underground*, features a central character whose exploits are based on those of a real person: Helene Deschamps, a member of the French Resistance during World War II, who was also a consultant for the game.

▸ *Medal of Honor* was parodied in episode 13 of *The Simpsons Game* **7**. The stage, called Medal of Homer, has you playing as Bart and Homer, collecting white flags from a French town and then rescuing stolen paintings from a warship.

❓ GWR QUIZ

Q7. Music from *Medal of Honor: European Assault* was used in a 2008 TV campaign supporting which US presidential candidate?

METAL GEAR

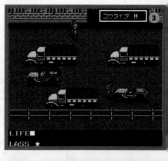

PLATFORMS

PC
XBOX 360
PS1
XBOX
PS2
X
PS3
DS
PSP
GAME BOY ADVANCE
Wii

SPEC

Developer:
Konami
Publisher:
Konami
Initial release:
Metal Gear *(1987),*
MSX2 home computer

GAMEPLAY

*Tactical espionage
action, as covert agent
Solid Snake uses
guile and gadgets
to infiltrate enemy
strongholds. His target:
enormous mechanized
weapons platforms
known as Metal Gears.*

First handheld
Metal Gear game

The first handheld *Metal Gear* title
was *Metal Gear: Ghost Babel* ①
for the Nintendo Game Boy Color,
released in April 2000 in Japan
and USA (it was released in the
United States under the title *Metal
Gear Solid*). The gameplay is a mix
of *Metal Gear Solid* and slightly
updated *Metal Gear 2: Solid Snake*
and is set seven years after the
events of *Metal Gear*.

First stealth video game

Created by Japanese designer
Hideo Kojima, *Metal Gear* ③ was
the first video game to fully utilize
stealth as part of the gameplay.
Although earlier adventure games
had used elements of stealth,
such as hiding and disguises,
Metal Gear was the first game
to concentrate solely on these
elements, effectively creating
the "stealth game" sub-genre.

Most bosses
in a Metal Gear game

The *Metal Gear* game with the
most bosses is *Metal Gear 2:
Solid Snake* ② in which there are
11 deadly encounters with major
enemies. These enemies, in order
of appearance, are: Black Ninja,
Running Man, Hind D, Red Blaster,
Four Horsemen, Jungle Evil, Night
Fright, Dr Drago Pettrovich Madnar,
Metal Gear D, Gray Fox and
Big Boss.

Best-selling stealth game

Until the release of *Grand Theft Auto*
games *Vice City* and *San Andreas*,
MGS2: Sons of Liberty was the
fastest-selling game on the PS2 in
the UK, having sold over 200,000
units in its first weekend.
It remains the biggest
seller in the stealth
sub-genre and the
sixth best-selling
game ever on the
PlayStation 2 with
worldwide sales of
over 7 million units.

IF YOU LIKE THIS...

... then you won't want to be left in
the dark when it comes to the *Splinter
Cell* series. Head to p.52 for a peek.

Most innovative use
of a video-game controller

During *Metal Gear Solid*, the
character Psycho Mantis addresses
the player directly, commenting on
the games saved on their memory
card and telling them to drop the
controller, which then "rumbles"
violently. To defeat Psycho Mantis
in battle, the player must break his
"psychic connection" by unplugging
the controller and reconnecting it to
the second socket on the console.

First turn-based
Metal Gear title

Metal Gear Ac!d ④
upset some Metal Gear
fans in 2004 when
it became

the first
game in the
series to veer away from
the traditional stealth-action
gameplay in favour of turn-based
strategy. While this radical change
in gameplay for what was also the
**first Metal Gear game on the
PSP** split opinion among *Metal
Gear* fans, it was still popular
enough to spawn a sequel.

1 hr 55 min 31 sec – the **fastest time to complete *Metal Gear Solid***, set by Rodrigo Lopes (Brazil) on 30 June 2000 and confirmed by record adjudicators at Twin Galaxies.

> *I am thinking of a totally new concept right now in the action-game genre. I don't know if it will be as popular as Metal Gear, but I hope I'll win another Guinness World Record award for it.*
> **Hideo Kojima [8], creator of Metal Gear Solid**

▼ **NEW RECORD**   ▽ **UPDATED RECORD**

▼ First PSP game to make use of Wi-Fi hotspots

Metal Gear Solid: Portable Ops [10] made imaginative use of the PSP's Wi-Fi capabilities. By using the built-in Wi-Fi (or by purchasing the GPS receiver [9] separately), players could download new bonus features including new characters that could be recruited as soldiers.

First interactive digital graphic novel for the PSP

Released on 13 June 2006 in the USA, *Metal Gear Solid: Digital Graphic Novel* is the first interactive comic for the PSP. Made by Kojima Productions, a company headed by *Metal Gear* creator Hideo Kojima, the graphic novel features character back-stories, the art of Ashley Wood and an original soundtrack. The aim of the digital novel is to bring to life the *Metal Gear Solid* comics produced by IDW publishing in a "digitalized, re-edited and recomposed cinematic presentation".

▼ First stereoscopic stealth game

Metal Gear Ac!d 2 is the first stealth game to use the "Solid Eye" [7], an add-on device for the PSP that transforms the game into a stereoscopic experience. In reality, the gizmo is less impressive than it sounds as it is actually a folding cardboard box with specialized lenses that fit over the PSP's screen to create a 3D image.

▪▪▶ **FACT**

Metal Gear Solid, released in 1998, benefited from a massive promotional push by publishers Konami. Costs for the launch, which included television and print advertising and an estimated 12 million demos distributed, cost in the region of $8 million (£4.85 million). The game shipped over 5.5 million copies worldwide.

ℹ TRIVIA

> Released worldwide on 12 June 2008, *Metal Gear Solid 4* [5] achieved impressive first-day sales [6] of 1.3 million units, according to VGChartz. Over 350,000 units of the latest game in Hideo Kojima's famous series were sold in Japan and over 400,000 units sold in the Americas.

> A movie based on the *Metal Gear Solid* series is in production and mooted to be released in 2009. Initial reports suggested that David Hayter, who voices Solid Snake in the video games and is also an acclaimed writer of movie adaptations, was penning the script for the film, but this was denied by sources close to Konami, the game's developer. This didn't deter Hayter's fans, however, who put together an online petition to try and persuade the film's producers to allow Hayter to write the script. At the last count, the petition had over 5,000 signatures.

TOM CLANCY

PLATFORMS

SPEC

Developer:
Ubisoft/Red Storm
Entertainment
Publisher:
Ubisoft
Initial release:
Tom Clancy's Rainbow
Six (1998), PC

GAMEPLAY

It was with the release of Tom Clancy's Rainbow Six 3 *in 1998 that Clancy's name became rooted with squad-level tactical action games, where the player plans, directs and controls a squad of combat operatives against international criminals. The Rainbow Six series spawned the overtly military Ghost Recon series* 2 , 7 *and then the stealth-infused Splinter Cell, all of which have evolved into multi-million-selling franchises.*

◢ Most successful writer in the gaming industry

Tom Clancy-branded games have sold more than 55 million units for publisher Ubisoft since 1998, making the novelist the most successful living author to be associated with the gaming industry. Such is the draw of the Tom Clancy name that Ubisoft paid an undisclosed amount to use his name exclusively, without having to pay future royalties to the author.

Largest mobile-gaming launch

Mobile-phone versions of *Tom Clancy's Splinter Cell Pandora Tomorrow* were launched on an unprecedented 48 different handsets in over 30 countries in 2006, making this the largest mobile-gaming launch. It also remains the UK's highest-rated shoot-'em-up in mobile gaming history, scoring over 90% in the majority of reviews.

Fastest Splinter Cell speedruns

Oskar Lundquist completed *Tom Clancy's Splinter Cell* 1 in 1 hr 21 min 45 sec on 27 August 2006. The fastest time for *Tom Clancy's Splinter*

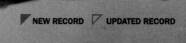

Cell Pandora Tomorrow is held by Wesley Corron, who blazed through normal difficulty in 1 hr 11 min 45 sec on 11 December 2004. The best completion time for *Tom Clancy's Splinter Cell Chaos Theory* is just 1 hr 16 min 34 sec by Mathew Thompson on 30 August 2006. This record is made even more impressive by the fact that Mathew played the game on the "expert" difficulty setting.

First game to use dynamic lighting technology on PS2

Tom Clancy's Splinter Cell Pandora Tomorrow was the first PlayStation 2 game to use moving dynamic lighting to create realistic shadows. This came in the form of a torch picking out details in the darkness.

◢ **NEW RECORD** ◺ **UPDATED RECORD**

▮▮▶ FACT

Tom Clancy games can help you fall in love and start a family – kind of. One unnamed couple met on Xbox Live while playing *Tom Clancy's Rainbow Six: Lockdown*. The couple disliked each other at first, but love soon blossomed and on 24 September 2007, the couple fired off their first child.

500% – the increase in activity on the GCHQ "Careers in British Intelligence" recruitment website due to in-game advertising in Tom Clancy titles *Splinter Cell: Double Agent* and *Rainbow Six: Vegas*.

> *Fighting wars is not so much about killing people as it is about finding things out. The more you know, the more likely you are to win a battle.*
> **Tom Clancy,**
> **author and war game guru**

Best-selling Tom Clancy game

The most successful commercial release of a Tom Clancy game is the original Xbox version of *Tom Clancy's Splinter Cell*, released in 2002. The game has currently sold 2.93 million units worldwide.

Best-selling squad-shooter

Originally released in 1998, *Tom Clancy's Rainbow Six* continues to outperform every other title in the squad-shooter genre. As of July 2008, the series has sold more than 20 million units on all platforms.

Longest continuous play of a first-person shooter

At the UK's largest multiplayer gaming event, I33, on 22 March 2008, all-girl gaming team the Frag Dolls ⑧ continuously played the Xbox 360 version of *Tom Clancy's Rainbow Six: Vegas 2* for 24 hr 4 min, marking the longest recorded session playing a first-person shooter. The team's American counterparts, the US Frag Dolls, are also recordbreakers, being the **first all-girl winners of a pro-gaming tournament**, coming first in a CPL *Rainbow Six: Vegas* competition in Dallas, USA, in December 2006.

First Tom Clancy game

The first game to bear the Tom Clancy name was *The Hunt For Red October* ⑥, released in 1987. A second, more arcade-orientated game with the same name came out in 1990 to coincide with the *Red October* movie launch that same year.

WAR GAMES ROUND-UP

👍 IF YOU LIKE THIS...

... then you should plan a visit to p.176 for all the best strategy and simulation records at a glance.

The game was the sixth in the *Delta Force* series and was inspired, like the unrelated book and film of similar names, by the events and aftermath of Operation Gothic Serpent in Somalia in 1993.

▌ Most players online at one time in a FPS war game
Game: *PlanetSide*
Publisher: Sony
In the online first-person shooter (FPS) *PlanetSide* ❺, players take the role of a soldier fighting for one of three factions seeking domination of the planet Auraxis. On 23 March 2003, a record 6,400 players logged on to the Emerald server for a mega-battle for control of the planet.

▌ Largest game area for a tactical shooter
Game: *Armed Assault*
Publisher: 505 Games
The fictional island of Sahrani in *Armed Assault* ❷ is the largest continuous land area to be created in a tactical shooter. At 400 km² (154 miles²), the island, which is divided into two hostile nations, can be fought over in its entirety by playing the multiplayer warfare game mode.

▌ Most popular online PS2 war game series
Game: *SOCOM: US Navy SEALs*
Publisher: Sony
Selling in excess of 8 million copies, the *SOCOM* ❶ (Special Operations Command) series of third-person military action games are the most popular online titles ever released for PlayStation 2. The *SOCOM* games focus on the exploits of a Navy SEAL team on missions around the world.

▌ First use of dynamic in-game advertising (PC)
Game: *SWAT 4*
Publisher: Sierra
The v1.1 update for *SWAT 4* ❼ in June 2005 featured dynamic in-game advertising for the first time in a PC game. Instead of being written into the game code before its release, dynamic advertising enables advertisers to insert new adverts into the game, both in the form of posters and other elements, on an ongoing basis.

▌ Most Xbox players online
Game: *Delta Force: Black Hawk Down*
Publisher: Novalogic
Delta Force: Black Hawk Down ❹ was the first Xbox game to allow up to 50 players per live session.

THE VIRTUAL BATTLEFIELD DOES EXIST

$5 million – the amount the US Army paid game developer Pandemic Studios for developing *Full Spectrum Warrior*.

First FPS to support more than 100 online players
Game: *Joint Operations: Typhoon Rising*
Publisher: Novalogic
In June 2004, *Joint Operations: Typhoon Rising* **10**, an online FPS game set in the near future and featuring a coalition of armies fighting against separatist forces in Indonesia, was the first FPS to allow for 150 players in a single game map in June 2004.

First game modified for use in army troop training
Game: *Bradley Trainer*
Publisher: Atari
On 2 June 1980, Atari's *Battlezone* featured the first truly 3D battlefield environment and impressed the United States Armed Forces so

▶ NEW RECORD ▷ UPDATED RECORD

much they commissioned Atari to build specially-modified versions for possible use in training gunners on tanks. Only two prototypes were produced and it remains uncertain if they were ever used in a training environment.

First massively multiplayer online war game
Game: *WWII Online: Blitzkrieg*
Publisher: Strategy First
In June 2001, servers went online capable of accommodating thousands of players across a massive scale map of Europe, either on foot, in vehicles or in the air, making *WWII Online: Blitzkrieg* **6** the first massively multiplayer online war game.

First "terrorist" video game
Game: *Special Force*
Publisher: Hezbollah
First published in 2003 by a group that has been declared a terrorist organization by some Western governments, *Special Force* **8** is a controversial shooter that tasks players with eliminating soldiers of the Israeli Defence Force. Despite being described by Israeli Foreign Ministry spokesman Ron Prosor as "part of an educational process which is preventing any chance of real peace," *Special Force* proved popular in Lebanon and Syria, selling out of all 8,000 copies of its intial run in a week. The game's success also led to the creation of *Special Force II*, a sequel set during the 2006 Lebanon war.

ⓘ TRIVIA

> With free updates based on events that may only be weeks old, *Kuma/War* **9** is a free tactical war game that provides players with missions based on current conflicts. Every mission available for the game – there are now more than 100 – is based on accounts of combat operations in theatres of engagement such as Afghanistan and Iraq.

> On 5 September 2008, EA gave away £20,000 of fuel in London, UK, to promote *Mercenaries 2: World in Flames*. Traffic congestion caused by the giveaway created misery for residents and a local politician reproached the stunt as "completely irresponsible and downright dangerous".

> Classic war game *Ikari Warriors* was the first run-and-gun game to feature limited ammunition. Players could find themselves without bullets deep in enemy territory unless they were careful with their resources.

POINT 'N' CLICK ADVENTURES

Sam & Max – the canine detective and his rabbit sidekick – have featured in two series of episodic games, spawning 11 different titles, the **most games in an episodic point 'n' click series**.

CONTENTS

POINT 'N' CLICK GAMES

WITH THEIR TESTING PUZZLES AND SPELL-BINDING STORIES, POINT 'N' CLICK GAMES EVOLVED FROM EARLY TEXT-BASED ADVENTURE GAMES TO BECOME THE SEDATE ALTERNATIVE TO FRANTIC BUTTON-BASHING SHOOT 'EM UPS.

EXPERT

David Crookes began writing about computers in 1993 for *Amstrad Action*. He has been news editor of *N-Revolution* and has written for many publications including the multi-award-winning *GamesTM*, *Retro Gamer* and *X360*.

OVERVIEW

A point 'n' click adventure game is story-heavy, relying on narrative rather than reflexes for game play. The player is immersed in the game environment, investigating, solving puzzles and interacting with game characters. This is done by moving a cursor around the screen, pointing at an object or character and clicking to enable an action to be carried out.

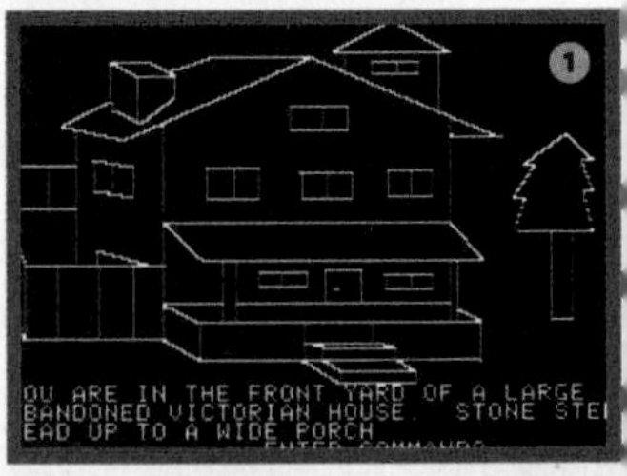

Although you can chart the history of point 'n' click adventure games back to 1984, when *Enchanted Scepters* came on to the scene as the **first point 'n' click adventure game**, the roots of the genre stretch back to the text-heavy adventure games of the 1970s.

Colossal Cave Adventure (*ADVENT*), the **first text adventure game**, was created in 1975 for the PDP-10 computer. With puzzles, an element of fantasy and a command system, it introduced much of the groundwork from which point 'n' click adventures drew their inspiration.

Players would read a description of their location, then choose what to do next by typing commands such as "enter building" or "go north". But as technology advanced, some adventure games began to incorporate professionally created graphics, with *Mystery House* (1) on the Apple II becoming the **first text adventure game with graphics** in 1980.

The rise of the ZX Spectrum in the early-to-mid-1980s helped build the foundations of point 'n' click adventures with successful graphic-text adventure releases such as *The Hobbit*. The P'n'C genre's defining moment came in 1984 with Silicon Beach's *Enchanted Scepters* for the Macintosh. In this adventure game, players wandered from screen to screen, clicking on objects and characters in order to interact with them, and choosing options ("Look", "Rest") from drop-down menus.

Enchanted Scepters' World Builder engine failed to generate a significant head of steam, however, and the next wave of popular P'n'C titles to emerge – among them *King's Quest* (4), *Police Quest*, *Space Quest* and *Leisure Suit Larry* – probably owe more to *Mystery House*.

Then, in 1987, Lucasfilm Games launched *Maniac Mansion*. It used SCUMM (Script Creation Utility for Maniac Mansion), a point 'n' click system created by Ron Gilbert that was inspired by the MacVenture games, *Déjà Vu* and *Uninvited*. Lucasfilm Games – later to become known as LucasArts – went on to revolutionize adventure games. Titles such as *The Secret of Monkey Island* did away with text parsing (by allowing your click on a verb such as "open" then click on a door). Games such as *Day of the Tentacle* (2) and *Sam & Max Hit the Road* in 1993 and later, in 1998, *Grim Fandango*, created a golden age for point 'n' clicks.

TIMELINE

1975 The text-only game *Colossal Cave Adventure* (*ADVENT*) is created by programmer William Crowther on the PDP-10.

1980 *Mystery House*, the **first adventure game to use graphics**, is released for the Apple II.

1984 *King's Quest* introduces an on-screen walking character.

1985 *Déjà Vu* is released on the Mac.

1987: *Maniac Mansion* and *Leisure Suit Larry in the Land of the Lounge Lizards* are released.

1990 *The Secret of Monkey Island* swashbuckles on to the scene and *Déjà Vu* (5) is ported to the NES.

200+ – the number of graphical scenes with interactive elements such as doors and characters in *Enchanted Scepters*, the **first genuine point 'n' click adventure game**.

packed titles. One of the last of the "old-school" adventures to receive critical acclaim was *The Longest Journey* ❾ in 1997 – and yet even that was criticized for its lack of action; a perfect example of a good game released in the wrong era. Today, however, they are making a comeback and the genre is once again becoming healthy with the Nintendo DS flying the flag.

i TRIVIA

> The original *Maniac Mansion* game could be played, pixel-perfect, on a computer inside the bedroom of one of the characters in the game's 1993 sequel *Maniac Mansion: the Day of the Tentacle*, the first time such a game-in-a-game facility had been offered.

They also eased the way for other games to enter the market: *Myst* in 1993 was a revelation and Revolution Software's *Broken Sword* ❼ series, which began in 1996, also proved hugely popular.

Classic literature, such as H.P. Lovecraft's 1926 short story *Call of Cthulhu,* lent itself perfectly to the genre, while titles such as *Shadow of the Comet* and *Prisoner of Ice* portrayed a darker, edgier slant.

Point 'n' click games spent some years in the wilderness following the 1990s, due mainly to changing trends among gamers with a desire for faster, more action-

1993	1998	2005	2007
Following cameos in *Monkey Island*, Sam & Max get their own game: *Sam & Max Hit the Road*.	LucasArts abandons the SCUMM engine for the 3D system GrimE in *Grim Fandango* ❿ .	*Phoenix Wright: Ace Attorney* ❸ comes out for the DS.	*Zack & Wiki: Quest for Barbaros' Treasure* ❽ hits the Wii.
1996: *Broken Sword* is released.		**2006:** The ▷ **first successful episodic point 'n' click game**, *Sam & Max: Season One*, is released.	**2008:** *Jack Keane* ❻ revitalizes the point 'n' click genre.

DISCWORLD

PLATFORMS

PC | 360 | PS1 | XBOX | PS2 | DS | PS3 | GBA | PSP | Wii

SPEC

Developer:
Teeny Weeny Games and Perfect 10 Productions
Publisher:
Psygnosis
Initial release:
Discworld *(1986), PC*

GAMEPLAY

Packed with wizards and dragons, Discworld *is based on the fantasy book series by UK author Terry Pratchett. It is set in a flat world balanced on the backs of four elephants, which themselves are standing on the back of a giant turtle.*

Despite high levels of surrealism, the gameplay for Discworld, Discworld II *and* Discworld Noir *will be very familiar to point 'n' click adventure gamers – earlier games in the series are more straighforward graphic adventure games.*

1

2

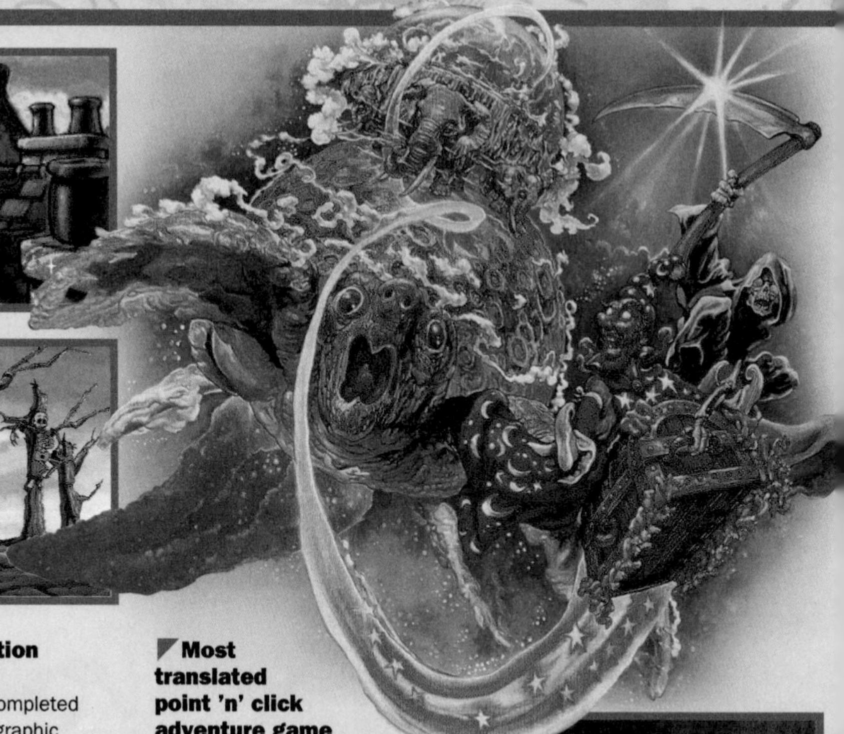

Fastest completion of Discworld

Nicko! from Belgium completed the first *Discworld* (1) graphic adventure in 1 hr 52 min 3 sec on 15 March 2007. He played it in a single session, according to adventure-speedruns.com, which also recorded Nicko! speed-running through *Discworld II: Missing Presumed...!?* (2) in 35 min 50 sec. He completed the sequel – also in a single, unbroken attempt – on 20 March 2007.

TRIVIA

Look out for film noir references in *Discworld Noir*, such as this classic inspired by the Bogart and Bacall movie *To Have and Have Not*: "You know how to howl don't you, Lewton? You just pull your jaws apart and blow."

Most translated point 'n' click adventure game

The first *Discworld* game was available in 11 languages, making it the point 'n' click game with the most translations from English. *Discworld* can be played in English, Dutch, Hebrew, Japanese, Korean, French, German, Italian, Spanish, Polish and Portuguese.

First 3D game based on the Discworld series

Discworld Noir (3) was the first 3D game based on the *Discworld* series. It parodies the film noir genre, one of only two point 'n' click games to do so – *Grim Fandango* being the other. It was released on the PC and PS in 1999.

3

Most faithful Discworld game

The Colour of Magic (11) game is the only *Discworld* game to be adapted directly from one of Terry Pratchett's novels. Taking the name of the book, it was released in 1986 for the Spectrum,

COMEDY ACTORS

4

5

6

7

8

9

10

The *Discworld* series has drawn on the talents of numerous actors and actresses with extensive experience of British comedy. Former *Monty Python* star Eric Idle (4) voiced Rincewind in *Discworld* while Tony Robinson (5), who played Baldrick in *Blackadder*, voiced many of the others along with ex-*Doctor Who* and *Worzel Gummidge* actor Jon Pertwee (6). Comedian Rob Brydon (7) and former *Spitting Image* impressionist Kate Robbins (8) voiced the rest. In *Discworld II: Missing Presumed...!?*, Idle continued to voice Rinceworld, with Brydon and Robbins joined by *Young Ones* actor Nigel Planer (9) for the rest. In *Discworld Noir*, Brydon, Robbins and Planer provided most of the characters and were joined by *Red Dwarf* actor Robert Llewellyn (10).

INTERVIEW WITH... PAUL KIDD

Paul Kidd wrote the scripts for *Discworld* and *Discworld II: Missing Presumed...!?.*

How did you get involved with the *Discworld* games?
I used to go to various sci-fi conventions across the world and I'd often end up chatting with Terry Pratchett. I also knew Gregg Barnett, who had set up a developer called Perfect 10 and he knew that I had contact with Terry. As a novelist, I could write dialogue swiftly and in the amounts required, so Gregg asked me to handle all the scripting for the game.

What was Terry Pratchett's contribution to the games?
The scriptwriting was all mine rather than Terry's. I have to say that in all the time I worked on both games, I never saw him or spoke to him. Terry gave the OK to the overall game design but he had his own work cut out for him just keeping up his output of the novels. So the humour you see in the first two games is mine rather than Terry's.

What elements are essential for a *Discworld* game?
A sense of humour and a sense of fun. I had to be able to write 80,000 words of comedy dialogue, but for me, writing for Eric Idle, Tony Robinson and Jon Pertwee was a thrill.

THE COLOUR OF MAGIC **11**

> *"My involvement was very high with the first game, and when I realized the guys knew what they were doing, I let them get on with it.*
> **Terry Pratchett, creator of Discworld**

▼ **NEW RECORD** ▽ **UPDATED RECORD**

ℹ TRIVIA

> The PC version of *Discworld* was heavily bugged and riddled with graphic and sound glitches. Although patches were released, publisher Psygnosis eventually released a Director's Cut version.

> Although some games today make liberal use of expletives, in the mid-90s it was relatively rare. So upon discovering an easter egg in *Discworld*, some players were shocked to hear Rincewind saying he "wants to be be first person in games to say f***." However, the word had been used a number of times in *Gabriel Knight: Sins of the Fathers* in 1993.

❓ GWR QUIZ

Q8. Which Monty Python actor was the voice of Rincewind in *Discworld*?

Commodore 64 and Amstrad CPC, three years after the book was published. Unlike other *Discworld* games, *The Colour of Magic* was a text-only adventure. (An action game inspired by the novel was released for mobile phones in 2006.)

▸ FACT

The text-only *Discworld MUD* (multi-user dungeon) allows for the creation of player-run clubs and families, of which there are at least 553. Each club is funded and run by the players themselves, and each group has its own set of aims and objectives. Some are used as social clubs, while others provide in-game services.

▸ TERRY PRATCHETT: CREATIVE GENIUS AND GAMER

Sci-fi and fantasy writer Terry Pratchett **12** has attracted a massive cult following since he published his first novel, *The Carpet People*, in 1971. Much of his appeal has centred around Discworld, with *The Colour of Magic*, published in 1983, becoming the first of many novels set in his strange, flat world.

Pratchett is keen to protect the Discworld franchise and so during production of the video games he worked with the developers on each of the titles, and also made a cameo appearance in a crowd scene at the end of the first game. Such was his close involvement with *Discworld Noir*, the developers jokingly credited him in the game... for causing far too much interference!

The author is a huge fan of video games and an avid PC gamer. He told *PC Zone* magazine that he enjoyed playing "anything that's intelligent and has some depth" including *Half Life 2, Far Cry, Call Of Duty, Thief!* and *The Elder Scrolls IV: Oblivion*. Pratchett began gaming with a Sinclair ZX81. He has written novels on an Amstrad CPC 464, which he replaced with a PC, and he has contributed to the Usenet newsgroup alt.fan.pratchett since 1992.

12

LEISURE SUIT LARRY

Most popular hint book

According to publisher Sierra On-Line and creator Al Lowe, more hint books were sold for *Leisure Suit Larry In The Land Of The Lounge Lizards* 5 than copies of the actual game itself. This is believed to be due to the large number of pirated copies made of the game following its release in 1987. In the first year, Al Lowe has claimed "millions" of books were sold yet only 250,000 copies of the game had been bought in that time.

First adult graphic adventure

The seedy nature of the series was obvious from the start and *Leisure Suit Larry In The Land Of The Lounge Lizards* was the first graphic adventure aimed at an adult audience. For this reason, the game had an age-verification system that asked gamers a series of (USA-centric) multiple-choice questions to which the developers thought only adults would know the answers.

Longest running graphical adventure series

The *Leisure Suit Larry* series spans 21 years. The first game was *Leisure Suit Larry In The*
Land Of The Lounge Lizards in 1987, with the latest, *Leisure Suit Larry: Box Office Bust* 6, slated for release in 2008 on various platforms. There would have been more games in the series but the scheduled eighth title, *Lust In Space*, was cancelled.

Biggest adventure game "sleeper hit"

For a game about encouraging women into bed, it is fitting that *Leisure Suit Larry In The Land Of The Lounge Lizards* is the biggest "sleeper" hit in adventure gaming history. It sold just 2,000 copies in the first month – the worst sales start of any Sierra game ever – but, over the first year, went on to sell 250,000 copies.

PLATFORMS

PC
PS1
PS2
PS3
PSP
360
XBOX
DS
GBA
Wii

SPEC

Developer:
Sierra On-Line
Publisher:
Sierra On-Line
Initial release:
Leisure Suit Larry In The Land Of The Lounge Lizards (1987), PC

GAMEPLAY

Larry Laffer is in his 40s and out to attract the attentions of young women, which sees him visiting the world's top hotels and casinos among many other locations. Despite the raunchy content, there is much tongue-in-cheek humour and some amusing scenarios.

£0 – the advertising budget for *Leisure Suit Larry In The Land Of The Lounge Lizards*. Sierra wasn't prepared to commit any money as it was unsure how the game would be received.

INTERVIEW WITH... AL LOWE

Al Lowe was the lead programmer on *King's Quest III* and *Police Quest I* in 1986 but is best known for starting the *Leisure Suit Larry* series of games. Now retired, Lowe refers to himself as the "world's oldest computer games designer". Lowe worked for Sierra On-Line for 16 years. He believes it is a record for the longest time spent designing games for one software company.

Why do you think the Larry series became so popular?
Every guy who played it had this belief that no matter how bad he was, he was better than Larry. Funnily enough, the game was also popular with women – probably because many could relate to dating jerks like that.

How did you take the controversy?
You know, I never got a lawsuit but we did get mentioned in the papers. Gaming was so juvenile at the time that anything mature stood out.

Were you surprised it did well?
Considering there was no advertising and no marketing for the game, yes. I remember the charts after 54 weeks when Larry was still in the top 10... and had actually climbed.

👍 IF YOU LIKE THIS...

...then keep your eyes peeled for the the upcoming release of *Box Office Bust* **6**, the latest addition to the *Leisure Suit Larry* franchise, due out on PC, Xbox 360 and PlayStation 3.

ℹ TRIVIA

> Al Lowe designed and wrote the original *Leisure Suit Larry* game and the next five sequels, ending with *Leisure Suit Larry 7: Love for Sail* **1**. He did not work on *Leisure Suit Larry: Magna cum Laude* **7** in 2004, later saying he was happy to see Larry was still alive but felt the character was "being tortured". He added: "Had I got involved, I would have wanted to change almost everything."

> The first few *Leisure Suit Larry* games **3** are all about the pursuit of women and featured 40-something Larry Laffer. However, more recent games have focused on Laffer's nephew Larry Lovage, a college student who shares his uncle's love of girls.

> *Leisure Suit Larry: Pocket Party* was to be the first handheld game to use cell-shading, a technique that makes graphics look hand-drawn and cartoon-like. Unfortunately, although announced in 2004 for Nokia's N-Gage, the game was later cancelled.

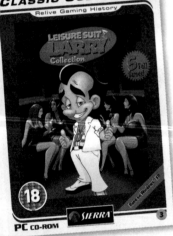

CLASSIC COLLECTION
Relive Gaming History

LEISURE SUIT LARRY Collection
5 full games!

18
PC CD-ROM   SIERRA   **3**

▌ **NEW RECORD**   ▷ **UPDATED RECORD**

▌ Fastest completion of Leisure Suit Larry 6

The fastest completion of *Leisure Suit Larry 6: Shape Up or Slip Out!* **4** was accomplished on 11 November 2007. "Spor" played the game without saves as a single segment in 24 min 2 sec, as verified by adventure-speedruns.com

▌ First graphic adventure to allow the player to switch roles

Leisure Suit Larry 3: Passionate Patti in Pursuit of the Pulsating Pectorals (1983) allowed players to see the story from another point of view. It was the first Sierra adventure game to permit this, letting gamers toggle between Larry and Passionate Patti, a girl searching for her dream man.

MONKEY ISLAND

⇄ GAMEPLAY

You control wannabe pirate Guybrush Threepwood, who begins the series of games washed up on the Caribbean island of Mêlée. The island's governor, Elaine Marley, has been kidnapped and taken to Monkey Island by ghost pirate LeChuck, and your task, using problem solving and and careful exploration, is to rescue her. Three sequels followed, each full of humour and in-jokes.

▸ First point 'n' click game to use character scaling

The Secret of Monkey Island was the first point 'n' click game to use a technique called character scaling ②. This allows a sprite – an image or animation that usually represents a character, for example the pirate Guybrush Threepwood – to appear nearer to or farther away from the player. The programmers "scaled" the sprite (that is, made it bigger or smaller), thus giving a crude feeling of perspective.

▸ First point 'n' click game to feature a full soundtrack

The Secret of Monkey Island ① was the first point 'n' click game to have a full soundtrack with different tunes tailored to specific parts of the game. Michael Land wrote the music and was the only musician to have a permanent job at LucasArts. The sequel, *Monkey Island 2: LeChuck's Revenge* ③,

went further and was the ▸ **first game to use LucasArts' iMUSE sound system**, which allowed music to be synchronized with the on-screen action. This heralded a new era of audio in gaming and truly brought the adventures of Guybrush Ulysses Marley-Threepwood to life.

▸ First point 'n' click game to offer the player two levels of puzzle difficulty

Monkey Island 2: LeChuck's Revenge allowed the player to work through the game in one of two difficulty modes. Gamers could play the regular game or choose the easier version that bypassed many of the puzzles.

▸ Easiest point 'n' click adventure to complete

The Secret of Monkey Island can be completed without even playing the game. All the player has to do is press CTRL-W on the computer keyboard to see the words "You Win" and the end credit sequence.

▸ Fastest completion time for The Secret of Monkey Island

One gamer known only as "Mike" ran through the first *Monkey Island* game in 39 min 12 sec as a multi-segment – i.e., saving his progress after each chapter. His time was verified by adventure-speedruns.com.

▸ Most controversial ending of a point 'n' click adventure

The surreal ending of *Monkey Island 2: Le Chuck's Revenge* massively split opinion, and the debate still rages today over whether it is the most frustrating or best ending ever created. At the end of the game, LeChuck casts a spell on Guybrush, convincing

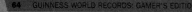

INTERVIEW WITH... RON GILBERT

Ron Gilbert designed *The Secret of Monkey Island* as well as *Monkey Island 2: LeChuck's Revenge* and *Maniac Mansion*. We caught up with him.

How did you come up with the ideas for the puzzles and humour in *The Secret of Monkey Island*?
There was lots of brainstorming and sitting around laughing and having fun. There is no other way to do it.

What are you most proud of with the *Monkey Island* series?
The puzzle structure. I spent a lot of time figuring out the "rules" for adventures before starting the game and then I adhered to them. I wanted a clear end objective with sub-goals and incremental rewards. I didn't want to create an interactive movie, that's for sure.

You weren't involved with the third and fourth *Monkey Island* games. What did you think of them?
I liked the third game (*The Curse of Monkey Island*) quite a bit. I thought the spirit and humour of the first two was captured very well.

I was not a big fan of the fourth, *Escape from Monkey Island* .

Would you be interested in producing a fifth game?
Yes, if I had the opportunity, I would love to make another.

What is the secret of *Monkey Island*?
Pi.

▐ FACT

One joke in *The Secret of Monkey Island* had a lot of people stumped – literally. It involved a tree stump in a forest that, upon examining, was found to be hollow and lead to a maze of caverns. When climbing into the stump, the game asked for a range of randomly numbered discs. The joke resulted in LucasArts being inundated with calls from gamers who believed they were missing discs. The joke was removed from the CD version of the game but was reused in the sequel.

him that LeChuck was not only his brother but that they were both children in an amusement park and that they had to meet their parents. LeChuck turns towards the screen, his eyes glowing, and Elaine is shown pondering Guybrush's whereabouts. This prompted a flood of angry mail to magazines and LucasArts at the time from a number of disappointed fans of the series.

▐ NEW RECORD
▽ UPDATED RECORD

▐ FIRST GRAPHIC ADVENTURE TO BECOME A STAGE PLAY

A live stage version of *The Secret of Monkey Island* was performed at Hammond High School in Columbia, Maryland, USA, between 21 and 29 May 2005. The production was organized by US student Chris Heady ⑤, a fan of the *Monkey Island* series, after he was granted permission from LucasArts.

MYST

⚙ PLATFORMS

✗ SPEC

Developer:
Cyan Worlds
Publisher:
Brøderbund
Initial release:
Myst (1993), Apple

⇄ GAMEPLAY

Although critics claim it is little more than an interactive slideshow, Myst's lush graphics proved to be a catalyst not just for people to buy the game but for the uptake of CD-ROMs in general. This first-person journey allows the player to explore the seemingly deserted Myst Island. Some players actually reported feeling lonely.

SIMPSONS IN THE MYST OF TIME

In *The Simpsons' Treehouse of Horror VI* ③, Homer Simpson appears in 3D in the Homer³ segment and walks past the library from *Myst* as music from the game plays in the background.

⚑ Best-selling graphic adventure

Released in 1993, *Myst* shot to No.1 in the PC and Apple Mac charts and continued to sell well for years. Even during the week ending 11 January 1998, some five years after it had been released, NPD Market Tracking said the game had sold more than any other title – including blockbusters *Quake II* and *Tomb Raider II*. *Myst* sold 6 million copies, the sequel *Riven* shifted 2 million and the series as a whole (*Myst I, II, III* ⑥, *IV, V, Riven* and *URU*) has sold more than 12 million. It was the best-selling computer game of all time until overtaken in 2002 by *The Sims*.

⚑ **NEW RECORD**   ⚐ **UPDATED RECORD**

⚑ Fastest-selling point 'n' click sequel

Riven ②, the sequel to *Myst*, became the top-selling game of 1997, even though it was only released on 29 October of that year. It sold almost 1.5 million copies in three months, making it the fastest-selling point 'n' click sequel ever. *Riven*'s success was recognized at the BAFTA's first Interactive Entertainment Awards in 1998, where it had the most nominations of any media: Sound, Moving Images and Design.

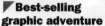

Fastest completion time for *Myst*

Student Dylan Guptill (USA) of South Berwick, Maine, USA, completed *Myst* in 3 min 18 sec on 22 August 2007.

Least violent adventure game

Myst features almost no dialogue, no enemies, no time limit and no way of dying, making it the least violent adventure game of all time. Many people attribute the game's popularity with women to its lack of violence and its logical puzzles. It is estimated that 25% of *Myst* players are female, making the game one of the most enjoyable graphic adventures for women.

Most widely-released graphic adventure

Appearing on 11 platforms, the original *Myst* shares the record with *Déjà Vu* as the most widely released graphic adventure of all time. The game has been ported across generations, made available on the Mac, PC, Amiga, CDi, 3DO, Jaguar, Saturn, PlayStation, PlayStation Portable, Pocket PC and Nintendo DS.

PURE GENESIS

Singer Peter Gabriel 5 lent his voice to *Myst IV*'s soundtrack and claimed to have become inspired by the calm, "zen" world of Serenia, one of the game's Ages. The former Genesis singer provided the voiceover for the gateway to Serenia. He said: "When *Myst* came out, I thought it succeeded well in creating a feeling of other worlds in which mystery and imagination were the compelling elements instead of the usual action-packed shoot 'em ups."

POINT 'N' CLICK ROUND-UP

▼ First game to use SCUMM

Game title: *Maniac Mansion* ①
Publisher: LucasArts

LucasArts' first full point 'n' click adventure was *Maniac Mansion*. Released in 1987, it was the first game to use the innovative SCUMM game engine. SCUMM stands for Script Creation Utility for Maniac Mansion. Over the next decade, the SCUMM engine was used to create 13 more games, including the *Monkey Island* series.

▼ Least successful point 'n' click launch

Game: *The Last Express* ②
Publisher: Brøderbund

Produced by *Prince of Persia*

creator Jordan Mechner, *The Last Express* cost $6 million (£3.6 million) to make and was released on 1 April 1997 to rave reviews. But Brøderbund's marketing department quit before the launch date and so there was no advertising for the game. Then Softbank, one of the title's distributors, pulled out of the games industry. Brøderbund was subsequently bought by The Learning Company and its games production ceased. *The Last Express* was pulled from the shelves after just a few months. Interplay bought the rights in 2000 and it was re-released as a budget title, but Interplay went bankrupt soon after. *The Last Express* sold just 100,000 units overall – well under its sales target of 1 million.

▼ First game to link directly to iTunes

Game title: *Broken Sword: The Angel of Death*
Publisher: THQ

The fourth game in the *Broken Sword* series contains a link that takes players directly to the game's

soundtrack album in the iTunes music store. The album features tracks by both the soundtrack's composer Ben McCullough and the UK electronic band Übernoise.

▼ Most voice samples for a point 'n' click game

Game: *The Longest Journey*
Publisher: Empire Interactive

The English language edition of the 1999 game *The Longest Journey* contains nearly 8,300 individual voice samples. The game has since been translated into 10 different languages.

▼ Most CDs for a point 'n' click game

Game title: *Phantasmagoria*
Publisher: Sierra Online

The Japan-only Sega Saturn release of *Phantasmagoria* in 1997 came on eight CDs. The PC version on which it was based spanned seven discs. The main reason for this was the amount of Full Motion Video (FMV) contained in the game. To prevent too much disc-swapping, game data was repeated on each CD.

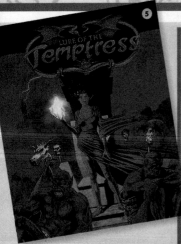

ℹ TRIVIA

> *Grim Fandango* **3** was originally going to be called *Deeds of the Dead* but the game's publisher did not want a reference to death in the title.

> Despite being best known as the creative force behind the legendary *King's Quest* series for Sierra Online, veteran games creator Roberta Williams **4** ranks *Phantasmagoria* the single game that best represents her achievement as a games designer.

WHATEVER HAPPENED TO POINT 'N' CLICK GAMES...

The point 'n' click genre faded into obscurity at the turn of the century, making games such as *Lure of the Temptress* **5** , the ▼**first game to use the Virtual Theatre engine**, and *Monkey Island* seem like ageing relics compared with today's titles. One of the reasons is that point 'n' click games are expensive to make since they require the creation of many game environments. They also tend not to port successfully to consoles because traditional joypad controllers have proven to be too fiddly for the precise cursor movements the games often require.

But the genre has recently begun to enjoy a revival, thanks in part to the Nintendo DS handheld console. The DS's stylus controller is perfect for such games, which may be why *Another Code: Two Memories* and *Hotel Dusk* have been so popular.

Games publishers are now looking at their back catalogues too, announcing revived franchises such as a planned *Broken Sword* game redesigned especially for the DS.

Point 'n' click games are also seeing something of a renaissance on the PC with releases such as *Agatha Christie: And Then There Were None* **6** and *Sam & Max: Season One*, the ▼**first PC point 'n' click game to be released in episodic form**. The Nintendo Wii is also getting in on the act with the brilliant *Zack & Wiki*. Point 'n' click games are definitely back in vogue.

SUPERHERO GAMES

The **first superhero to appear in a computer game** was Superman in the aptly named *Superman* on the Atari 2600 in 1979.

CONTENTS

SUPERHERO GAMES

LIVE OUT ALL YOUR SUPERHERO FANTASIES WITHOUT EVER LEAVING THE COMFORT OF YOUR SOFA (AND WITHOUT SQUEEZING YOURSELF INTO THAT CHAFING, SKIN-TIGHT COSTUME).

EXPERT

Dan Whitehead discovered games and comic books at roughly the same time, somewhere around 1982, as both the ZX Spectrum and Spider-Man crashed into his idyllic suburban childhood. These twin obsessions have fuelled him ever since, leading to a 17-year career in video-games journalism and far too many cardboard boxes stuffed with old comics. His own superpower is the ability to absorb and retain an infinite amount of useless information.

OVERVIEW

Superhero games are distinct from other action games in that the lead characters have their origins in the pages of a comic book, or draw influence from the style and format of superhero comic books. Key features include specific super powers, which may have to be toned down to keep gameplay balanced, and often – but not always – an iconic costume, preferably as skin-tight and brightly coloured as possible!

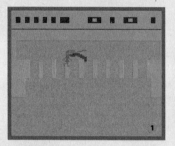

Superheroes go hand-in-spandex-glove with video games. Superhero stories are concerned with the triumph of good over evil, against all odds, and that's pretty much the driving force behind the majority of video games.

Superheroes had a head start on video games, with the modern incarnation stretching back to what fans call the Golden Age of comic books in the 1930s, then later in the Silver Age of the 1960s. By the time computer and video games arrived on the scene at the end of the 1970s, there were plenty of

IF YOU LIKE THIS...

...then you've probably already seen *The Dark Knight*, the **most successful comic-book movie adapation.**

new gamers itching to play as their favourite superheroes.

Superman was the first to touch down, his 1979 Atari game arriving on the back of the blockbuster Christopher Reeve movie and marking the ▶ **first official superhero game ❶**.

Spider-Man came next in 1982, followed by a trilogy of text adventures including *The Hulk* and another Spider-Man game (both in 1984), culminating in the first Fantastic Four game in 1985. Batman wouldn't debut until 1986, in a quirky isometric 3D adventure from British coding legend Jon Ritman.

1979
Superman – **the first official superhero game** – becomes available on the Atari 2600.

1982
Spider-Man makes his video-game debut in the aptly named *Spider-Man*, also on the Atari 2600.

1984
Adventure International release the *Questprobe* graphical adventure trilogy: *The Hulk, Spider-Man* and (in 1995) *Human Torch and The Thing* ❸.

1986
Batman, a quirky and very British adventure game, debuts on the ZX Spectrum and marks the caped crusader's first gaming outing.

1986
Seminal superhero adventure game *Redhawk* ❻ – in which text inputs are turned into comic-strip graphics – launches on the ZX Spectrum.

140 – the number of superheroes and villains featured in *Marvel Ultimate Alliance*, the video game with the **largest roster of licensed comic characters**.

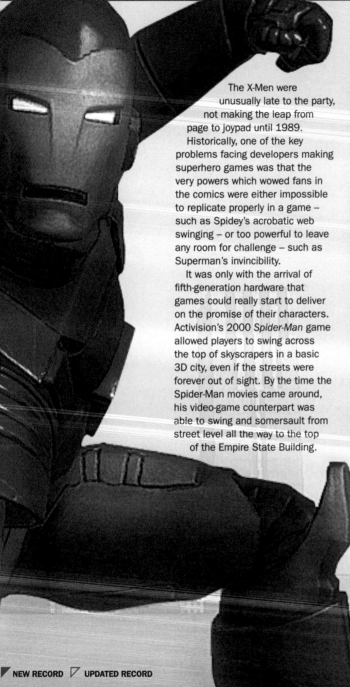

The X-Men were unusually late to the party, not making the leap from page to joypad until 1989. Historically, one of the key problems facing developers making superhero games was that the very powers which wowed fans in the comics were either impossible to replicate properly in a game – such as Spidey's acrobatic web swinging – or too powerful to leave any room for challenge – such as Superman's invincibility.

It was only with the arrival of fifth-generation hardware that games could really start to deliver on the promise of their characters. Activision's 2000 *Spider-Man* game allowed players to swing across the top of skyscrapers in a basic 3D city, even if the streets were forever out of sight. By the time the Spider-Man movies came around, his video-game counterpart was able to swing and somersault from street level all the way to the top of the Empire State Building.

Hulk: Ultimate Destruction, released in 2005 for PlayStation 2, Xbox and GameCube, went even further, giving players the freedom to rampage through both deserts and cities as the green goliath.

As consoles become more powerful, increasing numbers of heroes are making their video-game debuts, and the trend is now to include as many superheroes as possible in each game, such as *Marvel Ultimate Alliance* 9, the ▼ **first superhero game on PlayStation 3**.

The more superheroes we get, of course, means the risk of diminishing returns. *Iron Man* 4, for example, recently launched to coincide with the release of the movie of the same name, was universally panned, becoming the lowest-ranking game of all time (15%) according to the UK's *Official Nintendo Magazine*. And as for the 1999 N64 version of *Superman*, the less said about that the better!

i TRIVIA

> *Aquaman: Battle for Atlantis* 8 – the GameCube title based on the aquatic superhero – inspired the *X-Play* TV show to launch the Mullet Awards for "worst game of the year" (the "mullet" being a reference to Aquaman's hair!).

> With the release of *Catwoman* 2 – the game of the 2004 movie starring Halle Berry – Batman's feline foe became the **first female supervillain to star in her own video game**. Unfortunately, it was poorly received. GameTrailers.com ended their review with the classic line: "This game will make you want to drown kittens."

> One of the oddest superhero games of all time has to be *Superhero League of Hoboken*. In this quirky adventure-RPG – set in the New Jersey/New York/Pennsylvania tri-state area – you control superheroes such as Crimson Tape (special ability: making organizational charts), Iron Tummy (can eat really spicy foods) and Tropical Oil Man (can give his enemies high cholesterol)!

▼ **NEW RECORD** ▽ **UPDATED RECORD**

1989	1995	1996	1997	2004	2007
Marvel's mutant *X-Men* join the gaming world via the NES. **1989:** The game spin-off from Tim Burton's *Batman* (USA/UK) appears on 11 platforms.	The *Justice League Task Force* make their gaming debut in a one-on-one combat game for the SNES 7.	 *X-Men vs Capcom* released, the ▼ **first crossover fighting game featuring licensed superheroes**.	*Batman & Robin* take the lead roles in the ▼ **first free-roaming superhero game**, on PS. Comic character Turok appears for the first time on the N64 and the PC 5.	*City of Heroes*, the world's ▼ **first superhero-based MMORPG**, goes live on the PC.	*Marvel Ultimate Alliance* 9 is the first superhero game released on the PlayStation 3.

BATMAN

First Batman game

The legendary caped crusader's first video-game appearance came in *Batman*, published by Ocean Software in the UK in 1986 for the ZX Spectrum home computer. The devious isometric platform adventure was created by just two people – programmer Jon Ritman and artist Bernie Drummond.

🔧 PLATFORMS

✂ SPEC

Developer:
Bernie Drummond and Jon Ritman
Publisher:
Ocean Software
Initial release:
Batman (1986), ZX Spectrum

🔁 GAMEPLAY

Batman-licensed titles cover just about every game genre imaginable, so it's impossible to identify a common mode of gameplay. That said, though, the games are usually action-packed and feature the player taking on the role of the caped crusader battling against his regular enemies, such as The Penguin and The Joker.

First "cross-universe" Batman game

As well as his solo video-game outings, Batman has also been a key playable character in numerous Justice League games over the years. The first of these, *Justice League Task Force*, was a one-on-one fighting game, published for the SNES in 1995. Two Justice League games, *Injustice For All* and *Chronicles*, followed on the Gameboy Advance in 2002 and 2003 respectively. *Justice League Heroes*, meanwhile, was an action role-playing game released for the Xbox and PS2. However, *Mortal Kombat vs DC Universe* **①**, released in 2008 for Xbox 360 and PS3, marked the first time Batman and the other comic-book heroes had battled characters from outside their own fictional universe.

First Batman villain introduced in a video game

The villainous Sin Tzu, from the 2003 Ubisoft video game *Batman: Rise of Sin Tzu* **②**, was the first official Batman villain to be introduced in a video game, rather than in a comic book. The character was created by writer Flint Dille and artist Jim Lee, and DC Comics produced a promotional novel and toys to mark the event. However, Sin Tzu has rarely appeared in the comic series since.

Most villains in a Batman game

The game in the Batman franchise to feature the most villains is *LEGO Batman: The Videogame* **③**, which has 12 bad guys. The game features appearances from The Joker, The Penguin, Catwoman, Two-Face, Mr Freeze, Scarecrow, The Riddler, Clayface, Man-Bat, Harley Quinn, Killer Croc and Bane. All are playable, along with various good guys, which also makes it the **Batman game with the most playable characters**.

▌ NEW RECORD   ▽ UPDATED RECORD

▶ FACT

The development team behind *LEGO Batman: The Videogame*, is none other than TT Games, who also created *Guinness World Records: The Videogame*, the game that enables players to compete for the chance to get their names into this book! See p.8 for more.

47 – the number of years between Batman's first appearance in *Detective Comics #27* in 1939 and the **first appearance of Batman in a video game**, in 1986's *Batman* for the ZX Spectrum.

Widest release for a Batman game

The video-game tie-in for Tim Burton's blockbuster *Batman* (USA/UK, 1989) movie appeared on 14 different gaming platforms between 1989 and 1992. *Batman: The Movie* ④ was available for NES, Mega Drive/Genesis, ZX Spectrum, Amstrad, C64, Amiga, Atari ST, Game Boy, PC Engine, IBM PC, MSX, GX4000 and C64GS as well as arcade. Although based on the same source material, the gameplay often varied from format to format, depending on the technology.

First Batman game to feature exclusive animated scenes

The makers of television hit *Batman: The Animated Series* ⑤ created new cartoon scenes for the 1994 Sega CD release of *The Adventures of Batman & Robin* – the first time such material was produced exclusively for a video game. The scenes featured Kevin Conroy reprising his role as Batman, with Mark "Star Wars" Hamill as The Joker and Ron "Hellboy" Perlman as Clayface. The scenes form a complete storyline and are often referred to as the "lost episode" of the animated television series.

First free-roaming Batman game

The 1998 *Batman & Robin* video game ⑧, released to tie in with the movie of the same name, was the first to allow players to control the superhero in full 3D. The game required players to explore Gotham City, foiling crimes and looking for clues as to where Mr Freeze would strike next.

SUPERHERO, SPECIAL CAST

Batman Begins ⑦, the video-game tie-in for the movie of the same name, used the same cast as the film to record new dialogue, making it one of the most acclaimed voice casts ever in a video game. Both Michael Caine and Morgan Freeman are Oscar-winning actors, Liam Neeson, Ken Watanabe and Tom Wilkinson were all Oscar nominated, while Gary Oldman is a BAFTA winner.

⑦

ⓘ TRIVIA

> Despite his popularity, Batman has only ever appeared in two dedicated racing games. *Batman: Gotham City Racer* ⑥ was released in 2001 for PlayStation, and found the caped crusader driving around Gotham, rounding up supervillains after a breakout at Arkham Asylum. The other was the impressive *Batman Returns* on the Sega Mega CD in 1993.

> In *LEGO Batman: The Videogame*, Poison Ivy has the ability to blow love dust over security guards who then grant her access to places she's not supposed to enter...

BATMAN & ROBIN

PlayStation
PAL

A⊀laim

PlayStation™

⑧

CITY OF HEROES & CITY OF VILLAINS

PLATFORMS

PC, PS1, PS2, PS3, PSP, 360, XBOX, DS, GBA, Wii

SPEC

Developer:
Cryptic Studios
Publisher:
NCSoft
Initial release:
City of Heroes
(April 2004), PC.

GAMEPLAY

Players create their own superhero or supervillain and then join thousands of other players online to undertake adventures and missions by moving through zones within a constantly evolving gameworld. A series of free expansion packs have enabled players to create multiple active characters, meaning that their gameplay options can become ever-more complex and varied.

First superhero MMORPG

Launched in April 2004, *City of Heroes* (1) was the first multiplayer online role-playing game to focus on superheroes. The game is centred around Paragon City, with players taking on the role of their own superhero creations to protect the town from villainous plots and super-powered enemies. Traditionally, MMORPGs take place in more conventional fantasy worlds or a science-fiction setting.

First MMORPG to use adaptive difficulty

City of Heroes was the first MMORPG to adjust the strength of enemies (2) according to both the level of the players in the area and also how many players there are, taking the view that there is strength in numbers. Many other massively multiplayer games have since followed suit.

First MMORPG to use a mentoring system

In the tradition of great dynamic duos, *City of Heroes* (3) implemented a feature where superhero characters could recruit a sidekick (or "lackey" if they are a supervillain) who benefits from combat and level bonuses, providing he stays within a certain distance of his mentor. This allows casual or inexperienced players to team up with veterans and enjoy the game without having to grind their way up to high levels.

FACT

In 2004, Marvel Comics unsuccessfully attempted to sue the makers of *City of Heroes*, claiming that the game encouraged players to create unauthorized versions of famous Marvel characters. However, in 2006, after the case was settled out of court, Marvel even asked the *City of Heroes* team to help them develop an official Marvel Universe MMORPG for Microsoft, but the project was eventually cancelled.

32 million – the number of user-generated characters on the *City of Heroes* database in March 2008. Players in the USA are each able to create 396 active characters, while European players can create 144.

ISSUE 10
INVASION

◤ NEW RECORD ◸ UPDATED RECORD

◤ Most characters created by one player

MMORPG players are not restricted to playing as just one character and will often have many different active characters to choose from. Player "Jsocci" holds the record for the most characters created on a single *City of Heroes* account. By spreading the creations across the game's 11 US servers, Jsocci designed and played with a total of 149 different superhero and supervillain characters.

◤ Most successful City of Heroes supergroup

The US team BeeR DRiNKeRS uNiTed, playing on the Freedom server, is currently the most successful supergroup, or guild, in *City of Heroes*. The group have collected 109,335,990 Prestige points (the game's superhero currency) and have a further 239,372,200 invested in their superhero headquarters, making a total of 348,708,190 Prestige points.

◤ Most free MMORPG expansions

As well as the stand-alone *City of Villains* expansion, *City of Heroes* has so far offered subscribers 13 free updates, or "issues" 5, which add new content, play areas and storylines to the game. This is more than any rival subscription-based MMORPG. *Everquest* has offered 14 similar updates, but these required payments to access them.

◤ FIRST EVIL MMORPG EXPANSION

City of Villains 4, released in 2005, was a completely new and separate game in which players could create and play as their own supervillains. This marked the first time that a stand-alone MMORPG expansion had been dedicated to playing as the bad guys. The expansion is also notable as *City of Heroes* subscribers did not have to pay an additional charge to play *City of Villains*.

ⓘ TRIVIA

> *City of Heroes* has spawned many non-gaming spin-offs. Two novels set in the game's universe were published in 2005 and there have also been two separate comic-book series based on the game. It has also inspired a collectable card 6 game and a traditional tabletop RPG, while film and television adaptations are also being developed.

> The official *City of Heroes* comic book has attracted several well-known comic writers. When the title was relaunched in 2005, it was initially written by Mark Waid, whose credits include *Fantastic Four* and *Justice League*. Another *City of Heroes* three-issue storyline was written by Dan Jurgens, popular for his work on *Spider-Man* as well as contributing to the famous *Death of Superman* story.

CITY OF HEROES

CITY OF VILLAINS

SPIDER-MAN

⚙ PLATFORMS

✕ SPEC

Developer:
Parker Brothers
Publisher:
Parker Brothers
Initial release:
Spider-Man (1982),
Atari 2600

⇅ GAMEPLAY

As the theme tune to
the 1967 animated
Spider-Man series said:

"Spider-Man,
Spider-Man,
Does whatever a
spider can.
Spins a web, any size,
Catches thieves,
just like flies.
Look out! Here comes
the Spider-Man."

Which neatly sums up
the gameplay of most
Spider-Man games
– Spidey battles
against villainous foes
to win the day for the
good and the just,
usually by spinning
a web and swinging
across the city. From
platformers to action
games to virtual
pinball, the energy and
dynamism inherent in
the original Stan Lee
Spidey creation shines
through.

▰ First Spider-Man console game

Spider-Man's games debut
came in 1982, in the appropriately
titled *Spider-Man* ① on the Atari
2600. The game required players
to guide Spidey up the side of a
skyscraper, avoiding the Green
Goblin's bombs. It also has the
distinction of being the ▰ **first**
official Marvel Comics game.

▰ First playable villain in a Spider-Man game

The first game to allow players
to control one of Spidey's deadly
foes was *Spider-Man & Venom:*
Maximum Carnage ②, published
for the SNES and Mega Drive/
Genesis in 1994. In the game,

Spider-Man teams
up with Venom to stop
Carnage ③, and the game
allowed players to choose which
character they played as,
enabling them to control Venom
for the first time.

▰ Most Marvel heroes in a Spider-Man game

The 2000 PlayStation
Spider-Man ⑤ game features more
cameo appearances from fellow
Marvel heroes than any other solo
Spider-Man title. As well as the six
supervillains present in the game,
there are also cameo appearances
from Captain America, Black Cat,
The Punisher, Microchip, Daredevil,
Human Torch, Namor, Ghost Rider
and Uatu the Watcher.

▰ First true web-swinging game

Spider-Man 2 ⑦, the official
game of the 2004 movie, was
the first Spider-Man game to
offer true web-swinging, in
which Spider-Man's webs must
actually attach to buildings
and physically alter his
trajectory. This innovation
gave players greater freedom
of movement, and the ability
to swing from skyscrapers
all the way down to street
level. In all his previous 3D
games, Spidey's webs had

mysteriously attached to the sky
above him and only allowed him
to swing straight ahead.

⫘▶ SPIDEY FACTS

Secret identity:
Peter Parker, student
First appearance:
August 1962 in *Amazing Fantasy #15* ④
Published by:
Marvel Comics
Created by:
Stan Lee and Steve Ditko
Super powers:
Super strength, speed and agility,
spider sense.
Other abilities:
Chemistry genius,
mechanical
webshooters.

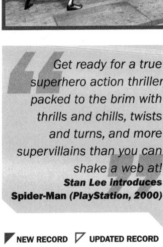

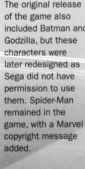

> *Get ready for a true superhero action thriller, packed to the brim with thrills and chills, twists and turns, and more supervillains than you can shake a web at!*
> **Stan Lee introduces Spider-Man (PlayStation, 2000)**

▼ Most popular video-game superhero

Spider-Man is by far the most popular superhero for video-game adaptations. From 1982 to 2008's *Web of Shadows* **6**, he has so far starred in 35 solo video games across 32 formats and appeared in nine other titles with other Marvel characters. He has also featured on pinball tables, handheld LCD games, PC activity packages and a plug-and-play TV game.

Chinatown level. The original release of the game also included Batman and Godzilla, but these characters were later redesigned as Sega did not have permission to use them. Spider-Man remained in the game, with a Marvel copyright message added.

▼ NEW RECORD **▽ UPDATED RECORD**

▼ First Spider-Man arcade game

Spider-Man's arcade debut came in 1991 in *Spider-Man: The Video Game*, a scrolling fighter with occasional platform elements. Up to four players could join in,

playing Spidey, Black Cat, Hawkeye and Namor. The storyline involved Doctor Doom creating an army of alien symbiotes – a plot that was recently re-used in the 2008 *Mighty Avengers* comic book.

▼ FIRST MARVEL GAME TO FEATURE STAN LEE

Spider-Man creator Stan Lee **9** appeared as a voice artist in *Spider-Man*, released in 2000 for PlayStation. The game featured enthusiastic narration from Lee, welcoming players with the line "Greetings, true believers and newcomers alike!".

Stan Lee created Spider-Man in 1962. The character first appeared in the comic book *Amazing Fantasy #15* before going on to become a huge international hit in his own comic-book series. Television, film, video games and mass-merchandising soon followed for the web-spinning wonder.

SUPERMAN

PLATFORMS

SPEC

Developer:
Atari
Publisher:
Atari
Initial release:
Superman *(1979),*
Atari 2600

GAMEPLAY

In the first video-game outing, up to two players controlled Superman's action. Challenges included capturing Lex Luthor and receiving kisses from Lois Lane to counteract the effects of kryptonite. Only three of Superman's powers were featured – X-ray vision, strength and flight.

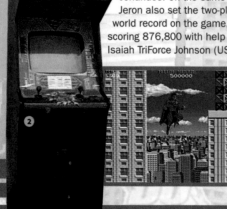

First superhero video game

Superman has the honour of being the first established superhero to get his own video game. The self-titled *Superman* was released for the Atari 2600 way back in 1979 and found a chunky representation of the hero racing to capture Lex Luthor before returning to the Daily Planet as quickly as possible.

Lowest-rated superhero game

The lowest-rated superhero game of all time is *Superman* for the Nintendo 64 ③. The game features the Man of Steel flying through rings in a city shrouded in green kryptonite mist. The game has an average rating of just 23% on GameRankings.com and was voted Worst Comic Book Game of All Time by GameSpy and the Worst Game Ever by GameTrailers.com.

Highest Superman arcade score

The highest recorded score on the *Superman* arcade game ②, as verified by Twin Galaxies, is 353,900 set by Jeron Grayson (USA) of Brooklyn on 31 May 2008. The game was played on medium difficulty with no continues. On the same day, Jeron also set the two-player world record on the game, scoring 876,800 with help from Isaiah TriForce Johnson (USA).

First superhero game to tie into a contemporary comic storyline

The Death and Return of Superman ④, released for 16-bit consoles in August 1994, was the first superhero video game that tied in with a comic-book storyline that was being published at the same time. As Superman, the player was defeated by Doomsday and then continued through the game as Superman wanabees The Cyborg, The Eradicator, Superboy and Steel. The game was released just a few months before the *Spider-Man & Venom: Maximum Carnage* storyline got its own spin-off game in 1994.

Least powerful video game Superman

The Superman who starred in the 1988 NES game *Superman* ① was a fairly wimpy specimen compared to his comic-book counterpart. Not only could he be damaged by bullets, turning back into Clark Kent when he became too badly injured, but he could only use one super power at a time by collecting the appropriate icons. Rather than flying, he could only leap! The game also featured cute graphics that looked nothing like the muscular hero fans expect.

First licensed superhero arcade game

As well as being the first superhero to get his own video game, Superman is also the first established superhero character to get an official arcade machine. Released by Taito in 1988, *Superman* was a scrolling shoot 'em up and fighting game, with Superman alternating between flying up the screen and battling his way from left to right. Gameplay involved fighting through five levels to battle the evil Emperor Zaas. If a second player joined in, they would play as a red Superman.

Largest superhero play area

Superman Returns ⑧, the Electronic Arts game released to coincide with the 2006 movie of the same name, features the largest single play area in a superhero video game. The game's virtual Metropolis covers the equivalent of 207 km² (80 miles²) and features 10,000 buildings. Superman is also able to fly up into the stratosphere and view the city from high in the air before flying back down to earth at 1,287 km/h (800 mph) – or "faster than a speeding bullet".

75 – number of orchestra members involved in the score for the game version of *Superman Returns*. There are around 120 minutes of music in the game in total.

IF YOU LIKE THIS...

...keep your eyes open for *DC Universe Online*, an MMO for PS3 and PC where superheroes battle classic baddies.

NEW RECORD / UPDATED RECORD

Most powerful Superman

In *Superman Returns* (6), Superman is endowed with more powers than in any other Superman game. In total, his seven super powers are X-ray vision, heat vision, flight, super hearing, super strength, super speed and super breath.

SUPERMAN FACTS

Secret identity:
Clark Kent, reporter
First appearance:
June 1938, Action Comics #1 (7)
Published by:
DC Comics
Created by:
Jerry Siegel and Joe Shuster
Super powers:
Flight, super strength, super speed, heat vision, X-ray vision, freeze breath, super senses, almost unlimited endurance and resilience

TRIVIA

> In the 1988 NES *Superman* game (1), the superhero's famous X-ray vision is actually used to make invisible enemies visible again. The game explains this change in Superman's powers by claiming that Lex Luthor has lined every building in Metropolis with lead!

> Superman's legendary invulnerability has often been ignored in his game adaptations, simply because an indestructible hero isn't much of a challenge. In Midway's *Mortal Kombat vs DC Universe* (5), the developers had an easy way around the problem – as well as kryptonite, Superman is officially vulnerable to magic, which many of their fighting characters already use!

"Superman is one of the toughest comic-book characters to accurately portray in a video game and Tiburon did get some things right, particularly Superman's mechanics."
ign.com game review, November 2006

FACT

It is possible to complete the Atari 2600 *Superman* game in less than one second by pausing the game as it starts and then resuming play when the Daily Planet building appears. Clark Kent then just has to touch the building to complete the game!

X-MEN

PLATFORMS

PC
360
PS1
XBOX
PS2
DS
PS3
GAME BOY ADVANCE
PSP
Wii

SPEC

Developer:
LJN
Publisher:
Acclaim
Initial release:
The Uncanny
X-Men (1989), NES

GAMEPLAY

From the very earliest incarnations, the X-Men games have taken advantage of multiple character play. Gameplay tends to centre around basic 2D and 3D combat, although later titles have RPG overtones. The more famous X-Men characters also appear in other Marvel games.

Most simultaneous players on an arcade game

Konami's 1992 X-Men fighting game is the only arcade beat 'em up to support six players at the same time. To accommodate this unprecedented number of players, the game used two screens side-by-side to create a widescreen effect. The playable X-characters were Cyclops, Colossus, Wolverine, Storm, Nightcrawler and Dazzler.

Most X-Men characters in a single game

The X-Men game featuring the most characters taken from the pages of the Marvel comic books is X-Men Legends II:

Rise of Apocalypse ④. The PS2 and Xbox versions of this epic action RPG feature 42 official X-Men characters, including 15 playable heroes, four unlockable secret characters and 23 villains.

Most spin-off X-Men games

Wolverine is the X-Men character with the most spin-off solo games. As well as appearing in 20 official X-Men games and numerous Marvel games, he has also starred in four video games of his own.

Wolverine for the NES was released in 1991, Adamantium Rage for the Megadrive and SNES arrived in 1994, Wolverine's Rage hit the Game Boy Color in 2001, while Wolverine's Revenge ⑦, based on the second X-Men movie, came out on five platforms in 2003.

Highest X-Men arcade score

The highest score on the X-Men vs Street Fighter ② arcade game is 2,098,100 points, scored by Clarence Leung of Michigan, USA, on 16 March 1999. The record was set under Twin Galaxies tournament conditions, with maximum difficulty, maximum damage and no continues.

X-MEN FACTS

Secret identity:
Various
First appearance:
September 1963 in X-Men #1 ⑥
Published by:
Marvel Comics
Created by:
Stan Lee & Jack Kirby
Super powers:
Various – such as weather control, flesh regeneration, optic blasting and so on – the result of genetic mutations
Other abilities:
Self-defense training.

IF YOU LIKE THIS...

...then you'll enjoy one-on-one combat games. Check out the **fighting games round-up** on p.178.

1.6 million – copies of Activision's *X-Men Legends* [8] shipped globally, making it the **most successful X-Men video game** yet.

EASTER EGG

Completing *X-Men Legends* unlocks a host of new costumes for the characters, including the original 1963 outfits for Cyclops, Beast, Iceman and Jean Gray. You also get Wolverine's Weapon X outfit, plus Storm's, Colossus' and Nightcrawler's 1980s costumes.

Most games based on a superhero group franchise

The X-Men characters have inspired more video game releases than any other group of comic characters, with at least 30 games available, trailing fellow Marvel superstar Spider-Man by five games. The first title in which the two sets of characters appear together is Acclaim's 1992 *Spider-Man/X-Men: Arcade's Revenge.*

▼ **NEW RECORD**   ▽ **UPDATED RECORD**

> The central development goal of this game was to really deliver on the Superhero experience.
> **Chris Palmisano, Associate Producer, X3: The Official Game, Activision**

has a cumulative rating of 85% on GameRankings.com, putting it slightly ahead of *X-Men Legends II: Rise of Apocalypse*, which has an average score of 82%.

Most popular X-Men video-game villain

The X-Men's arch-enemy Magneto [5] has appeared opposite the mutant heroes, and other Marvel characters, in 22 video games. He first appeared as the final boss in *X-Men*, released for the NES in 1989. Fans would have to wait for *X-Men 2: Clone Wars* in 1994, however, before he became playable.

First superhero first-person shooter

X-Men: Ravages of Apocalypse [1], released for the PC in 1997, was the first officially licensed superhero entry in the first-person shooter genre. Published by Marvel Interactive, the game was a conversion of *Quake* and required that game to run. The player took the role of a cyborg, created by Magneto, hunting down evil cloned versions of the X-Men characters.

Highest-rated X-Men game

Children of the Atom [3], the first of Capcom's Marvel-themed fighting games, is the highest-rated X-Men video game. The Sega Saturn version of the arcade machine

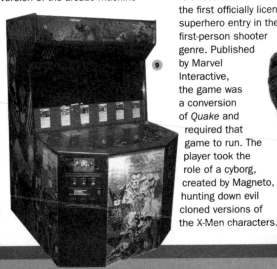

ℹ TRIVIA

> In *Wolverine's Revenge*, the spin-off game based on *X2* (USA, 2003), the second X-Men movie, the character of Wolverine was voiced by Mark Hamill, best known as Luke Skywalker in the *Star Wars* movies. Another sci-fi stalwart, *Star Trek*'s Patrick Stewart, reprised his role as Professor X for the game.

> Much of the bizarre dialogue from the *X-Men* arcade game has passed into popular video-game lore. Magneto's declarations "I am Magneto, master of magnet!" and "Welcome to die!" suffered in the translation from the original Japanese game, while completing the game gives the message "X-Men succeed to rescue Professor and return to Earth with the victory".

> The *X-Men* comic was one of the first to feature a superhero team made up from many different nationalities. Over the years, their ranks have included mutant heroes from Egypt, Ireland, England, Russia, Germany and Japan.

SUPERHERO ROUND-UP

FACTS

> Many superheroes aren't popular enough to sustain an entire series of games, but every now and then a few get lucky and are allowed to fly solo for one-off video-game outings. The Silver Surfer starred in an eponymous NES shoot-'em-up in 1990. DC Comics monster hero Swamp Thing earned himself a NES platform game in 1992, while Aquaman's solitary Xbox outing *Aquaman: Battle for Atlantis* sank without trace in 2003.

i TRIVIA

> The 1997 PlayStation platformer *Spawn the Eternal* ① contained a hidden treat for anyone who played the disc in a CD player: a hidden bonus interview with Spawn's creator, veteran comic artist Todd McFarlane.

▼ **NEW RECORD**
▽ **UPDATED RECORD**

■ Most licensed superheroes in a game
Game: *Marvel Ultimate Alliance*
Publisher: Activision
The superhero game featuring the most established comic-book characters is 2006's *Marvel Ultimate Alliance* ④. The game is an epic role-playing game (RPG) that makes use of 92 Marvel Comics characters, over 40 of which are available to the player – the **most playable characters in a superhero game**.

■ Most destructible environment in a superhero game
Game: *The Incredible Hulk*
Publisher: Sega
The superhero game with the most potential for destruction is the 2008 version of *The Incredible Hulk*, based on the green behemoth's latest movie. The game takes place in a virtual New York, in which every building, vehicle and item can be smashed to pieces – including famous landmarks such as the Empire State Building and even Marvel Comics' headquarters.

■■▶ FACT

The ▼ **first computer-generated comic** was *Shatter*, scripted by Peter B. Gillis (USA) with artwork by Mike Saenz (USA), published in June 1985 by First Comics. In 1988, Saenz created *Iron Man: Crash*, the ▼ **first computer-generated graphic novel**, featuring Iron Man from Marvel Comics.

INTERVIEW WITH... SCOTT ADAMS

American programmer and game developer Scott Adams pioneered the first superhero text adventure games. We caught up with Scott recently and asked him about his experiences working on the first superhero video games.

Why did you start with Hulk?
Hulk was just plain fun and easy to start with. He was a very well-known Marvel hero with an interesting alter ego. He really only had one major power and it was possible to come up with puzzles that would work well in his world.

What was your favourite part of making the games?
When I had the initial comic plot outlined, Marvel wanted to know how I wanted the new character that the series was introducing drawn. His name was Chief Examiner and he appeared in every comic for the series. I mentioned I thought it would be neat if they could base it off of me and they said "send a picture". I did and they replied that they thought it would work and so I became part of the comic.

Who is your favourite superhero?
My favourite superhero has always been Spider-Man. Someone with greatness thrust upon them, complete with the true frailty of humanity and all that it entails.

Highest-rated superhero game
Game: *Marvel vs Capcom 2*
Publisher: Sega
The most critically acclaimed superhero game is *Marvel vs Capcom 2: New Age of Heroes* ③, released in 2000 for the Sega Dreamcast. The fighting game achieved an average review score of 90% according to both the Metacritic website and GameRankings.com.

Most games based on a Japanese superhero comic
Game: *Dragon Ball*
Publisher: various
The most video game titles based on a Japanese superhero comic-book series is held by Akira Toriyama's *Dragon Ball* ⑤. *Dragon Ball* stars Son Goku, a monkey-tailed boy with superhuman strength and top martial arts skills. The series has included 81 titles between 1986 and 2008 for a vast selection of platforms from Game Boy to Xbox 360.

First text adventure game featuring a licensed superhero
Game: *Questprobe ft. The Hulk*
Publisher: various
The first text adventure game featuring a licensed superhero was *Questprobe featuring The Hulk* ⑥, released in 1984 on various formats. A similar game featuring Spider-Man followed, as did The Human Torch and The Thing. There were plans for 12 Marvel adventures, but developers Adventure International went bust before series completion.

Earliest superhero to feature in a game
Game: *Phantom 2040*
Publisher: Viacom
The earliest superhero to have been given his own video game is The Phantom, who debuted in a newspaper comic strip in February 1936. This makes the character 73 years old as of 2009, just over two years older than Superman. The Phantom made his games debut in *Phantom 2040* ②, released in 1995.

First superhero created for a game
Game: *Redhawk*
Publisher: Melbourne House
Redhawk, released for the ZX Spectrum in 1986, gave players the first comic-book superhero story created specifically for a game. Transforming into the mighty hero, thanks to the magic word "Kwah!", players typed their commands on the keyboard, and saw the actions come to life in an animated comic strip at the top of the screen.

Grossest superhero game
Game: *Boogerman*
Publisher: Interplay
The grossest superhero created for a video game is 1994's *Boogerman* ⑧. The game starts with our hero throwing bogies at the screen, before battling enemies using snot, burps and farts. He later appeared as a playable character in *Clayfighter* on the Nintendo 64, where his dialogue was provided by Dan Castellaneta ⑦, who is better known as the voice of Homer Simpson!

Star Wars: The Force Unleashed marks the **first games collaboration between LucasArts and Industrial Light & Magic**, the video games and special effects divisions of George Lucas's business empire.

CONTENTS

SPACE GAMES

DESPITE COUNTLESS STUNNING TECHNOLOGICAL ADVANCEMENTS, TWO FUNDAMENTAL THEMES HAVE REMAINED PIVOTAL THROUGHOUT THE EVOLUTION OF THE SPACE GAME GENRE: SPACE SHIPS AND ALIEN WORLDS.

EXPERT

BAFTA winner Martin Korda is the managing director of GameConsulting.com, a leading games consulting and scriptwriting company. He has provided expert advice to many of the world's leading games companies.

OVERVIEW

While often lumped together with science fiction and fantasy games, space games are a significant genre in their own right, and space ships are the key feature. Sometimes these ships are built for fighting, other times they are used for transport, trade and commerce, or even just to simulate the experience of flying through the void of space.

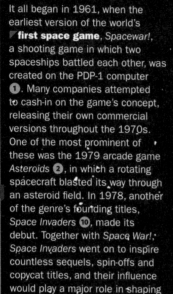

It all began in 1961, when the earliest version of the world's **first space game**, *Spacewar!*, a shooting game in which two spaceships battled each other, was created on the PDP-1 computer ❶. Many companies attempted to cash-in on the game's concept, releasing their own commercial versions throughout the 1970s. One of the most prominent of these was the 1979 arcade game *Asteroids* ❷, in which a rotating spacecraft blasted its way through an asteroid field. In 1978, another of the genre's founding titles, *Space Invaders* ❿, made its debut. Together with *Space War!*, *Space Invaders* went on to inspire countless sequels, spin-offs and copycat titles, and their influence would play a major role in shaping the space games genre over the next three decades.

During the early 1980s, arcade space blasters of the previous decade came to home consoles, and proved particularly popular on the Atari 2600. The success of the *Star Wars* movies meant that *Star Wars*-themed video games were inevitable, and the first such release, *The Empire Strikes Back*, emerged in 1982.

The real world also provided inspiration. Space Shuttle mission STS-1 launched in April 1981, although it would be two more years until we saw the **first Space-Shuttle sim**, *Space*

Shuttle: A Journey into Space; it would take another decade for the **first true space sim**, Microsoft's *Space Simulator* ❸, to arrive on the scene.

Space games entered new territory in 1984 with the release of *Elite*, the **first space trading game**. And in 1986, the genre enjoyed its first graphical adventure release in the guise of *Space Quest: The Sarien Encounter* ❹

Solid shaded vector graphics made their genre debut with the release of *Starglider 2* on the Amiga and Atari ST in 1988. The

⬦ NEW RECORD   ⬦ UPDATED RECORD

game was developed by Argonaut Software, who went on to work with Nintendo to create the SuperFX chip, an extra processor that could be inserted into a SNES cartridge to improve visuals. In 1993, the space combat game *Starfox* ❻, a.k.a. *Star Wing*, became the **first game to make use of the SuperFX chip** and made a huge impact on the console market.

However, the genre's pivotal moment probably came in 1990 with the release of *Wing Commander*, a PC-based space combat game that propelled both the genre and gaming to new levels of cinematic excellence that were unrivaled until the release of *Star Wars: X-Wing* ❺ in 1993.

The mid-to-late 1990s were dominated by *Wing Commander*, *Star Wars* and *Star Trek* games, with each series spawning myriad sequels, spin-offs and sub-series. In 1998, the *Star Trek* franchise

TIMELINE

1961
Spacewar!, the first space game is created on the PDP-1 computer. Two ships are flown around a sphere (the sun) while shooting string-like missiles at each other.

1980
Space Invaders, is released for the Atari 2600 and soon becomes one of the machine's must-have titles, driving sales of the console up.

1984
Mixing trading and combat, *Elite*, the first truly epic space game, lets players explore thousands of star systems and requires some 500 hours to complete.

1990
With its high production-value cutscenes and stunning space combat, *Wing Commander* marks the dawn of the space genre's cinematic age.

1993
Wing Commander spin-off title *Privateer* ❾ gives players the chance to pursue a career as a space pirate, a merchant, a mercenary or a mixture of all three.

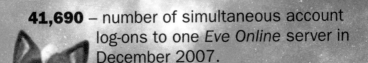

Wing Commander series or one of the established space games franchises.

The supremacy of *Star Wars* and *Star Trek* continued into the new millennium, with new movies and TV series driving the franchises' popularity. Among the most innovative of these releases was 2002's *Star Trek: Bridge Commander*, a game that could be upgraded for voice-activated ship commands. 2003's *Eve Online* **8** broke the mould by becoming the **first massively multiplayer online game based entirely in space**, while in recent years, space games have enjoyed a renaissance with the release of high-budget titles such as *Homeworld* **7** on the PC.

With production values continuing to soar and with the genre's founding principles of space ships and alien worlds still very much at the fore, the future of space games looks bright.

launched a first-person shooter; *Star Trek: The Next Generation – Klingon Honor Guard* on PC, followed by the *Quake III* engine-powered *Star Trek* game *Star Trek: Voyager* in 2000.

Between these two hits came the stunning and terrifying PC RPG *System Shock 2*, set on a derelict space ship. The game was a breakout hit and a rarity because it was not linked to either the

Ⅲ▶ FACT

Star Trek: Bridge Commander, Star Trek: Elite Force II and *Star Trek: Starfleet Command III* are considered unofficial limited editions, owing to the termination of Activision's *Star Trek* license in 2003 limiting the number of copies available.

ⓘ TRIVIA

> When *Spacewar!* was created in 1961, its battling space ships were controlled with trackballs, which were a forerunner to the world's first ever computer mice.

> You don't have to spend a fortune on subscriptions to live out an alternative life beyond the stars. Strange new worlds and mysterious aliens can be discovered for free if you join internet MMO DarkOrbit at www.darkorbit.com.

> *Space Quest: The Sarien Encounter* was the first Sierra graphical adventure not to be based in a fantasy setting.

> Developer Cheyenne Mountain Entertainment is working on *Stargate Worlds*, the first massively multiplayer game based in the Stargate universe. The game is due for release in late 2008.

1997	1999		2001	2005	2007	2008
Wing Commander: Prophecy is released.	*Homeworld, Unreal Tournament* and *X: Beyond the Frontier* **11** are released.		With *Independence War 2: Edge of Chaos*, Newtonian physics take space combat to a new level of complexity as gamers battle realistic natural forces as well as intelligent foes.	*Eve Online* and *Star Wars: Galaxies – An Empire Divided* bring the space genre into the massively multiplayer online age, allowing thousands to play together simultaneously.	*Wing Commander: Arena* is released for Xbox Live arcade. The first multiplayer *Wing Commander* game is not well received by fans and is not a hit with reviewers.	Realism within space games is propelled to new heights thanks to *Star Wars: The Force Unleashed*'s ground-breaking Euphoria and Digital Molecular Matter technologies.

PLATFORMS

PC · 360
PS1 · XBOX
PS2 · DS
PS3 · GBA
PSP · Wii

SPEC

Developer:
David Braben, Ian Bell, Frontier Developments
Publisher:
Various
Initial release:
Elite (1984), BBC Micro

GAMEPLAY

In 1984, most games were still simplistic affairs, short-lived arcade romps that were heavily reliant on repetitive game mechanics. Elite was the game to change all that. Epic on an unprecedented scale, Elite allowed players to assume the role of a space pirate and fly their spaceship through countless star systems, battling rival buccaneers and trading goods for profit in an attempt to earn the rank of Elite. September 2009 marks the series' 25th anniversary.

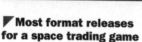

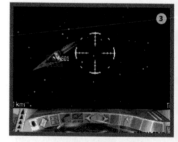

Most format releases for a space trading game
Elite ② was released on 25 formats: BBC Micro B (tape), BBC Micro B (disc), BBC Micro Master, BBC Micro Master Compact, BBC Micro Tube Enhanced version, Acorn Electron (tape), ZX Spectrum 48K (tape), ZX Spectrum 128K (tape), Amstrad CPC (tape), Amstrad CPC (disc), Commodore 64 (tape), Commodore 64 (disc), IBM PC CGA (5.25" disc), IBM PC EGA/VGA (5.25" disc) (as *Elite plus*), IBM PC EGA/VGA (3.5" disc) (as *Elite plus*), Tatung Einstein (disc), Apple II (disc), MSX (tape), MSX (disc), Acorn Archimedes, Atari ST, Commodore Amiga, Nintendo NES, NEC PC-9801 (5.25" disc) and NEC PC-9801 (3.5" disc). (A few unofficial versions exist such as the Commodore +4 and Commodore 128 versions, but these were never sold.)

Most star systems
Frontier: Elite II ① contains more star systems than any other space trading game. It features 100 billion unique systems that can be fully explored, with each system containing an average of 20 planets and moons. That's an equivalent of 300 planets or moons per person on earth!

First space trading game
On its release in 1984, *Elite* became the world's first space trading game, creating a genre that would go on to spawn hits such as *Privateer* ⑥, *X: Beyond the Frontier* ④ and *Eve Online* ⑧.

Longest-running space trading game series
The *Elite* series has been running for longer than any of its space trading competitors. *Elite* was first released in September 1984, and, with *Elite IV* currently in development, it means the series has been running for 25 years.

First game to use Lenslok copy protection
The ZX Spectrum version of *Elite* was the first Lenslok copy-protected game. A small plastic lens ⑤ was placed over the television screen to unscramble a two-digit code that appeared after the game had loaded. The fiddly device was notoriously unreliable and only 11 games used it.

IF YOU LIKE THIS...
...you will adore *Eve Online*, the natural evolution of the space trading game.

▼ NEW RECORD   ▽ UPDATED RECORD

100 billion – the number of unique, fully explorable star systems in *Frontier: Elite II*, more than any other space game.

> *Elite is about the freedom it puts in the hands of gamers. Perhaps Grand Theft Auto is the only other game to do this (so far).*
> **David Braben, co-creator of Elite**

have spawned three stand-alone games. The *Elite* trilogy consists of *Elite*, *Frontier: Elite II* and *Frontier: First Encounters*. The *X* trilogy consists of *X: Beyond the Frontier*, *X2: The Threat* and *X3: Reunion*.

▼ First space game to use procedural generation

Elite was the first space game to feature a procedurally generated world, while *Frontier: Elite II* was the first to feature procedurally generated star systems. *Frontier: First Encounters* was the first space game to contain procedurally generated terrain and textures.

Procedural generation uses random inputs to a computer "procedure" to create something unique that also adheres to certain rules, such as *Elite II*'s star systems. These were generated by the game aggregating the mass of material within an early solar system into planets and moons that obey the laws of physics, but which have slightly randomized material distribution in order to ensure each system's uniqueness.

▼ Most games in a space trading game series

The *Elite* series shares the record with the *X* series for being the space trading game franchise with the highest number of stand-alone games. Both series

THE DARK WHEEL

ELITE

Robert Holdstock

INTERVIEW WITH... DAVID BRABEN

British computer programmer and game developer David Braben created the original *Elite* with co-author Ian Bell, and went on to create *Frontier: Elite II* and *Frontier: First Encounters*, among many other career successes. We caught up with David recently and asked him about the huge success of the series.

How did the idea for *Elite* first come about?
Elite started off with just an expanding star-field and a few simple spaceships within it. Shooting at these spaceships was quite a

repetitive experience. We needed a justification to keep playing, so trading was added and *Elite* as we know it was born.

Did you ever envisage it being such a huge success?
Yes. Perhaps that was the arrogance that came with still being a teenager at the time, but I think my biggest worry was of someone else doing a game that somehow overshadowed it.

What are your future plans for the series?
We plan to bring out *Elite IV* after *The Outsider*.

Can you put your finger on what it is that makes *Elite* so popular with gamers to this day?
I recognize that there is still quite a big dose of nostalgia [connected with the game], but it's also about the freedom that *Elite* puts in the hands of gamers. Perhaps *Grand Theft Auto* is the only other game to do this (so far).

PLATFORMS

SPEC

Developer: *Various*
Publisher: *Various*
Initial release: *Star Trek: Phaser Strike (1979), Microvision*

GAMEPLAY

Since the late 1970s, Star Trek games have been entertaining gamers, with genres ranging from text adventures to titanic starship combat simulations. The nature of the series – with its space travel and planetary exploration – makes it suitable for almost any type of game. Over the course of its 30-year history, the series has been released across most formats and new games continue to be released.

Most games releases for a single IP in one year

In 2000, nine separate *Star Trek*-licensed games were released, the highest number of game releases for an IP in a single year. The nine games were *Star Trek: Voyager: Elite Force* ❶, *Star Trek: ConQuest Online* ❷, *Star Trek: Deep Space Nine: The Fallen* ❸, *Star Trek: Starfleet Command II: Empires at War* ❹, *Star Trek: New Worlds* ❺, *Star Trek: Armada* ❻ *Star Trek: Klingon Academy* ❼, *Star Trek: Invasion* and *Star Trek: Starship Creator Warp II.*

First Star Trek game to feature all five Star Trek captains

Released in 2006 on Xbox 360, *Star Trek Legacy* became the first *Star Trek* game to feature the voices of all five main *Star Trek* captains: James T. Kirk (William Shatner), Jean-Luc Picard (Patrick Stewart), Benjamin Sisko (Avery Brooks), Kathryn Janeway (Kate Mulgrew) and Jonathan Archer (Scott Bakula). *Star Trek Legacy* was also the first game of the *Star Trek* franchise to be released on a next-generation console.

First Star Trek game

Two games share the record of first *Star Trek* game. The first non-licensed *Star Trek* game was *Star Trek*, a text-based starship combat simulator created in 1971 by Mike Mayfield for the SDS Sigma 7 computer. The program was written in BASIC and cast the player as the commander of a Federation starship sent on a mission to eliminate a Klingon threat from the galaxy. The first officially licensed *Star Trek* game was 1979's action blaster *Star Trek: Phaser Strike* for the Microvision handheld console, in which you were tasked with destroying Klingon ships with phaser blasts.

First Star Trek strategy game to use tabletop game rule set

Released in 1999, *Star Trek: Starfleet Command* was the first *Star Trek* game to use a rule system based entirely on a tabletop game. *Starfleet Command's* rules were rooted in the *Star Fleet Battles* strategy ship-to-ship warfare board game, created in 1979.

First Star Trek first-person shooter

The 1998 PC release *Star Trek: The Next Generation – Klingon Honor Guard* ❽ is the first game in the *Star Trek* franchise to be released as a first-person shooter (FPS). While 1997's *Star Trek: Generations* did contain some FPS sections, it isn't considered a *bona fide* FPS.

First Star Trek game to feature the Borg

The assimilating alien race known as the Borg made their first game appearance in 1996's *Star Trek: Borg* ❾. This time-travelling adventure used full motion video (FMV) clips throughout, including clips of the Borg, who were played by real actors.

First Star Trek game to offer voice-activated commands

The 2002 tactical space combat simulator *Star Trek: Bridge Commander* was the first *Star Trek* game that could be configured for voice-activated ship commands. The game allowed players to issue attack, move and repair orders simply by speaking the correct words into their microphones.

9 – the number of individual *Star Trek*-licensed games released in 2000, the **most games based on a single intellectual property licence released in a single year**.

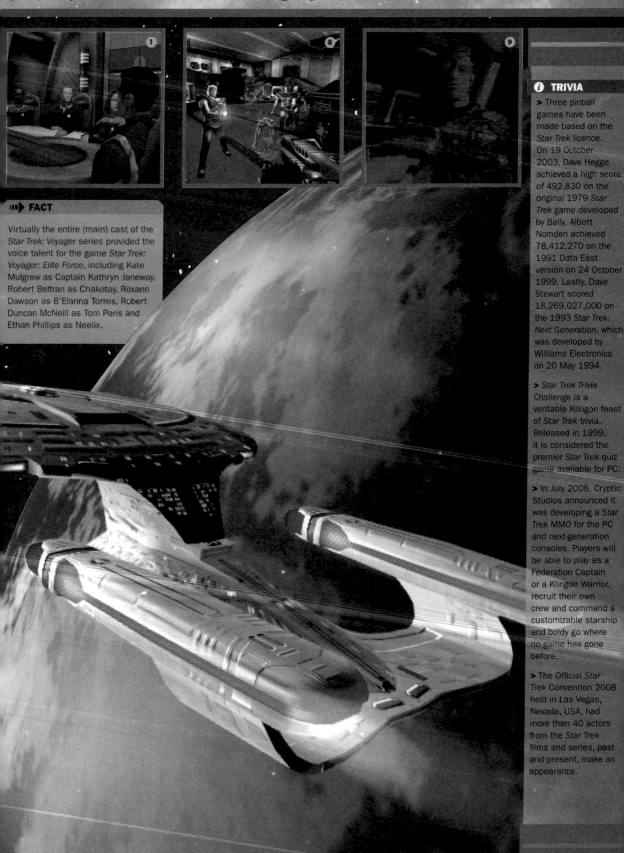

FACT

Virtually the entire (main) cast of the *Star Trek: Voyager* series provided the voice talent for the game *Star Trek: Voyager: Elite Force*, including Kate Mulgrew as Captain Kathryn Janeway, Robert Beltran as Chakotay, Roxann Dawson as B'Elanna Torres, Robert Duncan McNeill as Tom Paris and Ethan Phillips as Neelix.

ⓘ **TRIVIA**

> Three pinball games have been made based on the *Star Trek* licence. On 19 October 2003, Dave Hegge achieved a high score of 492,830 on the original 1979 *Star Trek* game developed by Bally. Albert Nomden achieved 78,412,270 on the 1991 Data East version on 24 October 1999. Lastly, Dave Stewart scored 18,269,027,000 on the 1993 *Star Trek: Next Generation*, which was developed by Williams Electronics on 20 May 1994.

> *Star Trek Trivia Challenge* is a veritable Klingon feast of *Star Trek* trivia. Released in 1999, it is considered the premier *Star Trek* quiz game available for PC.

> In July 2008, Cryptic Studios announced it was developing a *Star Trek* MMO for the PC and next-generation consoles. Players will be able to play as a Federation Captain or a Klingon Warrior, recruit their own crew and command a customizable starship and boldy go where no game has gone before.

> The Official *Star Trek* Convention 2008 held in Las Vegas, Nevada, USA, had more than 40 actors from the *Star Trek* films and series, past and present, make an appearance.

STAR WARS

PLATFORMS

SPEC

Developer:
Various
Publisher:
Various
Initial release:
Star Wars: The Empire
Strikes Back *(1982),*
Atari 2600

GAMEPLAY

*In 1977, the landscape
of the movie industry
changed forever with
the release of Star
Wars Episode IV:
A New Hope (USA).
Over the next three
decades, the Star
Wars franchise
would also have
an unparalleled
impact on the
space video game
genre, spawning
more games
than any other
licence in history.
With such a
broad range of games
to choose from the
gameplay for Star
Wars games varies
enormously and caters
for most gaming
tastes, but you can
rely on seeing your
favourite Star Wars
characters and lots of
lightsaber dueling.*

First Star Wars game
The first *Star Wars* movie did not
get its first video game outing until
after the film's sequel, *The Empire
Strike Back*, was released. The
first game in the franchise was
Star Wars: The Empire Strikes Back
(1982) on the Atari 2600; the first
arcade game based on the first
movie didn't arrive until 1983's
Star Wars.

3

First game to use
both Euphoria and DDM
technologies
Star Wars: The Force Unleashed
❸ is the first game to use both
the ground-breaking Euphoria and
Digital Molecular Matter (DMM)
technologies. Euphoria is a
behavioural simulation engine that
ensures the game's characters
move and act in lifelike ways, while
DMM is a physics engine that
adds realism to a game, dictating
the way that materials break and
how grass sways in the wind, for
example.

Most playable characters
in an action-adventure game
The most playable characters in
an action-adventure video game
are found in *LEGO® Star Wars II:
The Original Trilogy* ❷, which
features 50 characters unique
to the game, with a further 46
available if a saved game from the
original *LEGO® Star Wars* is loaded.
The game also allows players
to mix and match body parts to
create over 1 million customized
characters. It proved a massive
success and took over $1 million
(£535,000) in its opening week.

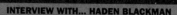

INTERVIEW WITH... HADEN BLACKMAN

**Haden Blackman worked on
classic games such as *Monkey
Island 2* and *Maniac Mansion*,
and was project lead for 2008's
ground-breaking *Star Wars: The
Force Unleashed*. We caught up
with him and asked about
working with such a revered
media franchise.**

**What makes *Star Wars*
games so endearing?**
I think the credit goes to the
characters and stories that George
Lucas created. We have such a rich
world to play with, and it allows us
to focus our energy into creating
a great game, rather than having
to come up with a setting that
people will be interested in.

**What have *Star Wars* games
added to the *Star Wars*
universe?**

Besides
new worlds,
characters
and stories,
the primary
addition is
the ability
to interact
directly with
the saga.
Movies are
great, but our games allow fans and
newcomers to experience the *Star
Wars* universe in an entirely different
way and be fully immersed in it.

**What does *The Force Unleashed*
bring to the *Star Wars* franchise?**
Unleashed tells the story of Darth
Vader's secret apprentice, and
acts as a bridge between the two
movie trilogies, giving players an
entirely new perspective on the
Star Wars saga.

FACT

The *Jedi Knight* first-person shooter franchise ran for eight years, from 1995 to 2003, which is longer than any other *Star Wars* series. Interestingly, the original game in the franchise *Star Wars: Dark Force* 4 didn't have Jedi Knight in the title.

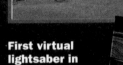

TRIVIA

Star Wars: Force Commander 6 was originally planned as a 2D strategy game before being completely redesigned for 3D play.

GWR QUIZ

Q12. What was the first *Star Wars* game to feature lightsaber action?

NEW RECORD   UPDATED RECORD

First Star Wars MMORPG

It was 21 years after the release of the original *Star Wars* game that the franchise spawned its first massively multiplayer online game: *Star Wars: Galaxies – An Empire Divided* 8 in 2003. *Star Wars: Knights of the Old Republic*, the **first *Star Wars* role-playing game**, was also released in 2003.

First Star Wars inter-licence game

In 1997, *Star Wars: Monopoly* 5 became the first *Star Wars* game to be based on two official licences. However, it would be 2005's release of *LEGO® Stars Wars* that would see the first ever inter-license *Star Wars* game based on the events of the *Star Wars* movies.

First Star Wars real-time strategy game

On its PC release in 1998, *Star Wars Supremacy* (a.k.a. *Star Wars Rebellion* in the UK) became the first ever *Star Wars* real-time strategy game. The very first *Star Wars* strategy game was *Star Wars Chess*, released in 1993.

First game to feature digitized speech exclusively from a movie

Atari's 1983 *Star Wars* arcade game 7 was the first in which all the speech was digitized from a movie. Speech was featured in *Discs of Tron*, which was based on the movie *Tron* (USA/Taiwan, 1982) and released three months before the *Stars Wars* game, but only some of the dialogue was taken from the movie; the rest was recorded specifically for the game.

First game to contain lightsaber action

Star Wars: Jedi Arena for the Atari 2600 1 was the first game to contain lightsaber action. While failing to accurately simulate lightsaber duelling, the game challenged the player to use a lightsaber to destroy enemies by deflecting laser bolts towards them and is based on the scene in the original *Star Wars* movie in which Luke Skywalker first learns to wield a lightsaber and feel the Force.

First virtual lightsaber in a video game

The first video game to let the player swing a virtual lightsaber in anger is *LEGO® Star Wars: The Complete Saga*, released for the Nintendo Wii in November 2007. The game utilizes the motion sensing capabilities of the Wii Remote, allowing players to control their lightsaber by swinging the controller.

WING COMMANDER

How goes the war against the Terrans?

⚙ PLATFORMS

PC
PS1
PS2
PS3
PSP
XBOX 360
XBOX
DS
GBA
Wii

✂ SPEC

Developer:
Origin Systems Inc.
Publisher:
Electronic Arts
Initial release:
Wing Commander
(1990), PC

💲 GAMEPLAY

In 1990, Wing Commander revolutionized PC gaming. The game was a deep, yet accessible, space combat game driven by a compelling plot, which charted humanity's conflict with an alien race called the Kilrathi. Wing Commander would go on to spawn numerous sequels and push countless boundaries, with Wing Commander III and IV even boasting a cast rivalling many Hollywood movies.

▸ First Hollywood star to top both film and video game charts

Mark Hamill was the first actor to star in both a No.1-selling video game and a box office-topping Hollywood movie. Hamill played the role of Luke Skywalker in *Star Wars* (USA, 1977). He returned to the role in the two sequels; *Star Wars: The Empire Strikes Back* (USA, 1980) and *Star Wars: Return of the Jedi* (USA, 1983), both of which were also No.1 box office hits. In 1994, Hamill played the role of Colonel Christopher Blair in the No.1-selling PC game *Wing Commander III: Heart of the Tiger* ❶. He resumed the role in *Wing Commander IV: The Price of Freedom* and *Wing Commander: Prophecy*, both of which were also No.1 sellers.

▸ Most expensive space combat game

The most expensive space combat game ever developed was *Wing Commander IV: The Price of Freedom* ❷, which cost $14 million (£9 million), $8 million (£5 million) of which was spent on Hollywood actors and the game's Full Motion Video (FMV) cutscenes.

▸ First space game to be made into a Hollywood movie

In 1999, *Wing Commander* became the first movie to be based on a space game. Its cast included Freddie Prinze Jr. and David Suchet. Chris Roberts – the creator of the *Wing Commander* franchise – also directed the *Wing Commander* movie ❺, becoming the **first game designer to direct a film version of a video game.**

▸ Longest-running space combat simulator

The *Wing Commander* series is both the **highest-selling** and **longest-running space combat game** of all time, selling five million units in total. *Wing Commander III: Heart of the Tiger* sold over one million units, making it the **first PC space game to break the one million sales mark.** The series ran for eight years, from 1990 (*Wing Commander*) to 1998 (*Wing Commander: Secret Ops*), longer than any other space combat series.

"Never work with animals, kids or animatronics! The animatronics sucked! I remade them for the *Wing Commander* film and they sucked again."
Chris Roberts, Creator of Wing Commander

▸ Most Full Motion Video footage in a space game

Wing Commander IV: The Price of Freedom holds the record for the greatest amount of FMV footage within a space game. The total combined length of all the cutscenes comes to an impressive 3 hr 52 min 7 sec – longer than most space-related movies!

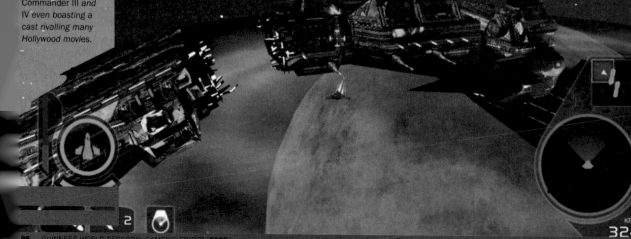

$14 million (£9 million) – the cost of developing the **most expensive space combat game**, *Wing Commander IV: The Price of Freedom*, which was released in 1996.

INTERVIEW WITH... CHRIS ROBERTS

Chris Roberts is the creator of the *Wing Commander* series. We asked him about his work.

What was the key inspiration behind *Wing Commander*?
Wing Commander was the natural result of my obsession with both video games and films. I always wanted to make a game that made me feel like I was inside *Star Wars*, fighting the good fight and saving humanity from impending doom. I wanted a game that wasn't about a high score, but more about living inside a cinematic environment, with your actions determining the outcome of the story.

Which game are you most proud of?
Probably the original *Wing Commander*. It certainly feels like the most perfectly designed and balanced game I ever made, and it's a world that still endures in people's imaginations.

What was it like working with animatronics while filming *Wing Commander III* and *IV*?
Never work with animals, kids or animatronics! The animatronics sucked! I remade them for the *Wing Commander* film and they sucked again. I should have used the dancer in a suit model that *Alien* (USA, 1979) used and shot them to look big – performers... with heavy animatronic heads can never move quickly.

you in... Commander.

First use of an animatronic character
In 1994, *Wing Commander III: Heart of the Tiger* became the first game to use animatronic characters in its FMV footage. These mechanized characters were used to depict the Kilrathi aliens and cost $200,000 (£130,000).

First game to release a speech pack
In 1991, *Wing Commander II: Vengeance of the Kilrathi* ❸ became the first game to release a speech pack, the *Wing Commander II: Speech Accessory Pack* ❻. This enabled owners of Sound Blaster sound cards to hear the characters, voiced by professional actors, speaking for the first time.

First multiplayer space combat gamey
On its release in 1994, *Wing Commander Armada* became the first 3D space combat game to feature multiplayer options, with players able to compete against each other in split-screen mode or over a network or modem connection.

> ▷ **NEW RECORD**
> ▷ **UPDATED RECORD**

Sound Blaster™ Compatible Version

WING COMMANDER
Vengeance 2 Kilrathi™

SPEECH ACCESSORY PACK

Disk # **1**

IBM 5.25" High Density

ORIGIN

SPACE GAMES ROUND-UP

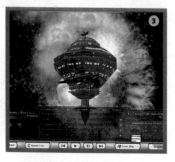

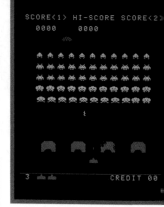

ℹ TRIVIA

> Tomohiro Nishikado, the creator of *Space Invaders*, originally wanted to use aeroplanes as the enemies, but found them too difficult to animate on a simple 8-bit processor.

> Back in 1983, the British novelist Martin Amis wrote a book entitled *Invasion of the Space Invaders*. "I knew instantly that this was something different," he wrote. "Cinematic melodrama blazing on the screen, infinite firing capacity, the beautiful responsiveness of the defending turret, the sting and pow of the missiles..."

> *Star Wars* games are many and varied and have covered virtually every gaming genre from racing game through to MMORPG. (See p.94 for more!)

> The acceleration that occurs in *Space Invaders* makes the game challenging: the fewer aliens, the faster they move and the harder they are to kill. A nice bit of gameplay, but it appears to have come around by accident. The programmers discovered that the fewer the aliens, the faster the processor could render them – a quirk the programmers decided to keep in!

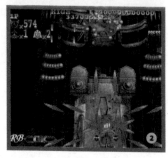

▶ First video game to feature animated aliens

Game: *Space Invaders*
Publisher: Taito
The original arcade version of *Space Invaders* ④ in 1978 was the first video game to feature an animated alien – in fact, it had four different species of them. This classic space-shooter became the first coin-op adapted for the Atari 2600.

▶ Longest game of Space Invaders

Game: *Space Invaders*
Publisher: Taito
Between 29 August and 2 September 1980, Eric Furrer (Canada) set a world record for the longest marathon session of *Space Invaders*. The machine on which 12-year-old Furrer played was fitted with a special button that he used to pause the game for bathroom breaks, which no doubt helped him set his impressive record time of 38 hr 30 min.

▶ First space racing game

Game: *F-Zero*
Publisher: Nintendo
The first exponent of the genre was Nintendo's *F-Zero*, a launch title for the SNES that made its debut in 1990. The game was later re-released for the Wii in 2006 through Virtual Console.

👍 IF YOU LIKE THIS...

... then you'll probably be a big fan of Fantasy and Sci-Fi games. Battle over to p.134 to begin your quest!

▶ NEW RECORD ▷ UPDATED RECORD

▶ First arcade game debated by government

Game: *Space Invaders*
Publisher: Taito
In 1981, George Foulkes, the Labour MP for Ayrshire South, UK, tabled a private members' bill to have *Space Invaders* banned, citing a connection between video-gaming and child "deviancy". The "Control of *Space Invaders* (and other Electronic Games)" bill was debated for 22 minutes before being narrowly defeated by 114 votes to 94.

▶ First sit-down arcade cabinet to use fresnel-lens projection

Game: *StarBlade*
Publisher: Namco
The first-person arcade shooter *StarBlade* (1991) featured quadraphonic sound and a vibrating cockpit seat ⑤. It was also the first sit-down arcade cabinet to use a fresnel lens to reflect the image from a standard 26-in monitor on to the interior of the "pod", giving a unique 3D wraparound "space" effect. A fresnel lens (named after its inventor, Augustin-Jean Fresnel) is a thin, lightweight lens composed of concentric rings, such as those used in lighthouses.

sold 4.03 million units, making it the best-selling third-person space combat game. *Starfox 64* was also the first game to use Nintendo's Super FX Chip, when it was built into the cartridge of the SNES version in 1993, and the first N64 game to feature filled solid vector polygons.

▽ Highest Giga Wing 2 score
Game: *Giga Wing 2*
Publisher: Capcom
On 27 February 2008, Rodrigo Lopez (USA) achieved history's highest ever video-game score playing on *Giga Wing 2*  for the Sega Dreamcast gaming console. On the Score Attack Mode – Stage 7, Lopez scored 13,617,120,714,066,509,130 points (that's 13 quintillion, 617 quadrillion, 120 trillion, 714 billion, 66 million, 509 thousand, 130).

The record for the **lowest high score** in video-game history was set on Cinematronic's *Space Wars* and is a mere 19 points.

> He cleared out the whole level one [of Space Invaders] basically on brain control... He learned almost instantaneously!
> **Eric C. Leuthardt, MD, on his patient – a teenager with epilepsy – who learned to play video games using mind control**

▼ Highest Space Invaders score using mind control
A team of neurosurgeons, neurologists and engineers at Washington University, St Louis, USA, have devised a hands-free system of playing the classic video game *Space Invaders* using brain power alone . As part of pioneering studies into brain activity in November 2006, they attached an electrocorticographic grid to the brain of a teenager suffering from epilepsy. Engineers then adapted Atari software to react to stimuli transmitted through this grid, so that the boy could control an on-screen cursor simply by imagining the movements he would have to make to do so. The boy reached the third screen of the game, amassing 5,000 points.

Highest Asteroids score
Game: *Asteroids*
Publisher: Atari
The highest score ever reached in a game of *Asteroids* ① is 41,336,440, set by Scott Safran (USA) in 1982. His classic score is one of the longest-standing world records in video gaming.

▼ Best-selling third-person space combat game
Game: *Starfox 64*
Publisher: Nintendo
According to VGchartz.com, the N64 3D space shooter *Starfox 64*

ⓘ TRIVIA
> In 1961, the illustrious-sounding Hingham Institute in Cambridge, Massachusetts, USA, sponsored the Study Group on Space Warfare. One of the aims was the "dynamic simulation of a weapons system"; the result was *Spacewar!*, the **first shooting game**.

> Hardcore turn-based space-strategy game *Galactic Civilizations II: Dark Avatar* ③ is the highest-rated space-strategy game on GameRankings.com, with an average of 92% scored from 26 reviews.

> It is impossible to complete or win the game *Asteroids* – it just keeps getting harder and harder until you give up exhausted or get totally smashed to smithereens!

RICHARD GARRIOTT – FIRST GAME DEVELOPER IN SPACE?

On 12 October 2008, *Tabula Rasa* creator Richard Garriott (USA) ⑦ hopes to become the first game developer in space after buying a $30 million (£16.6 million) berth aboard a Russian *Soyuz* spacecraft. Mr Garriott – who is currently undergoing an eight-month training regime – will dock with the ISS (International Space Station), which orbits the earth every 90 minutes at an altitude of 340 km (211 miles) at a speed of approximately 28,163 km/h (17,500 mph).

He will also become the first son of a NASA astronaut to go into space, following in the space boots of his father, *Skylab* veteran Owen K. Garriott ⑧.

Race Driver: GRID's Ego engine is the **most advanced damage-engine in a driving game**. Up to 70 components of each car can crumple, shatter, break or fall off and remain on the track as hazards!

CONTENTS

WHEELS & THRILLS

IF YOU LIKE TO LIVE YOUR LIFE AT HIGH SPEED, THEN RACING GAMES COULD BE FOR YOU. JUST CHOOSE YOUR RACER, SHIFT INTO GEAR, PUT THE PEDAL TO THE METAL AND HIT THE ROAD.

👤 EXPERT

A prolific freelancer, Simon Parkin has written extensively for *Edge* magazine, Eurogamer, Yahoo Games, *PlayStation Official Magazine* and other high-profile print titles and websites. He is also a game designer and producer working on both console and web-based titles.

↻ OVERVIEW

Racing games have existed almost as long as it's been possible to move a block of pixels around a screen. Their common aim might be straight-forward: get from A to B in the shortest possible time, but there are as many ways to go about it as there are vehicles in a game designer's imagination. From Mario's go-karts through Wipeout's streaking hover ships to Gran Turismo's meticulously recreated production cars, the number of ways to race in video games is matched only by the number of virtual tracks available to race them on.

The **first racing game** to emerge from gaming's primordial soup was Atari's *Gran Trak 10,* released in 1974. Looking at it now, the gameplay and visuals appear primitive, but back then controlling this boxy-looking car around a single, oval track was state-of-the-art.

A head-to-head rally with unbelievable sound effects!!
The most realistic car racing game

As the ▶ **first arcade game to use mask ROM chip**, *Gran Trak 10* was hugely expensive to develop and distribute. Nevertheless, the game spawned a handful of spin-offs, including 1974's *Gran Trak 20*, the ▶ **first two-player racing game**, and 1976's *Le Mans*, the ▶ **first game to offer multiple circuits**. Eight years after *Gran Trak*'s debut, Japanese developer Namco released *Pole Position*, a far more advanced driving game in which players control a Formula One car at the Fuji racetrack. Contrary to popular belief, it wasn't the ▶ **first game to utilize the "behind car" perspective** – that honour was bestowed upon *Sega Road Race* in 1976 – but *Pole Position* most certainly was the ▶ **first game to feature AI opponents on a 3D circuit**.

Pole Position's use of realistic graphics established the genre's popularity, and the following months saw driving games evolve with titles like Tatsumi's *TX-1* in 1983, which was the ▶ **first driving game to offer multiple routes** through a race by breaking

▐▶ FACT

In 1990, the tobacco conglomerate Philip Morris filed a lawsuit claiming copyright infringement against Namco, Atari and Sega for featuring Marlboro advertising billboards in the games *Super Monaco GP* and *Final Lap*. At the time, the board was on display at the real Suzuka and Monaco racing circuits, but its use had not been cleared for video games. As a result, Namco was forced to replace EPROM chips on the boards to remove Marlboro from the *Final Lap* games.

courses up into forked stages.

The tradition of arcade-style racing games developed apace through the early 1990s with Namco's 1993 *Ridge Racer* and

TIMELINE

1974	1982	1983	1986	1988
Gran Trak 10 and *Gran Trak 20* both released by Atari. **1976** *Le Mans* released by Atari.	Namco develop and release *Pole Position*, which goes on to become the **most popular arcade game of 1983** and the **most ported racing game**.	*Laser Grand Prix* uses a recording of a real track and overlays computer-generated cars on top. **1985** *Hang On* released by Sega.	Seminal racer *OutRun* released by Sega. Players get to choose one of three soundtracks to accompany their drive.	Taito's *Miami Vice*-inspired *Chase H.Q.* released. Atari's *Hard Drivin'* released. **1990** *F-Zero* released on Super Famicom.

SUZUKI'S FERRARI CHALLENGE

One of the toughest and most realistic modern racing games is Sega's *Ferrari F355 Challenge*. Released in 1999, some versions of the arcade cabinet utilize three screens and come with an H-shaped gear stick and three foot-pedals. Game designer Yu Suzuki ⑧ claims it's one of his favourite creations, not least because during the development he got to "fly to Italy, meet the Ferrari guys, drive around Ferarri's circuit and eat at a famous restaurant."

▼ **NEW RECORD** ▽ **UPDATED RECORD**

TRIVIA

> The **first racing game**, *Gran Trak 10*, was plagued by a multitude of problems during development and it took Atari many attempts to iron out the game's numerous bugs and control issues. *Gran Trak 10* was finally delivered at a cost of $1,095 (£467) per cabinet. However, its problems weren't over. Due to an accounting error, the finished game was sold for $995 (£424), meaning that, despite the fact the game was Atari's best-selling title of 1974, the company lost $100 (£42) on every unit sold.

Sega Rally ⑥, in 1995, providing high-octane racing that was full of the ever-more impressive thrills and spills that players had come to expect. However, 1989's *Hard Drivin'* ④, originally designed as a driving simulation, had seen driving games head down a slightly different track and go in search of a more realistic automotive experience with the **first use of a force feedback wheel**. This enabled the gamer to get a "feel" of the road with the steering wheel responding to the driver's actions.

This realistic approach was taken a stage further in 1997 with the birth of the *Gran Turismo* series, which recreated real-life cars in meticulous detail and replayed races in the style of TV footage. While in 2000, *Le Mans 24* ⑨ even allowed Dreamcast players to participate in the famous race in real time over a 24-hour period.

Of course, racing and driving games aren't just about cars – virtually every kind of vehicle, from multi-wheeled articulated trucks to two-wheeled

motorbikes have had their own racing games. Motorbike racers in particular have been popular since the likes of *Excitebike* and *Hang On* ③ hit the arcades in the mid 1980s; and truck titles, such as *18 Wheeler: American Pro Trucker* ⑦ in 2000 have also proved popular.

At the other end of the scale futuristic racers *Wipeout* (1995), *Rollcage* (1999) and *F-Zero* (1990) offered players a chance to leave the roads and experience races of the future, ensuring that there would be a racing game to suit every taste.

1992	1993	1997	2000	2007	2008
Virtua Racing released by Sega, one of the first games to use dedicated 3D hardware at 30 Hz. *Super Mario Kart* is the **first console kart-racing game**.	*Ridge Racer* and *Daytona USA* released. **1995** *Sega Rally Championship* enables players to race on different track surfaces.	*Gran Turismo* released; it goes on to become the **best-selling PlayStation game**. **1999** Release of *Driver*, *Crazy Taxi* and *Ferrari F355 Challenge* ⑪.	*Metropolis Street Racer* released. **2002** *Burnout 2: Point of Impact* released. **2005** *Project Gotham 3* released.	A bumper year for racing games as *Forza 2*, *Sega Rally Revo*, *Project Gotham Racing 4* and *Need for Speed: ProStreet* are all released.	*Race Driver: GRID* and *Gran Turismo 5 Prologue*, the precursor to the much anticipated *Gran Turismo 5*, released.

BURNOUT

⚙ PLATFORMS

PC · XBOX 360 · XBOX · PS1 · PS2 · DS · PS3 · GBA · PSP · Wii

🔧 SPEC

Developer:
Criterion Games
Publisher:
Acclaim
Initial release:
Burnout *(2001),*
PlayStation 2

⇅ GAMEPLAY

Burnout *has always
been about super-fast
cars weaving through
traffic at breakneck
speeds and the
eye-watering crashes
that result. The 2008
release* Burnout
Paradise *saw a new
free-form, open-world
structure set in the
fictional Paradise City.*

◤ First game to make crashing a high-score challenge

The primary aim in any racing game is to get from A to B in the fastest time possible, which usually means avoiding crashing. *Burnout 2* ③ turned this idea on its head, tasking players with driving as fast as they can into busy road junctions in order to cause the maximum amount of damage, in financial terms – a racing game first.

◤ First Xbox 360 title to take advantage of kiosk downloads

Following the release of the Xbox 360, Microsoft deployed a number of specially branded kiosks ④ in game stores across the world. Used primarily as demo machines, these consoles also allowed users to plug in their own memory unit and download additional exclusive game content for free. *Burnout Revenge* ⑤ was the first game to take advantage of kiosk downloads in the USA.

◢ FACT

In January 2008, in-game advertising network IGA Worldwide Inc. announced that it was working with leading brands to incorporate adverts – on radio stations, billboards and vehicles – into the *Burnout* series. IGA estimated that the in-game advertising market is worth $670 million (£335 million) annually.

◤ Most online multiplayer challenges

Burnout Paradise ② allows players to jump in and out of friends' cities at any point. Up to eight players can drive around Paradise City at

BURNOUT 2: CRASH MODE LEADERBOARD
CATCH UP CHAOS (ZONE 24)

The crash mode in *Burnout 2* assigns dollar values to the damage a player causes at each level. The object is to make the biggest pile-up possible, and the game keeps a running tab to show you just how much damage you've inflicted.

RANK	SCORE	GAMERTAG/USERNAME	NATIONALITY	VEHICLE USED	VERSION
1	$313,987,776	*Vieraldo*	NLD	Cop Car	Gamecube
2	$246,780,208	*Spade 234s*	USA	Supercar	Xbox
3	$233,389,344	*NitrousBlazer*	CAN	Custom Roadster	Xbox
4	$221,609,840	*Brainkiller007*	GER	Custom Roadster	Gamecube
5	$217,523,632	*Cool Wolfe*	GER	Supercar	Xbox
6	$213,712,128	*Drew22werD*	USA	Custom Roadster	Xbox
7	$202,979,216	*James2k5*	GBR	Supercar	Gamecube
8	$199,890,144	*Rock Denver*	GBR	Supercar	Xbox
9	$197,804,320	*Addyboy GBR*	Japanese	Muscle	Gamecube
10	$196,091,280	*bizarrojeb USA*	Japanese	Muscle	Xbox

once and there are 50 multiplayer challenges to be completed as they do so. As every group combination has its own set of 50 challenges, the game's total number of multiplayer tasks stands at 350, which is the highest number of any racing game.

▼ Most breakable billboards in a racing game

For years, billboards and advertising hoardings have acted as impenetrable walls at the side of the racing game's track, providing a useful buffer should a player spin off the road. *Burnout Paradise* uses billboards in a very different way, challenging players to smash through every single one of the game's 120 billboards in return for a bonus achievement.

▼ Most collectables in a racing game

There are 570 collectables in *Burnout Paradise* (items that must be found by exploring Paradise City). Split into Super Jumps, Smashes and Burnout Billboards, along with 35 Drive Thrus and 11 Car Parks, the game keeps a record of how many collectables are left to find at any time and offers multiple rewards for those players who manage to track them all down.

> *There are no drivers in Burnout. There never have been. Burnout is all about the fun, arcade experience. It's larger than life and it's not real.*
> **Nick Channon,**
> **Senior producer of Burnout**

NEW RECORD   UPDATED RECORD

FORZA MOTORSPORT

PLATFORMS

SPEC

Developer:
Turn 10 Studios
Publisher:
Microsoft Game Studios
Initial release:
Forza Motorsport (2005), Xbox

GAMEPLAY

As Microsoft's answer to the Gran Turismo series, the Forza games take an equally serious approach to recreating the real-life physics and complexities of motorsport. The first game was applauded for featuring licensed cars that degrade if involved in crashes, a feature carried over to the sequel in even more exacting detail **7**. Likewise, the game's massive range of downloadable cars and its extensive decal editor, which allows enthusiastic players to paint anything and everything on to the cars, has further marked the series out from its motorsports rivals.

Largest number of licensed cars featuring car damage

The first *Forza* **1** game was notable for convincing all of its licensors to permit car damage but *Forza 2* **2**, with 349 licensed in-game vehicles, has the largest number of real-life cars featuring car damage in a racing game.

Largest number of downloadable cars

Since *Forza 2*'s launch in May 2007 there have been four downloadable car packs for the game. The first, released on 1 August 2007, featured three free Nissan cars. Since then, a total of 39 vehicles have been added to the game, including the 2008 Audi R8 **6**, the SEAT Leon Supercup and the Ferrari FXX.

Most advanced decal editor in a racing game

Around 4,100 layers of graphics can be created with *Forza 2*'s decal editor, which allows multiple shapes and colours to be applied to the bumpers, sides **3** and hood of a car to build up complex customizations. The editor boasts 360 vinyl shapes (all of which can be stretched and shrunk), plus 150 manufacturer logos and nine alphabet fonts, allowing those with time, skill and patience to create almost any image for their car.

Most detailed telemetry readouts in a console game

Forza has the most detailed data, or telemetry, readouts **4** for any console driving game. The level of technical data revealed includes suspension travel, car-body G forces, traction patches and tyre flex. No other console driving game offers the player such advanced feedback.

IF YOU LIKE THIS...

... then you're a fan of proper driving games and will adore *GTR 2*, arguably the best racing simulation on the PC.

Longest set-distance race in a car racing game

The longest track featured in *Forza Motorsport* is Nürburgring Nordschleife at 20.99 km (13.04 miles). This is slightly longer than the length of the real Nürburgring Nordschleife's regular simple configuration, at 20.8 km (12.9 miles). The track has appeared in a variety of racing series, including *Gran Turismo*, *TOCA Race Driver* and *Project Gotham Racer*.

Most advanced AI drivers

In *Forza*, players can train computer-controlled drivers  to represent them in races. The "drivatars" are trained through a series of tests during which the player is asked to perform manoeuvres such as braking hard for a hairpin or taking a chicane at high speed. The drivatar then mimics the player's driving style to ultimately become an AI incarnation of the player, behaving in a very similar way. This drivatar technology is the most realistic player-driver mimicry ever created.

■ **NEW RECORD**   ▽ **UPDATED RECORD**

> *Just racing Forza will not make you a pro-racer, but if you take some racing classes first, and then go and play Forza, your racing skill will improve dramatically.*
>
> **Aaron Ogus, Turn 10 network coding engineer and racing consultant**

ⓘ TRIVIA

> *Forza Motorsport 2* uses the same simulation engine as the previous iteration of the game, however the physics update rate employed by the game now refreshes much faster, which makes the simulation of car behaviour more subtle and realistic.

> A bug in the initial release of *Forza Motorsport 2* gave the Lotus Elan a performance advantage over other vehicles, allowing players to put in extraordinarily fast times. A patch was released to downgrade the car and Turn 10 Studios began wiping scoreboard times and online rankings for players who had:

• A top 5,000 scoreboard time using a manual transmission vehicle set before 25 August 2007.

• A sub-10 second lap time.

• A top 2,000 scoreboard time using a Lotus Elan.

> The oldest car in *Forza Motorsport 2* is a 1954 Mercedes 300SL Gullwing Coupé. With a real-life top speed of around 260 km/h (161 mph), the 300SL was the fastest production car of its time.

TIME RECORDS*

RANK	GAMERTAG	LAP TIME	CAR TYPE	DATE
1	V12 BackONE AbS	01:24.4	#12 F333 SP	3 June 2008
2	R2P KimiMatt	01:24.6	#12 F333 SP	21 March 2008
-	V12 Fullspe3D	01:24.6	#12 F333 SP	5 March 2008
-	iCam v1	01:24.6	#12 F333 SP	6 June 2008
3	ooO x42x Ooo	01:24.7	#12 F333 SP	11 May 2008
4	Daveyskills	01:24.7	#12 F333 SP	5 June 2008
5	III LATTY III	01:24.7	#12 F333 SP	7 January 2008
6	iPicaso	01:24.7	#12 F333 SP	30 May 2008
7	xxD4RK SP33Dxx	01:24.8	#12 F333 SP	5 July 2008
8	V12 x TrAsGu x	01:24.8	#12 F333 SP	4 June 2008

Forza Motorsport 2, Europe: Donington – Grand Prix Circuit

GRAND THEFT AUTO

PLATFORMS

SPEC

Developer:
Rockstar Games
Publisher:
Take 2
Initial release:
Grand Theft Auto
(1997), PlayStation

GAMEPLAY

An epic free-roaming urban action series in which you undertake dangerous and often criminal missions. Although the game is controversial, the moral decisions each player makes have in-game consequences and affect the way other characters respond throughout the game.

Most successful entertainment product launch

On 29 April 2008, the release of *Grand Theft Auto IV*  generated $310 million (£159 million) of first-day sales worldwide. This is five times the $67 million (£33.5 million) revenue generated in the first 24 hours by *The Dark Knight* (USA, 2008), which is the most successful movie launch ever. The "Midnight Madness" launch ③ at thousands of stores worldwide made *GTA IV* the most successful entertainment product launch in history.

Longest marathon playing Grand Theft Auto IV

The longest continuous-play session on *Grand Theft Auto IV* is 28 hr 1 min, achieved by Jim Patton (USA) at the studios of Bushleague.tv in Los Angeles, California, USA, from 29–30 April 2008.

Most controversial video-game series

Grand Theft Auto has been the most consistently controversial video-game series in history. As of July 2008, over 4,000 news stories have been published about the game, including accusations of glamorized violence, alleged connections ②

with real-life crimes and the presumed corruption of gamers. Numerous lawsuits against *Grand Theft Auto* creators Rockstar Games have been put through the United States legal system since the first game was released in 1997.

In August 2008, the latest instalment, *GTA IV*, was banned in Thailand after an 18-year-old man murdered a taxi driver whilst alledgedly copying the gameplay. Thailand's Culture Ministry had already been pushing for tougher regulation of games like *GTA* and wants stricter age ratings and restrictions on the hours that people can play games in arcades.

Best-selling PlayStation 2 game

GTA: San Andreas ④ is the best-selling PlayStation 2 game of all time, with a massive 17.33 million copies sold.

GTA: Vice City is the third biggest with 14.2 million, and *GTA III* is fourth with 11.6 million. This makes *Grand Theft Auto* the most successful PS2 series ever.

Largest voice cast in a video game

GTA IV has a total credited cast of 861 voice actors, including over 174 actors playing named characters, radio DJs and TV voiceovers. The voices of Liberty City's many inhabitants were recorded by an additional 687 different performers, many of whom were *GTA* fans who volunteered their voices for a chance to appear in the game.

First computer-generated comedian

GTA IV is the first game to feature virtual versions of real comedians. Players can choose to go to a Liberty City comedy club and watch digital funny men performing stand-up routines edited especially for the game. One of the featured comedians is *The Office*'s Ricky Gervais ②.

IF YOU LIKE THIS...

... you might like *Scarface* (USA, 1983), a movie about a Cuban immigrant working his way up from street-level punk to Miami crime boss, a plot not dissimilar to that of *GTA: Vice City*.

Largest in-game soundtrack

GTA IV features 18 radio stations and 214 licensed tracks, beating the previous record of 156 songs in *GTA: San Andreas*. Players who register their copy of the game with the Rockstar Social Club website can opt to purchase MP3s of their favourite songs from Amazon.com by selecting them with the in-game mobile phone.

▷ Highest production budget

In an Interview with *The Times* dated 27 April 2008 Leslie Benzies, *GTA's* producer, estimated that production costs on *GTA IV* reached $100 million (£50 million), smashing the previous record of $70 million (£35 million) set by Sega's *Shenmue*.

Largest Grand Theft Auto environment

The *Grand Theft Auto* game with the largest playing area is *GTA: San Andreas*, which takes place over an area (which, because of its open-ended style, is known as a "sandbox") of roughly 44 km^2 (17 miles^2). Up to four times larger than other *GTA* titles, it contains three cities, 12 towns and many miles of virtual countryside.

▷ First Nintendo GTA game

GTA: Chinatown Wars, due in 2009, will appear on Nintendo DS with a new game engine, new characters and the DS's trademark stylus control.

Everything feels like it's moved on or moved up while still being very much part of the GTA series... And it's crazier than ever!
**Sam Houser,
President of Rockstar Games.**

¹₂₃ FIGURES

97.4% – The average rating on Game Rankings (www.gamerankings.com) for the PS3 version of *GTA IV*, the second highest-rated game of all time as of September 2008.

96.6% – The rating for the Xbox 360 version of *GTA IV*.

ⓘ TRIVIA

> A teaser site for WKTT, one of the in-game radio stations in *GTA IV*, invited people to call a telephone number to talk about how they felt about the current state of America in the style of a talk radio phone-in. The best rants were included in the final version of the game.

👤 EXPERT

> Most *GTA* experts agree that the fastest way to make money in any *GTA* game is to get a job. The most lucrative legal trade is being a cab driver. Stealing a police car, losing your wanted level and then embarking on dangerous vigilante missions is another slightly less legal way to get rich quick.

WORLDWIDE SALES – ALL FORMATS

RANK	GAME	UNITS
1	Grand Theft Auto: San Andreas	21.50 million
2	Grand Theft Auto: Vice City	17.50 million
3	Grand Theft Auto III	14.50 million
4	Grand Theft Auto IV	10.50 million
5	Grand Theft Auto: Liberty City Stories	8.25 million

BANNED & CONTROVERSIAL GAMES

VIDEO GAMES HAVE A LONG HISTORY OF CAUSING, AND SOMETIMES COURTING, CONTROVERSY. FOR LAW-MAKERS AND THE MEDIA, IT'S OFTEN NOT JUST FUN WITH GAMES.

USA

Originally titled *Pedestrian*, Exidy's 1976 game *Death Race* ➊ is usually cited as the ▸ **first controversial video game**. It was based on the movie *Death Race 2000* (USA, 1975), starring David Carradine, and was a simple driving game that challenged the player to run over as many "gremlins" as possible within a time limit. Many were concerned that it might inspire reckless driving and the game's notoriety provoked press coverage in the *National Enquirer* and television outrage on *60 Minutes*.

USA

Early pinball machines paid out cash prizes for high scores, which led to pinball being classified as gambling in the USA. In 1942, pinball machines were banned in New York, Los Angeles and Chicago. The mayor of New York City, Fiorello LaGuardia, even went so far as to smash pinball machines during a press conference ➎. Most bans were lifted by the early 1970s, but New York stood firm until 1976, which, at 34 years, makes it ▸ **the longest ban in gaming history**.

BRAZIL

Everquest ➏ was originally released in 1999 but was banned in Brazil nine years later in January 2008, which gives it the honour of having the ▸ **most belated video game ban**. Brazilian officials were reportedly upset that the game allowed players to choose to be either "evil" or "good" fantastical creatures. Judge Carlos Alberto Simões stated that the game encouraged "the subversion of public order" and was "an attack against the democratic state and the law and against public security".

MEXICO

Tom Clancy's Ghost Recon Advanced Warfighter 2 ➑ was banned in the state of Chihuahua, Mexico, because the state's governor was offended by the game's portrayal of the region and its people.

GREECE

On 30 July 2002, the Greek government hastily attempted to curtail illegal gambling by introducing law "3037" banning all electronic games. This, very briefly, led to Greece becoming the ▸ **first country to ban all video games**, including the innocuous *My Little Pony: Best Friends Ball* ➐. On 25 September 2002, the law was amended to allow the playing of all electronic and computer games providing there was "no financial gain for the player or any third party".

▶ FACTS

> After 11 September 2001, some elements of the media berated Microsoft, claiming that their *Flight Simulator* was so advanced that it could have been used by terrorists to learn how to fly and was therefore a "Terror Simulator".

> In some countries, games do not have to be banned to prevent people from buying them. In the UK, every game has to be submitted to the British Board of Film Classification (BBFC) before it can be sold in shops. If a game is not submitted for classification, it cannot be sold in shops in the UK.

UK

The image of scantily clad UK glamour model Maria Whittaker posing on the box cover led to games publisher Palace Software being accused of using inappropriate images to lure teenage boys into buying simple fighting game *Barbarian* **2** in 1987.

SAUDI ARABIA

Saudi Arabia's highest religious authority, the Higher Committee for Scientific Research and Islamic Law, issued a fatwa on *Pokémon* **3** in March 2001 because it had "possessed the minds" of Saudi children. The game has been equally criticised in other territories, with a Christian church in Mexico calling it "demonic".

CHINA

China banned the seemingly innocent *Football Manager 2005* **4** when Taipei of Taiwan, Hong Kong-Macao region and China's Tibet were represented in the game as independent countries. According to a Ministry of Culture circular in China, this "poses harm to the country's sovereignty and territorial integrity." Anyone caught selling the game is liable for a fine of 30,000 Yuan (£1,800; $4,400) and having their business licence revoked.

▼ NEW RECORD ▽ UPDATED RECORD

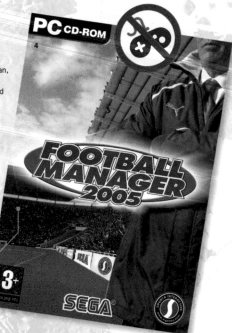

PC CD-ROM

FOOTBALL MANAGER 2005

3+

SEGA

i TRIVIA

> Many countries have their own ratings systems for game content, often evolved and adapted from laws relating to film classification and censorship. However, recently publishers have been attempting to create their own classification system designed specifically for the classification of video games.

> The 2001 winner of the IGN "Most Unnecessary Game of the Year" award went to *KZ Manager* – one of the four games in Germany banned for its support of the Nazi Party and use of the swastika. Sickeningly, this "resource management" game puts the player in charge of a concentration camp.

I am extremely disappointed in the Australian Government Classification Review Board's move to ban my video game.

**Mark Ecko,
US fashion designer**

AUSTRALIA

In Australia, the Office of Film and Literature Classification (OFLC) refused to classify *Marc Ecko's Getting Up: Contents Under Pressure* **9** . This dystopian urban action game, set in a future society where freedom of expression is suppressed, was refused classification, and therefore could not be sold in Australia, because it allegedly glorified graffiti. The fashion designer, lifestyle guru and grafitti enthusiast Marc Ecko **10**, who has attached his brand to the game, expressed his disappointment at the decision. The total number of games that have been refused classification in Australia is 14 as of August 2008, the ▼ **most games refused classification by a single country**.

GRAN TURISMO

GRAN TURISMO™
THE REAL DRIVING SIMULATOR

✖ SPEC

Developer:
Polyphony Digital
Publisher:
Sony
Initial release:
Gran Turismo (1997),
PlayStation

⇄ GAMEPLAY

The Gran Turismo series has always been about the relentless pursuit of motorsport realism. Players must earn their driver's licence before using credits to purchase cars, tune them up and enter a huge variety of races from around the globe.

◸ Best-selling racing game

On 9 May 2008, Sony Computer Entertainment Inc. announced that worldwide sales of the *Gran Turismo* franchise had reached 50 million units. This incredible figure was achieved just 10 years and 4 months after the launch of the first title in the franchise, *Gran Turismo* ①, in December 1997.

◸ First PlayStation 3 game to reach 1 million pre-orders

According to the website PlayStation Universe, *Gran Turismo 5 Prologue* ⑥, which is a kind of extended demo to the fifth entry in the *Gran Turismo* series, was the first PlayStation 3 game to generate 1 million pre-orders.

◸ Fastest-selling PlayStation 3 racing game

Following its release in March 2008, *Gran Turismo 5 Prologue* became the fastest-selling PlayStation 3 game ever with reported worldwide first-week sales of 639,548 copies (source VGChartz).

Since then, its first week sales have been surpassed only by *Grand Theft Auto IV* and *Metal Gear Solid 4* (which beat it by just 2,000 units), but it remains the fastest-selling racing game for the system.

◸ Oldest car in a racing game

Gran Turismo 4 ② features the Daimler Motor Carriage, which dates from 1886. Boasting a 462-cc (0.5-litre) engine and a stock weight of 290 kg (638 lb), it is the oldest drivable production car featured in any racing video game.

> " *It was actually surprising to us; the level of detail you can put into the cars and the detail on the screen – you can almost feel it in tangible form.*
> **Kazunori Yamauchi** ④ ,
> **Gran Turismo series creator**

◸ NEW RECORD   ◹ UPDATED RECORD

◸ Most post-release updates for a racing game

Since the Japanese release of *Gran Turismo 5 Prologue*, the game has undergone 11 iterative updates, bringing its version number to 2.10. The first game patch was released to the public on 25 December 2007 when the Japanese version's online game modes were activated. On 28 March 2008, a further update changed the game's name to *Gran Turismo 5 Prologue Spec II*. Another update in autumn 2008 introduced damage modelling to the game.

▐▶ FACT

A polygon is a 2D shape that can be coloured, shaded or textured. In video-game graphics, polygons are combined to make complex shapes. The cars featured in *Gran Turismo 5 Prologue* are made up of an average of 200,000 polygons. By contrast, the cars in *Gran Turismo 4* feature an average of 4,000 polygons. Polyphony Digital claims that a car in *GT 4* has the same number of polygons as a headlight in *Gran Turismo 5 Prologue*.

ℹ TRIVIA

> Series creator Kazunori Yamauchi designed the on-board computer for the real Nissan GT-R **7**. The Polyphony Digital logo appears on the dashboard screen when you start up the car.

> In *Gran Turismo 5 Prologue*, players can compete on six tracks with 12 total layouts, including Fuji Speedway, Suzuka Circuit and, for the first time ever in the series, Daytona International Speedway.

> The *Gran Turismo* series theme song "Moon Over The Castle" is arranged and performed by Vince DiCola, who also composed music for the movies *Rocky IV* (USA, 1985) and *Transformers: The Movie* (USA/Japan, 1986).

> The original *Gran Turismo* game features 178 automobiles, which can be raced over 14 race tracks.

▌ Most branded steering-wheel controllers

Peripheral manufacturer Logitech (known as Logicool in Japan) has launched no less than seven different official racing wheels for the *Gran Turismo* series, including the G25 Racing Wheel, the Driving Force GT **5**, the Driving Force Pro and the GT Force. All previous *Gran Turismo* wheels are supported by *Gran Turismo 5 Prologue* on the PlayStation 3.

Best-selling PlayStation game

The original PlayStation release of *Gran Turismo* sold 10.85 million units worldwide, making it the highest-selling game for the system. Its sequel, *Gran Turismo 2* **3**, is third on the all-time best-sellers list with recorded sales of 9.37 million units.

Largest Instruction manual for a racing game

The first Chinese and Japanese editions of *Gran Turismo 4* include a whopping 212-page reference guide. The book features a car index, an introduction to racing physics and theory as well as various tutorials written by professional drivers.

NEED FOR SPEED

⚙ PLATFORMS

✘ SPEC

Developer:
EA Canada
Publisher:
Electronic Arts
Initial release:
The Need For Speed
(1994), 3DO

⇄ GAMEPLAY

Originally more of a
simulation than an
arcade game, the Need
For Speed series has
changed format
numerous times over
the 15 years it has
been running. Recent
Need For Speed titles
have been an entirely
arcade-based
experience with stylized
imagery designed to
appeal to "modders"
– people who like to
modify their cars.

? GWR QUIZ

Q14. What is the
highest recorded
speed of a car in a
driving game?

▸ Most developers involved in a racing series

The Need For Speed ① was first
created in 1994 by Distinctive
Software, a.k.a. Unlimited
Software. In 1991, following
a buy-out from Electronic Arts
(EA), development passed to EA
Canada, who handled the series
for the next 11 years. In 2002,
Vancouver-based Black Box Games
was contracted to develop *Need for
Speed: Hot Pursuit 2*, a company
that was subsequently bought by
Electronic Arts to become EA Black
Box. In addition, spin-off titles *Need
for Speed: Porsche Unleashed* ②
and *Need For Speed: V-Rally* were
developed by Eden Studios, and
ports of the games have been

handled, variously, by EA Seattle,
EA Redwood Shores, EA Mobile,
EA UK and Exient Entertainment,
bringing the total number of
development studios who have
worked on the series to 10.

▸ Most releases in a racing game series

With no less than 17 different
titles bearing the *Need For Speed*
name, Electronic Arts' franchise
boasts the most separate releases
of any racing game series.

▸ Fastest recorded speed for a car in a driving game

A video posted on the internet on
4 May 2007 showed YouTube user
"Morettti" reaching 682 km/h

(423.7 mph) in *Need For Speed:
Carbon* ③, the fastest recorded
speed in a car for any driving
game. The record was achieved
in the Ford GT through a
combination of nitro use
and drifting.

▸ Most console platforms for a racing series

Need For Speed games have
appeared on no less than
13 different gaming platforms
(3DO, PlayStation, PS2, PS3,
GameCube, Wii, Xbox, Xbox 360,
Nintendo DS, Game Boy Advance,
PlayStation Portable, Sega Saturn
and Sega Dreamcast), more than
any other racing game franchise
to date.

AWARD SHOWS THAT PROSTREET FANS HAVE A REAL NEED FOR SPEED

GameTrailers (GT), an online provider of video for gamers,
announced on 30 June 2008 that *Need for Speed:
ProStreet* ④ had been granted GT's Diamond Award
for garnering ten million or more video views on
GameTrailers.com.

According to GameTrailers' video-tracking system
Stream Stats, *Need for Speed: ProStreet* follows
EA's *Crysis* in reaching this milestone, making
EA the first publisher to receive two GT Diamond
Awards. Other games to have received the award
include *Call of Duty 4: Modern Warfare*, *Assassin's
Creed*, *Metal Gear Solid 4: Guns of the Patriots* and
Super Smash Bros. Brawl.

FACT

Need For Speed 2 was the first racing game to feature Ford's exclusive Indigo model [5]. Developed by Ford in 1996 for the auto-show circuit, just two Indigos were produced, only one of which actually worked. The car went on to appear in the video games *Ford Racing 2*, *Ford Racing 3* and the Xbox 360 title *Project Gotham Racing 3* (as "Ford Super Car Concept").

▼ **NEW RECORD** · ▽ **UPDATED RECORD**

123 FIGURES

$6 billion (£3 billion) – the sales figure for Electronic Arts in 2011, as predicted by the company's CEO John Riccitiello at an analysts' meeting in February 2008, based on the expansion of key franchises such as *Need For Speed*.

▼ **First 3D MMORG**

EA's *Motor City Online* [6] was the first 3D Massively Multiplayer Online Racing Game. Available exclusively to PC players, the game's servers were closed on 29 August 2004, reportedly so that EA Games could focus on their next online project, *The Sims Online*.

▼ **First game to recreate gear-lever sound effects**

For the 1994 release of *The Need For Speed* on the 3DO, Electronic Arts teamed up with *Road & Track* magazine to replicate vehicle behaviour. One aspect to this work was mimicking the sounds made by a vehicle's gear-control levers – this was the first attempt to recreate the exact sounds heard in a car's interior.

ⓘ TRIVIA

> It is thought that the title *Need for Speed* came from a Tom Cruise line in the film *Top Gun* (USA, 1986), where Cruise's character, fighter pilot Maverick, announces "I feel the need… the need for speed," before boarding his F-15 aircraft.

> The 2007 release *Need For Speed: ProStreet* was accompanied by a soundtrack featuring over 35 songs from a range of different artists, along with an original score by Dutch DJ Junkie XL.

TOCA TOURING CAR/GRID

First licensed video game to be based on the British Touring Car Championship

Until *TOCA Touring Car Championship*'s release in 1997, players were used to driving only the fastest supercars in the world. *TOCA* **3** took a different angle, offering a variety of production cars that were available in showrooms across the country, including the Honda Accord, Vauxhall Vectra and Nissan Primera in the first video game recreation of the British Touring Car Championship.

First PlayStation game to feature four-player link-up

TOCA 2 **2** was the first PlayStation game to feature a four-player mode using the PlayStation's link cable. A two-console set-up allowed four players to race against one another via a split screen across two televisions. *TOCA 2* is one of only two games to use this PlayStation feature, the other being *Wipeout 3: Special Edition*.

First game to use Ordnance Survey modelling data

TOCA Touring Car Championship was the first video game to accurately model real-world race tracks using 3D landscape data obtained from the Ordnance Survey Solution Centre. All of the game's 10 tracks, including Donington, Silverstone, Thruxton, Brands Hatch, Oulton Park, Croft, Knockhill and Snetterton, were created using this technique, which was also employed for the sequel.

PLATFORMS

SPEC

Developer:
Codemasters
Publisher:
Codemasters
Initial release:
TOCA Touring Car Championships (1997), PlayStation

GAMEPLAY

Initially focusing on the British Touring Car Championship, the series later diversified to include Supertruck and Rallycross events as well.

> *Racing games, possibly more than any other genre, can treat realism as an end in itself, but for us the gameplay has to be the most important thing.*
> **Ralph Fulton, Chief Games Designer for Race Driver: GRID**

40,000 – the number of fully animated spectators that can be seen trackside in *Race Driver: GRID*, the **most animated spectators in a game**.

First driving game to offer "drop in" replays

Race Driver: GRID ❶ is the first game to allow players to rewind a race (up to 10 seconds) and drop back in to live play at any point. The mode is intended to allow players a second chance at taking a difficult corner or avoiding a collision, and forms the basis for much of *GRID*'s core strategy.

Most animated spectators

Race Driver: GRID, built with Codemasters' bespoke EGO graphical engine – an enhanced version of the Neon engine used in the *Colin McRae: DiRT* game – allows each of the game's tracks to be filled with up to 40,000 fully modelled, animated spectators ❹.

◥ **NEW RECORD** ◤ **UPDATED RECORD**

First game to feature in-car communication between driver and mechanic

TOCA Touring Car 2 (PS2, Xbox, PC) was the first driving simulation to feature an ongoing narrative – in the career mode – where your mechanic would offer advice and encouragement during the race.

EUROPE > DONINGTON > GRAND PRIX CIRCUIT (A GRADE)

RANK	GAMERTAG	LAP TIME	CAR	SPLIT 1	SPLIT 2	SPLIT 3	VERSION
1	GXR Karter	57.112	Audi R10 TDI	17.275	17.472	22.364	Xbox 360
2	Nutmar	57.518	Audi R10 TDI	17.048	17.914	22.555	Xbox 360
3	CTS Revolver	57.680	Audi R10 TDI	17.074	18.206	22.399	Xbox 360
4	uR Prospectz	58.217	Audi R10 TDI	17.155	18.420	22.642	Xbox 360
5	mchaggis08	58.472	Audi R10 TDI	17.148	18.084	23.239	PlayStation 3
6	team_stef	58.477	Audi R10 TDI	17.078	17.879	23.519	PlayStation 3
7	GAF Relentle	58.691	Audi R10 TDI	18.088	18.221	22.381	Xbox 360
8	Dave 1709	58.716	Audi R10 TDI	17.388	18.221	23.207	Xbox 360
9	Etonano	58.785	Audi R10 TDI	17.055	18.157	23.572	Xbox 360
10	FAF chinner	58.811	Audi R10 TDI	17.373	19.021	22.416	Xbox 360

ⓘ TRIVIA

> Every single piece of debris dropped from a vehicle in 2008's *Race Driver: GRID* ❺ remains in place throughout the race. While larger items of debris, such as bumpers, remain on the track throughout a race in games such as *Forza 2*, in *GRID* even tiny pieces of dropped carbon fibre stay put for the whole race.

⫸ FACT

Richard Darling (far right) and his brother David (far left) who, in 1986, co-founded Codemasters, creators of the TOCA/GRID series, were both appointed Commanders of the Order of the British Empire (CBE) in the Queen's Birthday Honours 2008 for services to the computer games industry. They are pictured here with the company's other co-founder, their father Jim Darling (second right), receiving the ELSPA Hall of Fame award in 2003 ❻.

WHEELS & THRILLS: EXTREME SET-UPS

The driving-game genre, perhaps above all others, has inspired games designers to look beyond the basic trackball or joystick-and-button controllers. That greatest of inventions – the wheel – was the obvious first choice for a controller. Indeed, the very **first racing video game**, Atari's *Gran Trak 10*, was also the **first game to use a steering wheel** for its controller.

Gran Trak 10 took its real-life driving analogy even further. As well as its steering wheel, it utilized a four-position gear shifter, accelerator and brake foot pedals – all firsts for the arcade industry.

Steering-wheel controllers soon became a feature of almost all arcade racing cabinets but it wasn't until 1986's *OutRun* – the ▼**first driving game to feature true force feedback** – that games made a significant shift closer to the reality of driving.

With authenticity being the holy grail of driving games – if not all video games – increasingly realistic feedback also became standard. One notable use was in Sega's *18 Wheeler: American Pro Trucker*, which was released into arcades in 2000 and later ported to the Dreamcast. The game employed dramatic force feedback to approximate the handling of the **largest drivable road vehicle in a video game**.

Sega's *Ferrari F355 Challenge* was one of the first racing games to employ a three-screen cabinet (that is, one in front and one to either side of the player). Multiple screens were nothing new, but this time players could look through the side windows as they would in a real car.

The resistance felt at the wheel while driving over gravel is different to that driving over asphalt.

FACT

2007's *Outrun 2* cabinet upgrade, dubbed *SDX Special Tours* ❹, is a mammoth cabinet consisting of four two-seat Ferraris (F50, Dino GTS, 360 Spider and the 512BB). Each car boasts its own 62-in monitor, the ▼**largest screen size of any four-player-linked arcade driving experience**.

This concept was then applied to Turn 10's *Forza Motorsport* on Xbox, where network-coding engineer Aaron Ogus, inspired by *Ferrari 355*, implemented a semi-secret mode to facilitate a triple-screen panoramic set-up by using three system-linked Xbox consoles with three televisions, a first for console gaming.

One of the most impressive and progressive driving arcade machines is the pneumatic Cycraft cabinet ❺ – a hulking machine with a suspended sit-in cockpit that replicates the G force of driving by hurling the player from side to side. Cycraft cabinets have been used with *F-Zero AX*, *Sega Club Kart* ❷ and Japanese drift-racing favourite *Initial D*.

Weighing in at 880 kg (1,940 lb) and with the option for eight cabinets to be linked, bringing the total weight to 8,000 kg (15,520 lb), this is the world's **heaviest arcade driving set-up**.

The **most comprehensive home-console driving set-up** record has to go to 2007's *Forza Motorsport 2*. As well as wireless force-feedback wheel support **3**, the game can be used with up to five screens, which display the windshield view, left window, right window, rear view mirror, and can show replays simultaneously. To facilitate this set-up, you'll need five Xbox 360s, five copies of the game and, of course, five screens to run them through!

If you can't be bothered to lug all of that home from the shops, VRX Design and Development produce an integrated racing kit with all of the set-up work (and more) done for you. Released on 29 May 2007, the "Mach 4" **6** is the **first universal triple-screen simulator for use with Xbox 360**.

The Mach 4 pushes the reality of driving to a new level – with a price to match! At $25,000 (£12,500), it's out of the range of your typical gamer's pocket money. But then, what would it cost you to tear round the Nürburgring in a real, brand-new Maserati MC 12 Corsa (and then write it off by smashing into a wall)?

If money's no object, then who can predict what games designers will think of next? Real-life speeding fines? Parking tickets? One thing's for sure: the driving-game peripheral hasn't yet reached the end of the road.

NEW RECORD
UPDATED RECORD

Virtual Wind System powered by two dual Honeywell fans with chrome shroud

Three Sharp Aquos 37-inch LC-D62U 1080p HD LCD displays

Adjustable rear-view Power Acoustik (PTM 750) 7-inch LCD display

Microsoft Force Feedback steering wheel

Universal triple-screen aluminium mounting bracket that accepts LCD displays from 20" to 40"

Beverage Containment System (that's "drink holder" to you and me!)

Polished aluminium screen mounts

Italian Sparco Monza racing seat (choice of red/black or black/silver)

Bose Acoustimass 10 series surround-sound system with subwoofer

1,500-watt Tactile Feedback System

Polished aluminium foot assembly that connects to the front of the VRX

Suspension seat base

CONTENTS

LittleBIGPlanet is the **first PlayStation 3 game to reward players with extra server space** – the amount of space is based on the popularity of the levels users create and upload for others to play.

GENRE-BUSTERS

NOT ALL GAMES ARE EASY TO CATEGORIZE. IS IT A PUZZLE GAME? IS IT AN ARCADE GAME? OR IS IT SOMETHING ELSE ENTIRELY? WHEN CATEGORIES COLLIDE WE CALL THESE GAMES GENRE BUSTERS.

EXPERT

David McCarthy has written extensively about games for a range of magazines and websites as well as co-authoring two books on gaming.

OVERVIEW

Genre busting games require a player to demonstrate an aptitude for logical problem solving and an ability to think strategically, often with a requirement to show lightning-quick reactions thrown in for good measure. From brain training to party quizzes via falling blocks and number grids, there are enough hybrid games out there to provide an absorbing challenge for any game player.

One of the first computer games to fuel the "what is it?" debate was A.S. Douglas's *OXO*, a version of tic-tac-toe created in 1952, which is also a contender for the disputed title of **first ever video game**. While puritans will call it a strategy game, others classify it as puzzle. In reality, it's a mathematical problem.

In the modern era, *Tetris* is undoubtedly the best-known puzzle game, thanks to its association with Nintendo's Game Boy. *Tetris* was created in 1985 by Alexey Pajitnov (Russia), who was inspired to create the game by traditional pentomino puzzles **5**. It is now the **most ported computer game of all time** and responsible for inspiring a multitude of falling block titles, such as *Mr Driller* **1** and *Lumines* **6**. However, some argue that *Tetris* is actually a strategy game because the player knows exactly what to do and the top players tend to have exceptional reflexes and

excellent planning – skills you would not ordinarily associate with puzzle solving. On that basis, *Tetris* could conceivably be classed as an arcade/strategy game.

There is a proliferation of games that do not fall into an established niche. They cover every aspect of logic, strategy, pattern recognition, rhythm, sound and beyond. Examples range from the simplicity of *Bejeweled* **2** to the bullet-blazing Japanese gunfest *Bangai-O* **3**.

One feature of such seemingly simple games is a lack of technological innovation. However, accurate physics implementation is starting to infiltrate into even the most obscure corners of the gaming world; new mainstream genre busters like *Boom Blox* and *LittleBigPlanet* rely entirely on physics, and it is purely because of new physics technology that these fusions exist at all.

While less action-orientated console games are just beginning to embrace realistic physics, it tends to be Internet titles such as *Line Rider* and *Rag Doll Kung Fu* that have championed the cause over the last few years. These independent offerings don't have huge budgets or advertising campaigns, but their slow viral infiltration, partly due to office workers surfing the web during their lunch breaks, has finally convinced publishers of their worth. There is no doubt that these low-budget,

5

TIMELINE

c.500	1952	1978	1979		1985
People in India play Chaturanga, an ancestor of games such as chess and shogi.	A.S. Douglas creates *OXO* for the EDSAC computer as part of his Ph.D.	Nintendo releases its first arcade game, *Computer Othello*, based on the board game of the same name.	Namco releases the classic maze game, *PAC-MAN*. Some 20 years later, Billy Mitchell (USA) records the **first perfect PAC-MAN score of 3,333,360**.	 **10**	Alexey Pajitnov, a Russian computer scientist at the Soviet Academy of Science, invents tumbling block teaser *Tetris* **10**.

15,207,353 – the **record high score for** *Centipede*, set by Canada's Darren Olson after his marathon on the Atari in 1982.

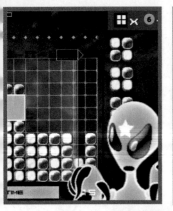

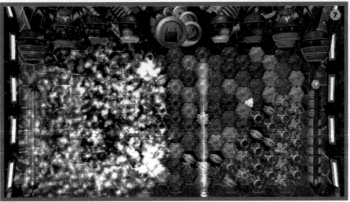

SUDOKU SUCCESS

The first ever puzzle named *Sudoku* was printed in Japan's *Monthly Nikolist* magazine in 1984. It was a version of a type of puzzle that had been known as *Suuji wa dokushin ni kagiru*, meaning "the digits must remain single", which was later abbreviated to the easier to manage *Sudoku*, which means "single number".

It is only a couple of years since the first video game appeared based on the Japanese puzzle phenomenon, yet there are now already over 50 different *Sudoku* games available for consoles and PC, with games for handheld players, such as the Nintendo DS ⑧, proving particularly popular.

yet highly inspired offerings have played a key role in the merging of video-game genres.

The rise of casual gaming websites and mobile phone gaming – as well as the success of PlayStation Network (see *PixelJunk Monsters* for example) and Xbox Live (*Rez HD*) – has also helped instigate a fusion of genres. Again, Nintendo has stimulated a renaissance in gaming – particularly among "non gamers" – with the DS inspiring electronic versions of pen-and-paper conundrums such as *Slitherlink* ④ as well as mind-expanding game, *Dr Kawashima's Brain Training: How Old Is Your Brain?*, released in Europe in 2006. Truly, game genres have never crossed over so often and so far. Genre busters are here to stay; the only problem is what to call them.

1989	**1992**	**1996**	**2001**	**2005**	**2008**
Tetris is bundled with Nintendo's new Game Boy handheld device.	Microsoft includes *Minesweeper* ⑪ as part of Windows 3.1.	*Tetris Attack* released by Nintendo for the SNES.	PopCap games releases *Bejeweled/ Diamond Mine*.	Nintendo of Japan releases *Dr Kawashima's Brain Training: How Old Is Your Brain?*	Nintendo and Steven Spielberg collaborate on physics mind-bender *Boom Blox* for the Nintendo Wii.
1991 *Tetris*-inspired *Puyo Puyo* released.	**1994** *Puzzle Bobble* (a.k.a. *Bust-a-Move*) released by Taito.	**1998** *Devil Dice* released for the PlayStation.	**2004** *Lumines* released by Bandai in Japan.		

BOOM BLOX

PLATFORMS

Wii

SPEC

Developer:
EA Los Angeles
Publisher:
Electronic Arts
Initial release:
Boom Blox (2008),
Nintendo Wii

GAMEPLAY

The simple but addictive gameplay requires players to knock over blocks by using the Wii remote to direct various objects, such as balls, guns and water hoses; or prevent blocks from being knocked over while using the Wii remote to remove blocks.

Most critically acclaimed puzzle game on the Nintendo Wii

According to the Metacritic and GameRankings websites, *Boom Blox* 1 by Electronic Arts is the most critically acclaimed puzzle game on the Nintendo Wii. The sites, which both publish an average of all of the review scores given to games, reveal that *Boom Blox* received average review scores of 85.37% (according to GameRankings) and 85% (according to Metacritic).

Most realistic physics in a puzzle game

Unlike the majority of puzzle games, which feature physics that are only realistic enough to control

2D objects falling down a screen, EA's *Boom Blox* uses the Havok physics engine to underpin its 3D block puzzles. According to the game's producer, Amir Rahimi, the game uses the majority of the Wii's CPU cycles solving physics so that every single block in the game reacts realistically to the forces acting upon it.

First multi-game deal between a Hollywood movie director and a video-game publisher

Steven Spielberg (2 pictured right) and Electronic Arts signed a long-term deal in October 2005 to jointly create three new original video-game franchises. *Boom Blox* is the first of these. There are currently no details on the other two planned franchises.

First game created by movie director Steven Spielberg

Boom Blox was the first game to be created in collaboration with Academy Award winner Steven Spielberg. However, it wasn't the film-maker's first foray into game development. In 1995, LucasArts released *The Dig* 3, which was based on an original story idea by Spielberg and credits him as writer.

450,000 – unit sales of *Boom Blox*, as revealed by game publisher Electronic Arts in July 2008.

INTERVIEW WITH... AMIR RAHIMI

Amir Rahimi, Senior Producer on *Boom Blox*, reveals the idea behind the game.

The idea was to leverage the ground-breaking motion-sensing Wii controller to tee off on a compulsion that is very simple and universal: the compulsion to stack something up (such as blocks, sand castles, bottles, etc.) and then smash them to the ground. With state-of-the-art physics and the imagination of Steven Spielberg, we were able to deliver on this promising concept like never before.

How much involvement did Steven Spielberg have in the project and what was it like to work with him?
First of all, it was his idea. He came up with it after he played the Wii for the first time with Shigeru Miyamoto. He then brought the idea to us and, needless to say, we loved it! Steven provided artistic and creative direction throughout the project. The collaboration was a dream-come-true for me as his work in the film industry has been a huge inspiration. As a collaborator, he was extremely approachable and had very impressive video-game instincts. One thing that I learned about Steven is that he loves to play video games and has a broad knowledge of game mechanics as well as the history of the industry.

> *I really wanted to create a video game that I could play with my kids.*
> **Steven Spielberg, creator of Boom Blox**

▼ **NEW RECORD** ▽ **UPDATED RECORD**

ⓘ TRIVIA

> *Boom Blox* was very nearly the first puzzle game to feature headtracking, where the game tracks the player's head movements and adjusts the camera to reflect those motions. At the Game Developers Conference in 2008, executive producer Lou Castle revealed that headtracking would activate by using two Wii remotes and some sort of headset or camera, but the feature never made it into the final game.

> *Hook* ④, released in 1992 was based on Spielberg's movie of the same name.

⏵ FACT

Havok is the physics engine of choice for game developers since the release of next-generation consoles. It's hardly surprising when you can buy a bespoke Havok package to deliver exactly what you need. Separate building blocks include Havok Behavior, Havok Physics, Havok Animation, Havok Cloth and Havok Destruction. To date, Havok has been used in over 200 games, including *Halo 3*, *Super Smash Bros. Brawl* and, of course, the more cerebral *Boom Blox*. Modified versions of the engine have also been used in big Hollywood CGI movies such as *Poseidon* (USA, 2006) and *The Matrix* (Australia/USA, 1999).

▷ Best-selling puzzle game on the Wii
Wii puzzlers are still quite rare and so *Boom Blox* is actually the best-selling puzzle game on the platform with 450,000 units sold up to July 2008, according to Electronic Arts.

LEMMINGS

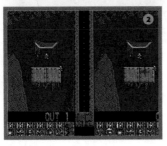

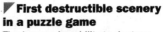

PLATFORMS

SPEC

Developer:
DMA Design
Publisher:
Psygnosis
Initial release:
Lemmings (1991),
Commodore Amiga

GAMEPLAY

*Try to stop a tide
of lemmings from
walking to their doom
by guiding them to a
predetermined exit
in each of the 120
hazardous levels.
The levels fall into
one of four difficulty
categories known
as Fun, Tricky,
Taxing and
Mayhem.*

Most successful UK game developer in 2008

Thanks to the unprecedented success of *Grand Theft Auto IV*, *Lemmings* ② developer, DMA Design (⑩ first offices pictured), a.k.a. Rockstar North, was the most successful British game developer in 2008, both commercially and critically.

First game to use indirect control

Lemmings was the first game to introduce "indirect control", where the player issues orders to AI-controlled automatons by using a mouse to click on a series of icons. This is now a core component of most realtime strategy (RTS) games, making *Lemmings* one of the earliest RTS outings.

> *Mike Dailly had this animation... it was a constant stream of these little guys marching up to their death. I saw that and it sparked the idea for Lemmings.*
> **Dave Jones, Lemmings creator**

First destructible scenery in a puzzle game

The impressive ability to destroy nearly everything on a level, whether through straightforward digging or more deadly explosive methods, makes *Lemmings* the first puzzle game to offer destructible scenery.

▮ NEW RECORD ▽ UPDATED RECORD

Funniest deaths in a video game

Lemmings was the first game to encourage the player to watch their charges die by making their deaths so amusing it didn't matter if you failed to complete the level.

INFLUENTIAL ADDICTION

Best-selling author Terry Pratchett turned his addiction to *Lemmings* to good use when he came up with the red army for his novel *Interesting Times* ⑦ – an army of digging, marching, climbing golems controlled by an icon-driven interface reminiscent of that used in *Lemmings*. When pressed about the matter, he replied: "What? *Lemmings*? Merely because the red army can fight, dig, march and climb and is controlled by little icons? Can't imagine how anyone thought that... Not only did I wipe *Lemmings* from my hard disc, I overwrote it so's I couldn't get it back."

65,000 – the number of units that *Lemmings* sold on its first day of release in 1991.

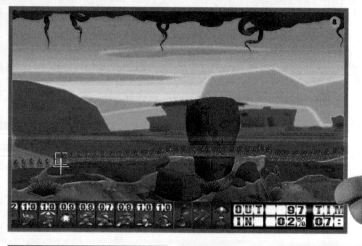

2 10 10 09 09 07 09 10 10

OUT 97 TIM
IN 02% 078

¹²³ FIGURES

> In 1991, with just three games to its name, DMA Design released *Lemmings* for the Commodore Amiga. With a hint of the success to come, it sold **65,000** units on the day of its release – the series has gone on to notch up sales of over **20 million**, having been ported to over 30 platforms including ZX Spectrum, Sega Mega Drive, Super Nintendo Philips CD-i, Apple, PC and Sony PSP ⑧.

LEMMINGS: PLAYSTATION 3 HIGH SCORES

The PlayStation 3 version ⑤ of *Lemmings* features over 40 levels, divided across four difficulty settings. The following are the fastest times achieved on the hardest level of each difficulty setting as of 14 July 2008.

DIFFICULTY SETTING	LEVEL NAME	PLAYER NAME	TIME
Fun	Beam me up Lenny	FunksTONe	0:46.04
Tricky	Don't send me up there	michaelseagull	1:00.54
Taxing	Lend me your ears	FunksTONe	2:25.66
Mayhem	The lengthy level	Flying Fudge	1:11.52

◤ First Lemmings game to feature "fast forward"

The original game did not include a fast-forward option, meaning the player would have to wait in realtime for the lemmings to either die or exit the level. It was only after working on the ultimately doomed attempt to create a *Lemmings* arcade cabinet for Data East in 1991 that the fast-forward icon was included in *Lemmings* on the Atari Lynx and *Lemmings 2* and the process was sped up.

◤ First split-screen, mouse-controlled game on the Commodore Amiga

Lemmings was the first Amiga game to offer simultaneous two-player action on a split screen ②, on the same computer, with both players using separate mice. Although the multiplayer mode was fun, the two-player head-to-head option has been missing from every version since.

❶ TRIVIA

> Apart from several sequels that kept the overall design of *Lemmings* intact, there were also two spin-offs: *Lemmings Paintball* ③, an isometrically viewed action game; and *The Adventures of Lomax* ④, a side-scrolling platform game.

> *Lemmings* includes several levels based on other Psygnosis games from the period, such as "A beast of a level" ①, which is a take-off of the Amiga classic *Shadow of the Beast*.

? GWR QUIZ

Q15. *Lemmings* developer DMA Design went on to create which record-breaking gaming series?

⑪▶ FACT

Lemmings are notable for their green hair and blue shirts, and the inexorable way they advance across each level, paying little heed to their own personal safety. But there are various skills that can be assigned to different lemmings:

Climbers can climb vertical surfaces
Floaters ⑨ can safely fall from great heights by using their umbrellas
Bashers can dig horizontally through destructible sections
Miners ⑥ can dig diagonally downward through destructible sections
Diggers can dig directly downward through destructible sections
Builders ⑪ build stairways to reach higher areas
Blockers reverse the direction of any lemmings that walk into them
Bombers explode after five seconds, taking destructible scenery with them.

REZ/LUMINES

⚙ PLATFORMS

✕ SPEC

Developer:
United Game Artists
Publisher:
Sega
Initial release:
Rez (2001),
Dreamcast

⇄ GAMEPLAY

Inspired by the
Russian painter
Wassily Kandinsky,
Rez is a rail shooter
that features a
blend of hypnotic
audio-visual effects
with elements of
shooting games,
rhythm action and
puzzle play. Its creator
also claims to take
inspiration from the
neurological condition
synaesthesia, which
is a crossover of the
senses – that is,
when one "hears"
colours or "sees"
musical sounds.
Gameplay is
enhanced by
a peripheral
known as a
Trance Vibrator,
which pulses
in time with the
sound effects
and adds an extra
sensory element
to the game.

◤ Highest score for Lumines Live!

The highest score on the Xbox
Live Leaderboard for the Lumines
Challenge Mode "Base" is
7,117,904. The highest score for
"Advance" mode is 6,005,100.
Both scores were set by a gamer
known as zrvan.

◤ Most critically acclaimed Xbox Live shooting game

The highest-scoring shooter
on Xbox Live according to the
GameRankings website, which
aggregates game review scores, is
Rez HD ①. It received an average
review score of just under 90%
as of July 2008. According to
Metacritic, another website that
aggregates scores, the most well-
reviewed shooter on the Dreamcast
was Rez, which achieved an
average review score of 91%.

◤ First video game inspired by synaesthesia

Synaesthesia is a medical condition
and literary technique that causes
senses to become mixed up. In the
medical condition, people literally see
sounds, while the literary technique is
exemplified in phrases such as "loud
shirt". In Rez, the condition is manifest
in a unique interplay between sound,
vision and action – hence the game's
slogan: "Rez will open your senses...
let's go to synaesthesia".

> " With Rez, or the first
> Lumines... With those
> games, the sound has a
> very important role. Sound
> has a power. Sound controls
> your emotions. "
> **Tetsuya Mizuguchi,**
> **creator of Rez**

◤ First virtual pop star to launch a global fundraising event

In July 2007, the Live Earth Tokyo
concert was launched by a hologram
of former US Vice President
Al Gore, who had been introduced
by Lumi, the lead singer of Genki
Rockets. The surprising thing is
that Lumi is an 18-year-old girl who
was born on 11 September 2037.
She's actually a virtual-reality
construct, created by Tetsuya
Mizuguchi ② and musician Kenji
Tamai, and she made her debut in
Mizuguchi's puzzle game Lumines II.

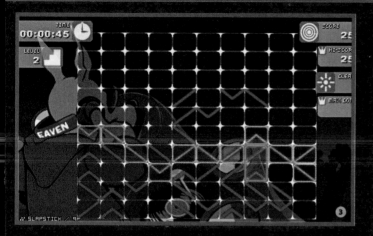

MIZUGUCHI: CREATIVE GENIUS

Rez is the brainchild of Tetsuya Mizuguchi, the former head of Sega's United Game Artists studio, where he was responsible for titles such as *Sega Rally Championship* and *Space Channel 5*. After leaving Sega, he set up Q Entertainment, where he updated Gunpei Yokoi's *Gunpey* ③ as well as adding several other audio-inspired puzzle games to his repertoire. *Lumines*, *Meteos* and *Every Extend Extra* are all furiously addictive games that combine fiendish design with cutting-edge music and kaleidoscopic images.

Mizuguchi even wrote and directed the music and video for the song *Heavenly Star*, which was performed by the virtual band Genki Rockets ⑤ in *Lumines II*. In 2002, his creative genius achieved wider recognition when *Rez* received a special award from the Japan Media Arts Festival.

Highest score for Rez HD

The highest score on the Xbox Live Leaderboard for the Direct Assault mode of *Rez HD* is 1,788,770, set by a gamer called TrueBluBomber. The highest scores for each of the game's five game areas are as follows:

Area 1	300,270	MisoraHebari
Area 2	311,540	TruBluBomber
Area 3	354,520	Rien Vayle
Area 4	328,040	Misora Hebari
Area 5	1,264,660	mumumu992·

First video game inspired by abstract expressionism

Wassily Kandinsky (Russia, 1866–1944) was a Moscow-born artist who helped to found the Bauhaus art movement and was among the first modern painters to explore abstract art. Kandinsky wrote that "music is the ultimate teacher", and his work explored the coming of a New Age – both themes that would influence the creator of *Rez*, Tetsuya Mizuguchi.

First musical shooting game

Every action that you take while playing *Rez* produces a sound and the game synchronizes each one of those sounds with a soundtrack created by a plethora of stars from Japan's underground dance scene and beyond. Playing the game therefore produces ever-evolving soundscapes.

Most critically acclaimed genre-buster on the PSP

Lumines ④ is the most critically acclaimed genre-buster on the PSP. Created by the genius behind *Rez*, Tetsuya Mizuguchi, it features a similar fusion of sound, vision and puzzling action, although the design itself is similar to *Tetris*. It was the highest-rated game to appear on Sony's handheld platform, according to Metacritic and GameRankings websites, until the release of *God of War* pushed it into second place – a position it still occupies as the most well-reviewed genre-buster on the platform.

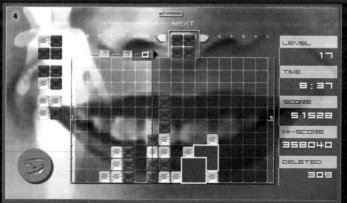

ℹ TRIVIA

> The *Rez* gaming experience can be enhanced by using a USB peripheral called a Trance Vibrator ⑥. According to the game's creator, Tetsuya Mizuguchi, the device was intended to simulate the feelings of vibration you might experience if you were to stand next to a very, very loud speaker, by vibrating in time to in-game noises and sounds.

GENRE-BUSTERS ROUND-UP

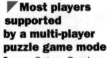

⏵ Most expensive maze game

Game: *Mr Boston Clean Sweep*
Publisher: Mr Boston
Copies of *Mr Boston Clean Sweep*, for the Vectrex home console ❷, exchange hands for as much as $3,000 (£1,510). *Clean Sweep* is a *PAC-Man*-style maze game, which was rebranded by the Mr Boston liquor store as a promotional item.

Best-selling puzzle-game series

Game: *Tetris*
Publisher: Various
Since the original *Tetris* was created on the PC in 1985, the ensuing series of games based on Alexey Pajitnov's creation has sold over 70 million units worldwide ❶.

Best-selling puzzle game on Nintendo hardware

Game: *Tetris*
Publisher: Nintendo
The Game Boy version of *Tetris* alone has sold a staggering 33 million copies – largely because it was bundled with the console itself. This figure dwarfs all of the other puzzle games available on Nintendo hardware – even *Wii Play*, which, bundled together with a Wiimote controller, has so far sold a lowly 11.5 million copies.

⏵ Highest score for *Bejeweled 2*

Game: *Bejeweled 2*
Publisher: PopCap Games
Nik Meeks (USA) scored a record 148,350 on *Bejeweled 2* ❸ – played as part of the *PopCap Hits! vol. 1* compilation, on the PS2 – on 4 February 2008.

> *Tetris is a game that playfully satisfies one of the most basic human drives: that is, to create order out of chaos.*
> **Tetris Friends, Facebook (Tetris Online, Inc.)**

⏵ Most players supported by a multi-player puzzle game mode

Game: *Saturn Bomberman*
Publisher: Hudson Soft
Released for the Sega Saturn in 1996 and starring Hudson Soft's eponymous mascot, *Saturn Bomberman* supports up to 10 players – although it requires the use of two of the Saturn's multi-tap peripherals for a game this size to take place.

⏵ Most critically acclaimed puzzle game on PS3

Game: *PixelJunk Monsters*
Publisher: Sony
The most critically acclaimed puzzle game on Sony's PS3 is *PixelJunk Monsters* ❺, which received average review ratings of 83% (according to the Metacritic website) and 83.78% (according to GameRankings.com).

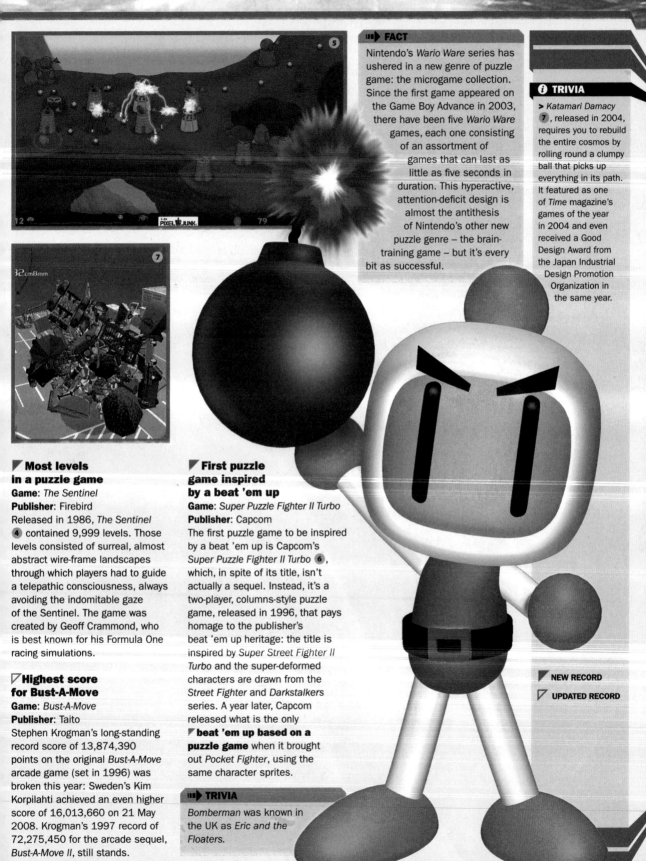

9,999 – the number of levels in Geoff Crammond's uniquely eerie 3D thriller *The Sentinel,* published in 1986 for 8-bit home computers.

12 79

32cmBmm

III▶ FACT

Nintendo's *Wario Ware* series has ushered in a new genre of puzzle game: the microgame collection. Since the first game appeared on the Game Boy Advance in 2003, there have been five *Wario Ware* games, each one consisting of an assortment of games that can last as little as five seconds in duration. This hyperactive, attention-deficit design is almost the antithesis of Nintendo's other new puzzle genre – the brain-training game – but it's every bit as successful.

ⓘ TRIVIA

> *Katamari Damacy* 7, released in 2004, requires you to rebuild the entire cosmos by rolling round a clumpy ball that picks up everything in its path. It featured as one of *Time* magazine's games of the year in 2004 and even received a Good Design Award from the Japan Industrial Design Promotion Organization in the same year.

◤ Most levels in a puzzle game

Game: *The Sentinel*
Publisher: Firebird
Released in 1986, *The Sentinel* 4 contained 9,999 levels. Those levels consisted of surreal, almost abstract wire-frame landscapes through which players had to guide a telepathic consciousness, always avoiding the indomitable gaze of the Sentinel. The game was created by Geoff Crammond, who is best known for his Formula One racing simulations.

◤ Highest score for Bust-A-Move

Game: *Bust-A-Move*
Publisher: Taito
Stephen Krogman's long-standing record score of 13,874,390 points on the original *Bust-A-Move* arcade game (set in 1996) was broken this year: Sweden's Kim Korpilahti achieved an even higher score of 16,013,660 on 21 May 2008. Krogman's 1997 record of 72,275,450 for the arcade sequel, *Bust-A-Move II*, still stands.

◤ First puzzle game inspired by a beat 'em up

Game: *Super Puzzle Fighter II Turbo*
Publisher: Capcom
The first puzzle game to be inspired by a beat 'em up is Capcom's *Super Puzzle Fighter II Turbo* 6, which, in spite of its title, isn't actually a sequel. Instead, it's a two-player, columns-style puzzle game, released in 1996, that pays homage to the publisher's beat 'em up heritage: the title is inspired by *Super Street Fighter II Turbo* and the super-deformed characters are drawn from the *Street Fighter* and *Darkstalkers* series. A year later, Capcom released what is the only ◤ **beat 'em up based on a puzzle game** when it brought out *Pocket Fighter*, using the same character sprites.

III▶ TRIVIA

Bomberman was known in the UK as *Eric and the Floaters*.

◤ **NEW RECORD**
◁ **UPDATED RECORD**

FANTASY & SCI-FI GAMES

It took just nine days for the demo of *Bioshock* on Xbox Live to be downloaded 1 million times, making it the **most popular download demo**.

CONTENTS

FANTASY & SCI-FI GAMES

DRAGONS, GHOSTS, GOBLINS AND ELVES ARE AMONG SOME OF THE COLOURFUL CHARACTERS YOU'LL ENCOUNTER IN THE IMAGINERY LANDSCAPES OF FANTASY AND SCIENCE-FICTION GAMES.

EXPERT

Dave Hawksett has a background in astrophysics and planetary sciences, and is the science and technology consultant for GWR.

OVERVIEW

Science fiction and fantasy covers a wide spectrum of topics, many of which have found their outlet through computer games. While they overlap, sci-fi and fantasy are not quite the same as each other. Fantasy often includes elements of magic and other planes of existence; sci-fi relies on ingredients that evolve from real-world science and could one day be possible.

The rise of video games in the 1970s coincided with the revolutionary escapism of *Dungeons and Dragons*. Created by Gary Gygax and Dave Arneson in 1974, the evocative pencil and paper exploits of heroic wizards and warriors battling hideous monsters immediately attracted the attention of Gary Whisenhunt and Ray Wood who conjured up *dnd*, the **first computer RPG** on the PLATO mainframe in 1974.

The 1970s also saw an explosion of modern science-fiction on television and in the cinema. *Star Wars* and *Star Trek* (see the Space Games section on pp. 86-99 for a more detailed look at both these series) inspired game designers to create new worlds featuring amazing technology and strange new races. In 1979 Edu-ware's *Space* became the **first RPG to appear on a PC**, while a year later *The Prisoner* for the Apple II, also by Edu-ware and based on the British television series of the same name, became the ▶ **first published science-fiction text-adventure**. As the 1970s drew to a close, fantasy games and fledgling

home computers blended together perfectly. In 1979, the *Dunjonquest* series was released for the Commodore PET and became the ▶ **first fantasy game trilogy**. Infocom's *Zork* arrived in 1980 and was the ▶ **first interactive fiction game to be a major commercial success**. In total, 15 *Zork* games were released, even making it on to the PlayStation and Sega Saturn.

Benchmarks of the early 1980s were set by *Balrog Sampler* on the TRS 80, a sample of the Maces and Magic series; the

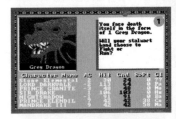

▶ **NEW RECORD** ▷ **UPDATED RECORD**

Apple II's *Ultima,* which eventually became the **longest-running RPG franchise**; and *Cyborg*, the ▶ **first cyberpunk game**, a 1982 text-only adventure in which the player had to find an energy source after merging with a life-draining artificial intelligence. This particular brand of sci-fi featuring body modifications and augmentation would go on to inspire games such as *Syndicate, Shadowrun, I Have No Mouth and I Must Scream, Bioforge* and the classic *Deus Ex* by Warren Spector in 2000.

The Hobbit was released in 1982 for most home computer formats, and in 1983 Anne McCaffery's *Dragonriders of Pern* also made the

1975
Adventure is the **first text adventure game**, but is known as *ADVENT* due to the 6 character filename limit. The game is improved and becomes *Colossal Cave.*

1982
The Hobbit released by Melbourne House.

1985
Four player fantasy classic *Gauntlet* released in arcades by Atari.

The Bard's Tale **1** (Interplay/EA) released.

1987
Final Fantasy is a massive hit, virtually saving Squaresoft from bankruptcy.

1994
Magic Carpet developed by Bullfrog and published by Electronic Arts. It was one of the first games to use Intel's new Pentium Processor.

1997
Diablo becomes a fantasy blockbuster, signalling Blizzard Entertainment's arrival on the world stage. The first sequel arrives two years later.

FACT

When *The Legend of Zelda* appeared in the 1980s, its mix of exploration, character development and puzzle solving set new gameplay standards in fantasy RPGs. TSR's *Heroes of the Lance* and *Pool of Radiance* offered a more statistics-based approach but it wasn't until Bioware Corporation released *Baldur's Gate* in 1998 that D&D-based games began to reach their full potential – but by this time the Zelda series had become one of the greatest fantasy series ever after the release of *Ocarina of Time* on the Nintendo 64. However, the release of *Neverwinter Nights* in 2002 and *Mass Effect* for the Xbox 360 in 2008 have now established Bioware as one of the finest producers of fantasy and science-fiction games.

transition from page to computer screen and became the ▶**first fantasy multiplayer strategy game**. That same year, *Atic Atac*'s pioneering mix of colourful graphics and fast-paced action gave fantasy games a whole new lease of life, and within a couple of years arcade classics *Dragon's Lair*, *Gauntlet* **2** and *Ghosts 'n Goblins* were drawing crowds around the world.

Meanwhile, in 1984, Lucasfilm's futuristic one-on-one robotic soccer game *Ballblazer* and Martech's *Zoids* showed sci-fi games on home computers such as the ZX Spectrum and Commodore 64 had

come a long way from the days of blasting rows of aliens. *Zoids* introduced a revolutionary new icon-based command system that would form the basis of modern real-time strategy game interfaces. Incentive's first-person thrillers *Driller* (1987) and *Dark Side* (1988) were also notable for generating tension in distant outposts and whose influence can be felt in FPSs such as *Quake*, *System Shock* and *Half-Life*.

Today, sci-fi and fantasy dominate the most dynamic market in gaming: the MMORPG. Practically all the big titles owe much of their inspiration to Gygax, Lucas or Tolkien, who are still the most influential figures in fantasy and sci-fi games.

> *...much of the blood that courses through the veins of [the video game] industry was transfused directly from Tolkien and his works.*
> **Ron "Grumpy Gamer" Gilbert on gaming's prime influence**

ℹ TRIVIA

> Drinking wine in the text adventure game *The Hobbit* gets you drunk – at which point the text instructions become slurred, with s replaced with sh ("You drink shome wine.")

> *Ballblazer* (1984) by Lucasfilm featured a funky jazz soundtrack created using fractal algorithims; this ensured that the musical top line never repeated itself, giving the "score" an improvized feel.

? GWR QUIZ

Q16. The original 1985 arcade version of *Gauntlet* can support how many players at once?

1999	2001	2004	2005	2006	2007	2008
Everquest launched and goes on to spawn a further 26 games or expansion packs in just nine years.	Lionhead Games' first release, *Black and White* **3** , makes its debut; it is massively delayed but features ground-breaking creature intelligence.	*World of Warcraft* released by Blizzard and goes on to become the mother of all MMORPGs.	*God of War* released by Sony Computer Entertainment, pushing the PS2's aging hardware to the limit.	Bethesda's *The Elder Scrolls IV: Oblivion* **5** takes single-player fantasy RPGs to beautiful new horizons.	*The Lord of the Rings Online: Shadows of Angmar* launched.	The much-anticipated third instalment in the *Diablo* series, *Diablo 3* **4** is announced. *Fable II* **6** (Lionhead/ Microsoft) released.

AGE OF CONAN

⚙ PLATFORMS

✕ SPEC

Developer: *Funcom*
Publisher: *Eidos Interactive*
Initial release:
Age of Conan:
Hyborian Adventures
(2008), PC

💲 GAMEPLAY

In the age-old tradition of MMORPGs, Age of Conan follows that most simplistic of philosophies: the more you play, the more powerful your character becomes.

? GWR QUIZ

Q17. Who wrote the series of books that *Age of Conan* is based on?

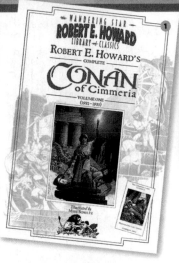

▰ First mature-rated MMORPG in the west

Released in May 2008, *Age of Conan: Hyborian Adventures* 4 was rated M for mature by the Entertainment Software Board in the USA and rated 18 by the Pan European Game Information System. Running from 2004 to 2007, the Japanese game A3 was the ▰ **first MMORPG with an adult rating**.

👍 **IF YOU LIKE THIS...**
... you should try out Jolt's widescreen fantasy MMO *Archlord*, available to play for free at archlordgame.com

▰ Largest city in Age of Conan

With an area of 4 km² (1.5 miles²), Tarantia 6, the capital city of Aquilonia, consists of several regions, the most famous of which is Old Tarantia. King Conan's palace is here and the area is patrolled by the Black Dragons – the king's elite bodyguards.

▰ Largest beta sign-up for an MMORPG

Beta testing is the last stage in a game's development before it is officially released. Usually conducted by gamers outside of the development company who sign up, it enables players to try out an advance version of a game and help its developers spot and correct any problems and glitches they have missed in the game code. Over 1 million people signed up to beta test *Age of Conan*, making it the largest MMORPG beta sign-up in history and helping establish the game among MMORPG fans.

▰ Most Motion Capture Animations in an MMORPG

Age of Conan: Hyborian Adventures contains around 7,000 individual animations created from motion capture – more than any other MMORPG. During development, the design team also filmed motion capture footage of a horse and its rider 3 to help them create the ▰ **first motion-captured horse animation in an MMORPG** 2.

⫸ FACT

Robert E. Howard's Conan started life in pulp magazines and books 1 before making the transition to film in *Conan The Barbarian* (USA, 1982), starring Arnold Schwarzenegger 7.

$25 million – the reported development budget at Funcom for *Age of Conan: Hyborian Adventures* during a five-year production process that culminated in the game's launch in May 2008.

INTERVIEW WITH... ERLING ELLINGSEN FROM FUNCOM

Erling Ellingsen is the Product Manager of *Age of Conan* at Funcom. Erling worked as a gaming journalist for a number of years before joining Funcom and recently took time to talk about his work on the eagerly awaited *Age of Conan*.

What games did you play when you were a kid?
I started playing games at an early age, so I've been through everything from the old Atari machines to the first computers. I remember playing the *King's Quest* games on an old 286 – at least that's what I think

it was – and we had to warm the computer up for half an hour before it would run! I have always been a huge fan of adventure and role-playing, and some of my most favourite games are the early *Monkey Island* games, *Might & Magic*, *Lands of Lore*, *Police Quest* and so on. I still play them, actually!

What are you most proud of in *Age of Conan*?
We managed to push the boundaries of what is possible with an online game, and that's something we are very proud of. We managed to set a whole new standard for graphical realism, mature content, interactive

combat and, of course, story-telling. *Age of Conan* is very much an online game that does not try to copy the success of other similar games; instead we tried to go our own way. And that definitely paid off for us and the gamers who were able to log in and try a different MMO experience.

> **TRIVIA**

> In June 2008, Funcom confirmed that many of the female player characters had their breast size accidentally reduced in a game patch. The company issued a statement promising to fix it in a subsequent patch.

¹²₃ FIGURES

60 – Different ways to dispatch your opponent in *Age of Conan* ⑤.

◤ **NEW RECORD**   ◺ **UPDATED RECORD**

◤ **First to kill Vistrix**
Vistrix, the last of the Tier 1 raid bosses, is a female demon who has taken on the form of a dragon ⑧. Considered one of the toughest mobs in the game, Vistrix was first defeated by Ebonlore from the Tyranny PvP server in summer 2008.

Games for Windows

AGE OF CONAN
HYBORIAN ADVENTURES

18+

BIOSHOCK

⚙ PLATFORMS

🛠 SPEC

Developer:
2K Games
Publisher:
2K Games
Initial release:
Bioshock (2007),
Xbox 360

💲 GAMEPLAY

A powerful narrative
drive combined with
an advanced AI means
that no two games of
this atmospheric,
Art-Deco-
styled,
actioner
are
ever the
same.
Set in
Rapture,
a mysterious
underwater
"utopia" in an
alternative 1960,
Bioshock offers the
gamer a compelling
storyline – a moralistic
sci-fi mystery par
excellence – inspired
by the writings
of novelist and
philosopher Ayn Rand
(Russia/USA).

Fastest time to secure 1 million demo downloads

Released via Xbox Live Marketplace on 12 August 2007, the
BioShock demo contained the first
45 minutes of the game along with
the tutorial and cinematic opening
sequence. It achieved one million
downloads in just nine days.

▼ Most nominations at the Interactive Achievement Awards (game)

The 11th annual Interactive
Achievement Awards were held
in Las Vegas in February 2008.
Bioshock ② received an incredible
12 nominations and won in four
categories, including Outstanding
Achievement in Story Development.

▼ Most realistic water effects

The water effects ① in Bioshock
are widely acclaimed as the
best ever seen in
a video game. As well as realistic
splashes, water gushes into the
city through broken glass panels.
Sections of tunnel can collapse
under pressure and even internal
tanks of water are designed to
break and inundate the area
with realistic water. Effects artist
Stephan Alexander and graphics
artist Jesse Johnson were hired
as "water gurus" to create all the
water effects.

👍 IF YOU LIKE THIS...

... would you kindly check out Deus Ex
(Ion Storm/Eidos), a futuristic, dystopian
action role-player for PC, Mac and PS2?
Set around 2050, in fantastical versions
of real places such as New York City and
Hong Kong, Deus Ex has the same dark,
brooding atmosphere as Bioshock and
also garnered many "Game of the Year"
accolades when launched in 2000.

▼ Highest-rated Xbox game of 2007

Bioshock scored a then-record 96%
on Metacritic.com, becoming the
site's highest-rated game of all
time (now surpassed only by Grand
Theft Auto IV, with 98%). Metacritic
averages the scores from more
than 50 critical review sites and
publications – and the high scores
for Bioshock secured "Universal
Acclaim" status for the game.

▼ First use of "Ecological" Artificial Intelligence

Bioshock's developers created
a bespoke AI engine dubbed
"ecological", which gives non-
playable characters in the game,
including the Big Daddies ④,
naturalistic relationships with the
environment and other characters.
Rather than the usual "see
player, kill player" mechanism,
the characters in the game
have, according to the creators,
"interesting and consequential
relationships with one another".

2.2 million – units of *Bioshock* shipped, across PC and Xbox 360 formats, between August 2007 and June 2008.

▶ AWARDS

Bioshock scooped up an armful of Best Games awards in 2007:

- Best Action/Adventure game (Game Critic, E3)
- Best Game (Associated Press)
- Game of the Year (Spike VGAs)
- Best Game (BAFTA)
- PC Game of the Year (IGN)
- Game of the Year (XPlay)
- Best Xbox 360 game (Leipzig Games Festival)
- Game of the Year (GameSpy, 2006)

First next-generation FPS with multiple endings

There are three endings to *Bioshock* ⑤, depending on how you choose to play the game. To achieve a "happy" ending, you must rescue all the Little Sisters; if you harvest some of the Little Sisters for the Adam drug in their bodies and kill the Boss, at the end, you'll experience the "sad" ending that sees the splicers unleashed, capturing a submarine equipped with a nuclear missile. If you harvest *all* the Little Sisters, you witness an "evil" ending that is similar to the "sad ending" but with a slightly different voiceover.

◢ NEW RECORD
◸ UPDATED RECORD

▶ FACTS

> A week before *Bioshock*'s official launch date, the web was flooded with stories that the retailer Toys "R" Us were already selling the game. The "accident" was quickly corrected!

ⓘ TRIVIA

> The city of Rapture is modelled in part on the philosophical system known as "objectivism", as developed by the Russian writer Ayn Rand (1905–1982). Rand wrote: "My philosophy, in essence, is the concept of man as a heroic being, with his own happiness as the moral purpose of his life, with productive achievement as his noblest activity, and reason as his only absolute." The name of Rapture's founder, Andrew Ryan, is a play on Ayn Rand.

> In March 2008, Take-Two Interactive announced the development of *Bioshock 2* by the recently formed 2K Marin studio – and the early rumour is that it's a *prequel* to the original game.

> Gore Verbinski, director of the *Pirates of the Caribbean* trilogy, has been signed by Universal Pictures to direct the big-screen version of *Bioshock*. At the time of going to press, a script had been prepared by John Logan, writer of *Gladiator* (UK/USA, 2000).

> *It was not impossible to build Rapture ③ at the bottom of the sea; it was impossible to build it anywhere else.*
> **Andrew Ryan, creator of Rapture in Bioshock**

GOD OF WAR

⚙ PLATFORMS

✕ SPEC

Developer: *SEC Studios Santa Monica*
Publisher: *Sony Computer Entertainment*
Initial release: God of War (2005), PlayStation 2

⇄ GAMEPLAY

Action-adventure in which players assume the role of Kratos, a ruthless Spartan warrior. Acquiring weapons and spells, players travel through a fantasy world, battling mythical creatures such as the Hydra, Cyclops and Medusa to earn powers that help towards the ultimate goal of killing Ares, god of war.

👍 IF YOU LIKE THIS...

... and own a PlayStation 3, then *Heavenly Sword* is the epic big-production adventure you've been waiting for.

◤ Best PlayStation 2 game of all time

In a study by games news and reviews website IGN.com, *God of War* ③ was rated as the best-ever game for the PS2, topping their charts of the greatest 25 PS2 games of all time. *God of War* has also won more than a dozen Game of the Year awards.

> Stunning artwork, addictive gameplay, compelling storytelling and a narrow learning curve all contribute to make God of War one of the most gratifying gaming experiences available today.
> **Tom Lane, CNN, 7 April 2005**

◤ NEW RECORD   ◸ UPDATED RECORD

◤ Most successful fantasy series based on Greek mythology

Since its initial launch, *God of War* has sold more than 2.3 million copies in the USA alone. *God of War II* ⑦ has also sold more than 2 million copies in the USA. No other action game focusing around the exploits of the Greek gods has sold as much or been as critically acclaimed.

◤ Most powerful god in a video game

Considered the most powerful of the Greek gods, and the most powerful within *God of War*, Zeus is the king of all the gods. Initially he befriends Kratos ④ in *God of War*, giving him the magical ability "Zeus's Fury", but in *God of War II*, Zeus ② tricks and betrays Kratos and impales him on the mighty Blade of Olympus.

93% – the GameRanking.com ratio for *God of War II*, based on 81 reviews. In total, 10 reviews awarded a maximum 100%.

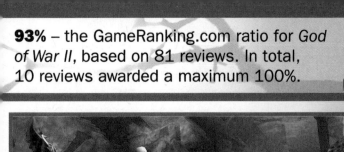

Most successful PS2 exclusive title (2007)

Released in March 2007, *God of War II* reached sales of 833,000 units in its first month, a coup for PlayStation 2. The franchise looks set to continue releasing games on a platform exclusive basis with *God of War: Chains of Olympus* launched exclusively for the PSP in March 2008.

FACT

The game engine for the original *God of War* made such efficient use of aging PS2 hardware that it was used for the sequel with no improvements or amendments to the code, the only PS2 sequel to do so. This surprisingly rare achievent was possible mainly because the PS2 was already a mature platform by the time the first game in the series was released in 2006 and the console's architecture had been exploited to the maximum.

First 3D action game to reveal its ending at the start of the game

God of War is something of a curiosity in that during the game's opening sequence, the player is shown what happens to Kratos at the end of the adventure. *God of War* is also one of a small number of games in which the main protagonist dies at the start of the game!

MYTHOLOGICAL CHARACTERS

The characters in *God of War* are based on legendary creatures from Greek mythology. Each creature has distinguishing features that give it a unique role within the game.

Minotaur: Part man, part bull, sealed in the legendary Labyrinth. Kratos must kill tougher axe-wielding minotaurs as he progresses.

Cyclops 6 **:** One-eyed humanoid monster, the son of Poseidon and Thoosa in Homer's *Odyssey*. In *God of War*, Cyclops lives on the Island of Creation and guards Pandora's Temple.

Siren: Beautiful women who lure sailors to their deaths. Occasionally, they are encountered by Kratos in pairs and attack using magic.

Gorgon: Three serpent-like sisters, Medusa, Stheno and Euryale. Only Medusa was mortal. Kratos meets several groups of gorgons with differing appearances and kills them by ripping their heads off.

Centaur: Servants of Hades, these monsters are half man and half horse. Kratos must kill eight in order to make a blood sacrifice for Hades.

Cerberus: A huge three-headed dog, with a snake for a tail, who guarded the gate to Hades. Kratos encounters several Cerberi as well as their smaller litters.

Hydra: An ancient serpentine water dweller with lots of heads. Kratos is ordered to kill the monster by Poseidon, god of the ocean.

Medusa: The only mortal of the three gorgons, Medusa was killed in mythology by Perseus. In *God of War*, Kratos kills Medusa and uses her head to freeze enemies.

TRIVIA

> Ares, the God of War, was the son of Zeus and Hera and features as a major character in the game. He was responsible for Kratos's murder of his own family. In revenge, Kratos kills Ares at the game's end, using Pandora's Box.

> When fighting boss mobs, in certain situations Kratos is able to enter a Quick Time Event 1 killing sequence. These highly cinematic sequences give the player partial control of Kratos and, if successful, Kratos dispatches the enemy in a gory, yet spectacular, display.

> Kratos's main weapons are the Blades of Chaos 5, which are twin curved swords on chains that are fused to the hero's forearms. The chains allow him to swing the swords in increased-range attacks. After Kratos becomes a god, he is awarded the Blades of Athena, by the goddess of the same name. Similar in appearance to the Blades of Chaos, the Blades of Athena also glow golden due to their divine magic.

THE LORD OF THE RINGS ONLINE

PLATFORMS

SPEC

Developer:
Turbine Inc.
Publisher:
Codemasters
Initial release:
The Lord of the Rings
Online: Shadows of
Angmar (2007), PC

GAMEPLAY

*The Lord of the Rings
Online series is based
on the books of J.R.R.
Tolkien. Players can
experience the most
famous fantasy
world of all time,
playing
with their
heroes, while
adventuring
through the
vast reaches of
Middle-earth in
the fight against the
forces of the Dark
Lord Sauron.*

Most complex music system in a MMORPG

*The Lord of the Rings Online:
Shadows of Angmar (LOTRO)* ③ is
the first MMORPG to allow players
to use their keyboard to play tunes
of their own choosing – either
by composing their own tunes
or arranging versions of existing
compositions. The number keys
1–8 correspond to playing an
octave of musical notes, and total
of nine different instruments can
be bought from a Bard.

The music system has proved to
be so popular that *LOTRO* players
have taken to making complex
compositions and posting them on
video-sharing website YouTube.

IF YOU LIKE THIS...

... then you're very likely to enjoy the
wonderful escapism of other MMORPGs,
World of Warcraft and *Age of Conan*.

First Player v Monster play zone in a MMORPG

The Ettenmoors ① is a region
around the same size as The Shire,
where gamers can take part in
monster play – a concept unique to
LOTRO. Monster play enables
gamers to
take part in
Player vs Monster Player battles
either as members of the Free
Peoples of Middle-earth, or as
one of the monsters. Players can
choose from monsters including
Orcs, Wargs and Uruks.

First LOTRO in-game hobby

Introduced in the *Book
13* update, fishing ② was the
first of many hobbies available to
inhabitants of Middle-earth. This
can be done anywhere in the world
with a large variety of fish available
to catch. The largest fish that a
player can land is the 50-lb (22.6
kg) salmon, while the hardest
fish to catch is the 20-ft
(6.1-m) white sturgeon.

INTERVIEW WITH... JEFFREY STEEFEL

Jeffrey Steefel is Executive Producer of *The Lord of the Rings Online* (*LOTRO*). We quizzed him about the popular MMORPG.

What were the first games you played?
I played a lot of Nintendo early on, as well as pinball machine and games like *Marble Madness* – there wasn't any other way of playing games back then apart from pumping quarters into an arcade machine.

What have been your favourite games?
I remain obsessed with *Warcraft 3*, which I played for many late-night hours doing endless campaigns! I played *World of Warcraft* until my fingers were bloody and I played *Everquest* while I was at Sony.

What makes *LOTRO* special?
This is the only persistent representation of Tolkien's world anywhere. It's the natural progression and extension from these books and movies and now it's a real place you can go. I don't know of any fantasy that exists like this.

I like the way we have created an immersive online Middle-earth. We've had lots of feedback that we did a great job. It's been hard in the industry at large to work out how to do storytelling online but *LOTRO* has given us a great opportunity to do that. Humans relate to storytelling. As an MMORPG, *LOTRO* is best of the breed! It's the best of what is good about a modern MMORPG... [with] our music system and deeds, we've brought MMORPGs to the next level... But this is just the beginning.

What other gaming world records would you most like to achieve?
The fastest-growing MMORPG would be good!

As a former actor, which character would you liked to have played in the *LOTR* movies?
If I was younger then probably Frodo, but right now I'd go for Aragorn. In the future, when I am a wise old man, it would have to be Gandalf.

ⓘ TRIVIA

> The original launch of *The Lord of the Rings Online: Shadows of Angmar* covered the region of Eriador, which includes the Shire, Rivendell and Breeland; Eriador provided a gameplay area of approximately 50,000 km² (101,893 miles²).

> The first retail expansion of *LOTRO*, *The Lord of the Rings Online: Mines of Moria* was announced in Birmingham, UK, which was the childhood home of J.R.R. Tolkien, author of the original *The Lord of the Rings* books.

> Amongst other features, *The Lord of the Rings Online: Mines of Moria* expansion introduces 200 new enemies, two new character classes and the ability to advance characters up to level 60.

> The two deeds in *LOTRO* regarded as the hardest to achieve are the Chicken, in which a player has to run around the world as a mostly defenceless chicken, and the Giant Slayer, in which a player must kill 120 giants.

208 games played and a skill point of 32,767; Eleventy-seven morsels: FragKiller67133, with 762 games played and a skill point of 1,110.

▶ Most difficult pipeweed to manufacture
Smoking pipeweed ⑤ is a purely recreational activity in *LOTRO*. There are three types of seeds available in the game: buying from vendors, looting from mobs, and cross-breeding with other seeds. The tobacco known as "Wizard's Fire" is the only pipeweed that requires two cross-bred variants to craft and is the only tobacco that needs a master crafter to make it.

▶ Toughest enemy in LOTRO
With a grand total of 316,961 health and 52,699 power, Thorog, a mighty dragon who has been resurrected by Fell spirits, is considered the hardest enemy to defeat in *Shadows of Angmar*.

▶ NEW RECORD ▷ UPDATED RECORD

▶ Largest dungeon in a MMORPG
Released in late 2008, *Mines of Moria* ④ is the first retail expansion for *LOTRO*. It contains the famous Mines of Moria, the home of the dwarves, which has an area of approximately 10.24 km² (4 miles²) beneath the mountains, the largest underground space in any MMORPG.

▶ Highest scores in LOTRO mini-games
Three mini-games have been released as the prelude to the *Mines of Moria*, with rewards available in-game for the highest-ranking. As of 30 July 2008, the players in the lead of the three games were as follows: King Under the Mountain: allrues, with 439 games played and a skill point of 188; Swig and Toss: uadan, with

❓ GWR QUIZ
Q18. What is the hardest fish to catch in *LOTRO*?

MASS EFFECT

⚙️ PLATFORMS

🔧 SPEC

Developer:
BioWare
Publisher: *Microsoft
Game Studios
(Xbox 360) & EA (PC)*
Initial release:
*Mass Effect (2007),
Xbox 360*

💲 GAMEPLAY

*It is the year 2183 AD
and mankind has
managed to break
free of the solar
system to establish
colonies within the
Milky Way. Playing
as the role of
Commander
Shepard,
Mass
Effect
combines
real-time
combat, artificial
intelligence,
space travel
and colonization
within a man-
Vs-machine
gameplay.
Influences on
the game include
the movies Aliens
(UK/USA, 1986),
Blade Runner (USA,
1982) and Star Wars
(USA, 1977).*

▶ Largest space station
The millennia-old Citadel
Station ①, at the centre of the
Serpent Nebula, is home to the
Citadel Council. Measuring some
44.7 km (27.7 miles) long, and
with a total mass of 26.4 billion
metric tonnes, it has a population
of over 13 million inhabitants.

👍 IF YOU LIKE THIS...
... you should try out BioWare's epic
Star Wars RPG series, *Knights of the
Old Republic* on Xbox.

▶ Most powerful
playable class
By completing various
"achievements" in-game, the
player, as Commander Shephard
②, is able to train and become a
Spectre – an agent of the Special
Tactics and Reconnaissance
branch of the Citadel. Shephard
becomes the very first human
Spectre in history in the year 2183.

▶ Stealthiest ship
in Mass Effect
The SSV *Normandy SR-1 Systems
Alliance* ③ frigate is the ship on
board which Commander Shepard
is Executive Officer. It is the only
ship in the galaxy to include
advanced prototype stealth
technology, which uses internal
lithium heat sinks to reduce
the heat emissions generated
by the craft to zero. The SSV
Normandy can maintain
stealthy "silent running"
for a couple of hours
before having to
vent heat into
space.

▶ First Mass Effect
novel – Revelation
Mass Effect: Revelation ④ was
written by Drew Karpyshyn, who was
also lead writer for the game. It was
published in 2007 by Del Rey Books
and fills in some of the background
of the game. Its sequel, *Mass
Effect: Ascension*, also by Karpyshyn,
was published in July 2008.

▶ First downloadable
content in Mass Effect
Bring Down the Sky, the first
downloadable content for *Mass
Effect*, was released in March
2008 initially for the Xbox 360. It
includes a new uncharted world in
the Asgard system and a new alien
race, the Batarians ⑥. Consisting
of roughly an extra 90 minutes of
gameplay, *Bring Down the Sky* pits
Shephard against the aliens who
have hijacked a mobile asteroid
station and have set it
on a collision course with a nearby
human colony.

4 million – the number of registered users at bioware.com

Fastest-selling RPG on Xbox 360

Mass Effect sold 1 million copies in the three weeks after its launch on 20 November 2007, which is faster than any other RPG on any Microsoft console.

Most productive RPG community

Neverwinter Nights, released in 2002, is a role-playing game that generated the most fan-created content in BioWare's history. Fans produced over 4,200 stand-alone adventures, thousands of new monsters and dozens of worlds. An example of the enormity of this fan-created content can be found in a single piece of content called the Community Expansion Project, or CEP. At over 750 MB in size, it has been downloaded over 500,000 times by fans from around the world.

Best-selling Sci-Fi RPG on Xbox 360

After selling nearly 2 million units worldwide, *Mass Effect* ⑤ is officially the best-selling sci-fi RPG on the Xbox 360. Microsoft's epic space adventure also held the record for the best-selling RPG exclusive to the Xbox 360 before the game was released on PC in May 2008.

Most advanced character face generator

The facial animation software developed by artists and programmers at BioWare is the most powerful of its type. The system blended together over 150 different models of facial features, including colours, skin, hair models and scars to create one billion unique faces for the expressive Commander Shepard. More challenging, however, was ensuring that all of these variations could be brought to life equally convincingly through *Mass Effect*'s digital acting system, which turned this complex assembly of art into a character that could perform scenes that appeared to portray lifelike emotion and personality.

¹²₃ **FIGURES**

130 – *Mass Effect* production team (peak size)

306 – Man-years spent in development

3.75 – Years in production

58 – Voice actors required

210 – Number of speaking characters

26,527 – Lines of dialogue featured

135 – Animated points of articulation in each human character

40 – Animated points of articulation in each human face

4 million – Number of people belonging to developer BioWare's *Mass Effect* online community

④ The thrilling prequel to the award-winning video game from BioWare!

MASS EFFECT

REVELATION

DREW KARPYSHYN
New York Times bestselling author and lead writer of the Mass Effect video game

FANTASY & SCI-FI ROUND-UP

◤ First game to feature full Quick Time Events

Game: *Dragon's Lair*
Publisher: Cinematronics
Quick Time Events are graphical, cinematic sequences that occur at critical story points in a game. They are usually characterized by graphical sequences that are of higher quality than the game at large and allow the player limited control over their avatar. *Dragon's Lair* ①, released in 1983 on Laserdisc, is best remembered for having practically all of its gameplay as Quick Time Events.

Longest-running fantasy video-game franchise

Game: *Ultima* (series)
Publisher: Various
The *Ultima* series of games began with the original *Ultima* in 1980. Since then, 11 sequels have been released, the final being *Ultima IX: Ascension* ② in 1999. Including *Ultima Online*, which was released in 1997, and its expansions, the series has been in publication for 27 years, with *Ultima Online: Kingdom Reborn* ③ being the last published to date, in 2007.

◤ **NEW RECORD**
◸ **UPDATED RECORD**

◤ First Pentium-optimized game

Game: *Magic Carpet*
Publisher: Electronic Arts
Published in 1994, *Magic Carpet* ⑥ was the first PC game to be advertised as being optimized for the (then) new Intel Pentium processor. The 3D graphics and effects were widely praised for being way ahead of their time, and the game was one of the first to be sold on CD-ROM ⑦, rather than a set of floppy disks.

◤ Greatest evolutionary scope in a video game

Game: *Spore*
Publisher: Electronic Arts
Released in September 2008, *Spore* ④, developed by Maxis and designed by Will Wright of *SimCity* and *The Sims* fame, has been described as having elements of god games, real-time strategy and life simulation. The game allows a player to control the evolution of a species, which begins as bacterial in nature and evolves through gameplay into multicellular organisms and then complex lifeforms that can eventually colonize planets and star systems.

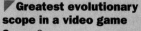

1 million – the number of incredible creatures created and shared by fans of *Spore* in just one week, following the release of the *Spore Creature Creator* in June 2008.

CATS : ALL YOUR BASE ARE BELONG TO US.

> "We've got almost 3,000 employees worldwide now, and the majority of that growth is due to the success of World of Warcraft. **Frank Pearce, co-founder of Blizzard Entertainment, talking in 2008 about the company's continued expansion.**

¹₂₃ FIGURES

> **$161 million (£90 million)** – invested in 16 virtual-world companies during the second quarter of 2008, bringing this year's total investment up to **$345 million (£192 million)**, according to figures from Virtual World Management.

> **$50 million (£28 million)** – amount of funding secured by *Crackdown* developer, Realtime Worlds, in 2008.

> **$40 million (£22 million)** – the next biggest securing of financing by Turbine, the developers of *The Lord of the Rings Online* MMORPG, led by Time Warner and GGV Capital.

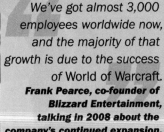

time strategy game, praised for its cinematic graphics and moody atmosphere. It was the first of the increasingly popular RTS games to incorporate full movement in the z-axis along with the x and y axes.

First motion capture animation in a video game
Game: *Prince of Persia*
Publisher: Broderbund
Prince of Persia, created in 1989 by designer and programmer Jordan Mechner (USA), is the first game to use motion-capture to create animation. Mechner first filmed his brother David performing acrobatic moves and then traced over each frame to create the Prince's smooth, realistic animation.

Gamer's Edition Records Manager Gaz Deaves is pictured presenting a certificate for this achievement to Chis Easton of Ubisoft, Montreal, Canada.

? GWR QUIZ

Q19. Who is the gaming legend responsible for creating *Spore*?

▶ First game mistranslation to spark an internet phenomenon
Game: *Zero Wing*
Publisher: Sega
The sci-fi shooter *Zero Wing*, released in arcades in 1989 and on the Sega Mega Drive in 1991, became famous in 2001 for its opening cutscene, which featured the phrase "All your base are belong to us". This mistranslation from the original Japanese transcript amused many gamers and spread across the internet to become a global phenomenon.

▶ First dungeon crawl
Game: *Pedit5*
Creator: Rusty Rutherford
Pedit5, written in 1974 by Rusty Rutherford, was run on a mainframe computer and involved players navigating a dungeon, fighting monsters and gathering treasure. Its name was designed to disguise the fact that it was a game, as the mainframe operators at universities regarded games as a waste of resources. Eventually, though, *Pedit5* was discovered for what it was and deleted.

▶ First real-time 3D sci-fi strategy
Game: *Homeworld*
Publisher: Sierra Entertainment
Released in 1999, *Homeworld* was an epic space-based real-

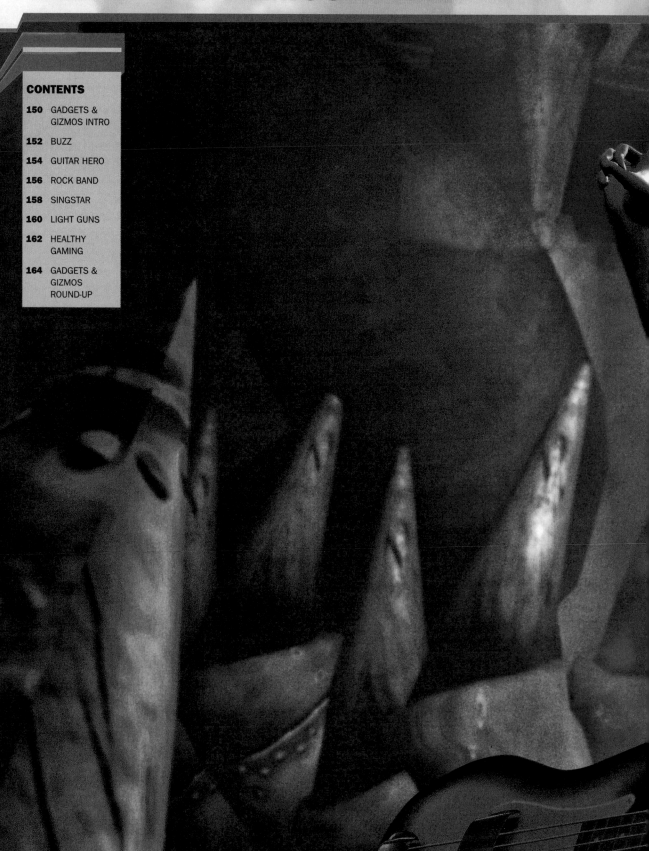

CONTENTS

The *Guitar Hero* franchise broke through the billion-dollar mark after just 26 months on sale in North America – the **fastest time for any game series to make $1 billion (£500,000,000)**.

GADGETS & GIZMOS

SINCE THE INVENTION OF GAMES CONSOLES, PEOPLE HAVE BEEN LOOKING FOR THE BEST GADGETS AND GIZMOS TO GET MORE FUN OUT OF THEM, FROM GUNS THAT SENSE LIGHT TO PLASTIC GUITARS.

EXPERT

Gaz Deaves has been a gamer ever since *Captain Comic* for the PC rocked his world when he was seven years old. He has been a games publicist and commentator for four years and is currently the video-gaming adjudicator for Guinness World Records. His proudest gaming achievement is beating the editor of *PC Gamer* in a *Doom 2* death match. His apartment is filled with an assortment of games consoles, as well as plastic musical instruments, dance mats, light guns, control pads and all the cables necessary to connect them.

OVERVIEW

Plugging in an external device, or peripheral, to get more out of your console is one of the oldest traditions of video-gaming, and it is a tradition that is still alive and well, as the huge successes of Wii Fit and Guitar Hero testify. But it's not just about unusual controllers: games consoles are often designed to be expandable and manufacturers have come up with some unique ways of making their machines do more through the use of innovative add-ons.

Games consoles have a long history of offering added extras that allow them to do that little bit more, from the light gun that was tested by Ralph Baer on the first home games console to the Wii MotionPlus, the latest super-sensitive upgrade to Nintendo's motion-sensing controller.

The ▶ **first commercially successful games console to include extra peripherals** was the Atari 2600, which not only came pre-packaged with two joysticks, but also two dial-based paddle controllers more traditionally used for playing pong and simple racing games. A short-lived balance-board accessory was also released for the console, more than 20 years before Nintendo released a similar device with *Wii Fit*.

However, Nintendo have been responsible for a lot of innovation in video-game controllers and peripherals. Included with the Famicom was the ▶ **first console joypad** a controller that was arguably more suited to platform and puzzle games than the joysticks used on earlier consoles.

Nintendo's core joypad design has changed little in the 25 years since the Famicom first launched, with the only major changes being the loss of a microphone component, the addition of analogue control sticks to make it easier to control games in 3D and extra buttons to allow a wider range of in-game actions.

The iconic NES joypad even inspired a team led by David Randolph and David Ledger (both USA) to create

the ▶ **world's largest video-game joypad** ⑧. Their joypad measured 2.43 m x 1.01 m x 0.22 m (8 ft x 3 ft 4 in x 9 in) and weighed 68 kg (150 lb).

Both the Famicom and the NES boasted strong catalogues of peripherally enhanced video games, with the Zapper light gun and Duck Hunt, as well as the ▶ **first robot peripheral** in the form of the Famicom Robot add-on for *Gyromite* and *Stack-Up*. The robot, called the R.O.B. (Robotic Operating Buddy) in the West, watched monitor-received commands via optical flashes during the games.

In 1989, Mattel released the Power Glove for the NES. It was the first Nintendo-approved, motion-sensing peripheral for the console. However, gamers criticised

TIMELINE

1968	1983	1985	1989
Ralph Baer invents the first light-gun game for his prototype console, the Brown Box.	Nintendo Famicom ④ comes with a controller that is the blueprint for modern joypads.	The Famicon Robot or R.O.B. (Robotic Operating Buddy) ⑤ peripheral comes to the Famicom and NES.	The Power Glove is released for NES in the US.

765 – number of schools in West Virginia outfitted with *Dance Dance Revolution* in a bid to combat childhood obesity.

it for being imprecise and Nintendo showed little concerted interest in motion control until the Wii was released 17 years later.

Throughout the 1990s, support for innovative controllers was left to unofficial add-on manufacturers, while the console makers concentrated on making more powerful machines. NEC produced the ▶ **first CD-drive console attachment** for the PC Engine (released in the USA as the TurboGrafx-16), which allowed gamers to play the first *Street Fighter* game for a home console. Sega were next with the Mega-CD **6** attachment that clipped in under the Mega Drive/Genesis system. The success of these CD attachments prompted Nintendo to negotiate an arrangement with Sony to develop a CD drive for the Super NES; however, the deal fell through and Sony took their work on the project as the starting point for a development process that led to the first PlayStation.

The real explosion of peripheral-based gaming happened during the PlayStation era, with the launch of *Dance Dance Revolution* (*DDR*) in 1999, a game that came with a roll-out dance mat that replicated the foot controllers of the *DDR* arcade machine **1**.

While rhythm games were already popular in arcades in Japan and South Korea with titles such as *GuitarFreaks*, it wasn't until the release of *Guitar Hero* in 2005 that such games made a significant impact in the West. The game and its sequels were massive hits and inspired *Rock Band*, which adds vocals and drums, making it the

👍 **IF YOU LIKE THIS...**
... then you should look at the add-ons that could help you achieve healthy living through gaming on p.162.

▶ **NEW RECORD**   ▷ **UPDATED RECORD**

▶ **first co-operative four-player console music game**

The most influential change to video-game gadgetry in recent years has to be the Wii Remote, or Wiimote, which promotes the greatest range of movement of all the standard next-generation controllers **3**. Nintendo's decision to adopt a completely different controller type from its competitors has played a part in making the Wii the ▶ **fastest-selling console in history**.

With the success of a variety of different controller peripherals for the Wii and the growing popularity of all kinds of console add-ons generally, gamers can expect to see more and better gaming peripherals for their consoles in the future.

see p.162

ℹ TRIVIA

> In October 2007, Nintendo introduced a silicon sleeve **2** for the Wii Remote to help improve gamers' grip on their controllers. There have been widespread reports of people causing damage to various household objects after losing grip of their Wiimotes. One gamer's website, wiihaveaproblem.com, keeps a tally of damage caused by flying Wiimotes. As of August 2008, it had documented 25 televisions damaged by over-enthusiastic gamers.

> In July 2008, Nintendo announced the Wii MotionPlus add-on for Wii Remotes. The device plugs into the end of the Wii Remote and enhances the Wii Remotes ability to track a player's arm position and orientation.

> Nintendo have released five official peripherals to enhance the Wii Remote so far, but fans expect more in the future.

1991	1996	1999	2004	2006	2008
Sega launches the first internationally successful CD-drive add-on for a home console, the Mega-CD.	Sega release *Sega Ski Super G* **9**. **1997** Sony launches its DualShock **7** controller for PlayStation.	*Dance Dance Revolution* is released for PlayStation by Konami.	Dance-mat games are officially recognized as a sport in Norway.	Wii is launched by Nintendo, bringing motion-sensitive gaming to the masses.	The Wii Balance Board is released; Nintendo predicts the Wii will be in short supply at Christmas, for the third year running.

BUZZ!

⚙ PLATFORMS

✂ SPEC

Developer:
Relentless
Publisher:
Sony
Initial release:
Buzz!: The Music Quiz
(2005), PlayStation 2

💲 GAMEPLAY

Players take part in
a virtual gameshow,
answering trivia
questions over a series
of rounds. The game
is played using special
buzzer controllers
❸, which each feature
a big, red button. The
questions are asked by
the gameshow's host,
Buzz, and there
are different
player
characters
and
buzzer
sounds
to choose
from. Buzz!
Quiz TV,
the first PS3
instalment
in the series,
works with wireless
buzzers and allows
players to create
and share quizzes
online.

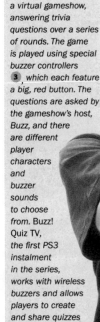

▷ Longest-running video game console quiz series
There have been 13 Buzz! games released so far. That figure includes four Buzz! Junior titles, which feature mini-games instead of quiz questions. The quiz games have featured themes such as music, movies and sport. Nine have now been released, making Buzz! the world's longest-running video-game quiz series.

▷ Best-selling video-game quiz series
More than 6 million Buzz! games have been sold in Europe alone. This makes Buzz! the best-selling video-game quiz series of all time.

▷ First quiz game to win a BAFTA award
On 5th October 2006, Buzz!: The Big Quiz won a BAFTA at the British Academy Video Games Awards. It took the trophy for Best Game in the Casual & Social category. Other nominees included Guitar Hero, SingStar Rocks! and Dr Kawashima's Brain Training, but Buzz! saw off the competition – becoming the first quiz game ever to win the award.

▷ First video game endorsed by the UK Government
In 2006, Sony unveiled Buzz!: The Schools Quiz. Designed for use in classrooms, it features more than 5,000 questions based on subjects covered by Key Stage 2 of the National Curriculum – from "Ancient Egypt" to "Weather". Buzz!: The Schools Quiz was the
▷ first home console game to be created in partnership with the UK Government. It's now used by thousands of children in primary schools across the UK, and was launched in Spain in 2007.

▷ Most popular Buzz! quiz pack
On 4 July 2008, Buzz!: Quiz TV ❶ launched in Europe. It was the first PS3 instalment in the series and the first to let users download new quiz packs from the PlayStation Store. This meant an additional 4,000 questions could be downloaded. The most popular offering during the first month after launch was the Sci-Fi Movies quiz pack.

▷ Longest development time for a Buzz! game
It took more than 700 man-months to produce Buzz!: Quiz TV, which is equivalent to nearly 60 man-years. That's twice as long as it took to develop any previous instalment in the Buzz! series.

1 million – the number of user-created quizzes downloaded by players of *Buzz!: Quiz TV* within one month of the service launching.

INTERVIEW WITH... DAVID AMOR

In 2003, David Amor **6** co-founded Relentless Software with Andrew Eades. The studio, which is based in Brighton, UK, has enjoyed great success with the *Buzz!* series.

What inspired you to create a quiz game in the first place?
We had seen *EyeToy* and *SingStar*, and saw that these new "social" games could be popular. Sony contacted us with the idea of making a quiz game and we felt that, if we designed it carefully, it might be popular for the same reasons that *EyeToy* and *SingStar* were.

What was the biggest challenge you faced when developing *Buzz!*?
Keeping it simple. It took some discipline to avoid falling into old video-game habits, which would have resulted in a game that only video gamers understood how to play.

Were you surprised by how successful the game was?
In 2003, it seemed very unlikely that a small game made by a team of 12 people in Brighton would end up being Sony Europe's biggest-selling game of 2005. During development, we held informal play-testing sessions and it became clear that the game was a lot of fun. But we didn't expect to get this far!

So, what's next for the *Buzz!* series?
We're a long way from running out of ideas, so you can expect to see more from the series. We're also working on another social game – but it's a little too early to talk about that just yet.

NEW RECORD   ### UPDATED RECORD

> *Good heavens! We're in the presence of what can only be described as off-the-scale stupidity. I don't know whether to weep or have a statue made.*
> **Buzz's funniest remark, as voted for by the game's development team**

▶ FACT

According to the game's publisher Sony Computer Entertainment Europe, each copy of *Buzz!* has been played a dozen times on average and 70 questions are answered in each gaming session. With more than 6 million copies sold, that means the number of *Buzz!* questions answered is just over 5 billion.

▶ First video game to support user-created quizzes

Buzz!: Quiz TV was the first video game to let users create their own quizzes and share them online. Within three months of the game launching, more than 70,000 quizzes had been uploaded to the MyBuzz! website. During the same period, *Buzz!* players downloaded user-created quizzes more than 5 million times. The most popular quiz was the "Trick Question Quiz", which was created by user "merlinpants".

▶ Most popular *Buzz!* online options

During July 2008, the most popular buzzer choice for online *Buzz!: Quiz TV* players was "Squeaky", which was picked 158,000 times. The most popular character was "Overlord" **2**, who was chosen 218,000 times.

👍 IF YOU LIKE THIS...

... then you'll love the **GWR Quiz** in this book! Find the answers at www.guinnessworldrecords.com/gamers

ℹ TRIVIA

> Buzz **5** is the wise-cracking host of the *Buzz!* gameshow. In the UK, his voice is provided by Australian actor and singer Jason Donovan **4**, who likes to play the *Buzz!* games with his children.

> A keen follower of fashion, Buzz has worn nine different outfits since the first game's release.

> The *Buzz!* games feature a wide range of player characters, from a mime artist to a Mexican wrestler. There are also plenty of wacky virtual prizes to be won. The funniest prize, as voted for by developers Relentless Software, is a horse in a jacuzzi.

¹₂₃ FIGURES

1 in 11 – number of European PlayStation 2 owners who possess a set of *Buzz!* controllers.

❓ GWR QUIZ

Q20. Which multi-talented Australian celebrity is the voice of the gameshow host in *Buzz!*?

GUITAR HERO

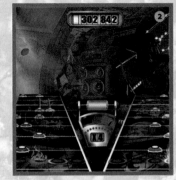

PLATFORMS

SPEC

Developer:
Harmonix (GHI and II),
Neversoft (GHIII)
Publisher:
RedOctane/Activision
Initial release:
Guitar Hero (2005),
PlayStation 2

GAMEPLAY

*Players use a special
guitar-shaped
controller to play notes
as they appear on
the screen, using the
strum bar to get the
timing right.*

▽ Single track high score on Guitar Hero III

The record for highest score for a single track on *Guitar Hero III* ③ is 899,703 points, achieved on the Dragonforce song "Through the Fire and Flames" by Chris Chike ④ (USA) in Minnesota, USA, on 29 August 2008. With 3,722 notes, this massive track is the **hardest song on *Guitar Hero*.**

▽ Single track high score by team of six on Guitar Hero II

The highest score for a single track played by a team of six on *Guitar Hero II* ② is 129,660 points achieved on the song "Beast and the Harlot" by Imran Akhtar, Adam Araim, Annis Araim, Saad Choudri, Phil Davies and Aleks Gakovic (all UK) at Zavvi, Oxford Street, London, UK, on 6 February 2008 ⑥.

▽ Largest audience for a video-game performance

The largest audience for a video game performance is 9,600 people, achieved by Lyndon Jones and Renos Georgiou, who played *Guitar Hero III* at the Give it a Name festival, Earl's Court, London, UK, on 11 May 2008 ①. The pair played "Welcome to the Jungle" by seminal hair-metal band Guns N' Roses.

> *It's what we would consider the pinnacle of difficulty, the guitar shredding in there is just insane.*
> **Kai Huang, President and co-founder of RedOctane describes the Guitar Hero III track "Through the Fire and Flames".**

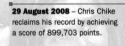

29 August 2008 – Chris Chike reclaims his record by achieving a score of 899,703 points.

11 March 2008 – Chris Chike smashes the record with a score of 880,920 points.

17 May 2008 – Danny Johnson (USA) breaks the record with 890,971 points.

31 January 2008 – Busking record-breaker Luke Albiges kicks off the year with a score of 380,908 points.

2.1 million – number of times Chris Chike's first flawless performance of "Through the Fire and Flames" has been viewed on YouTube as of September 2008.

unofficial controller, it can't be used for record attempts.

Youngest gamer to 5-star Through the Fire and Flames on Expert

Ben Eberle (USA) is the youngest person to achieve a 5-star rating on the hardest song on *Guitar Hero III* on expert difficulty. On 24 November 2007, Ben blasted through the Dragonforce track aged just 9 years and 167 days.

▶ **NEW RECORD**   ▷ **UPDATED RECORD**

👍 **IF YOU LIKE THIS...**
... then you'll love *Rock Band*. Rock up to p.156 for a full-on jam session with the greatest *Rock Band* records.

Longest relay marathon record on Guitar Hero III

The greatest number of passes in a relay on *Guitar Hero III*

First wireless bass guitar peripheral

The Widow Maker is the first wireless bass guitar-shaped peripheral for the PS2 and PS3 versions of *Guitar Hero* and *Rock Band*. The extra length and weight gives gamers a more authentic bass playing experience when playing in co-op mode, although since it's an

is 42, achieved at Zavvi, Oxford Street, London, UK, on 6 February 2008. Every player who participated had to complete their song or the attempt would fail. Players could select any song and the whole attempt lasted 165 minutes.

First video-game busking session

On 6 April 2006, Luke Albiges ⑤ (UK) played *Guitar Hero* for two hours at Leicester Square tube station in London, UK. He thrashed his way through all 30 songs featured in the game and donated all the money he raised to charity.

ROCK BAND

PLATFORMS

SPEC

Developer: Harmonix Music Systems, Inc.
Publisher: MTV Games
Initial release: Rock Band (2007), PlayStation 3 & Xbox 360

GAMEPLAY

Developed by Harmonix, creators of Guitar Hero, Rock Band challenges players to pick up their instruments and go in search of the rock 'n' roll lifestyle. Instruments available to players are guitar, bass, drums and microphone (for vocals) as they hit the road as either an aspiring solo act, or form a band and jam together in multiplayer action from home or anywhere in the world.

IF YOU LIKE THIS...

... then you might like *Donkey Konga*, the **first console game to come with a drum controller**.

Most difficult song in Rock Band

Each track in *Rock Band* ① gives a difficulty rating for each of the four instruments (guitar ②, vocals, drums ⑤ and bass). The ratings range from one to nine, with "Run to the Hills" by Iron Maiden the only song to rate a terrifying "nine" for every instument.

Longest track listing for a music game

With 90 tracks available out of the box on the Wii edition and over 100 downloadable songs (including some complete albums), *Rock Band* has more playable tracks than any other music game with 244 total songs as of 22 July 2008.

First song to sell more on Xbox Live than iTunes

Real-life rock band Mötley Crüe ③ released the song "Saints of Los Angeles" simultaneously on iTunes and via Xbox Live for *Rock Band* players to download. The track shifted 47,000 copies in its first week on Xbox Live, outselling the 10,000 downloads for the iTunes version by almost five to one!

Highest score for a full band in Rock Band

The highest combined score for a full four-piece band playing *Rock Band* is 3,686,599, achieved by UHR (USA) ④ on the song "Green Grass and High Tides" by Outlaw. The scores were broken down as follows: Draktyr (Guitar) 97%, raunch99 (Bass) 99%, GurnKiller (Drums) 99%, CowShark (Vocals) 100%.

FACT

US fans of *Rock Band* bought and downloaded 2.5 million extra songs in just two months after the launch of the game in November 2007, according to reports on website GamesIndustry.biz.

> *One thing I love about* Rock Band *is that it's co-operative, it's not a fight between people. It's this thing where everyone is pulling together and you can save somebody out of the fire.*
> **Chris Foster, Harmonix**

Most expensive peripheral-enhanced game in the UK

With a recommended retail price of £179.98 ($356.69) in the UK, *Rock Band* was the most expensive peripheral-enhanced game to be commercially released. When it launched in May 2008 it was cheaper to buy a new Xbox 360 Arcade console than stump up for the game; however, gamers in the USA weren't as hard-done by – *Rock Band* was on sale six months earlier in the United States and only cost $169 (£85.77), less than half the price paid by Europeans. In September 2008 the UK retail price was reduced to £110 (€140).

Longest drum marathon on Rock Band

The longest marathon playing drums on *Rock Band* is 26 hr 40 min, achieved by Sean "Phr34k" Feica (Canada) in London, Ontario, Canada, from 26–27 July 2008.

Feica played every song available on *Rock Band* at the time (a total of 243 songs) in order of difficulty. He achieved a 5-gold-star rating on 141 songs, of which 56 were full combos. Once every song was completed, Sean finished with an encore of the appropriately titled "Still Alive" by Jonathan Coulton, more commonly known as the *Portal* end theme.

SINGSTAR

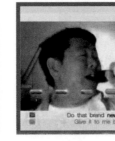

The way you move so scandalous
It's all about the two of us

Do that brand new thing
Give it to me baby

A guy like you
Should wear a warn - ing - -

You made me feel - - like - - the one
Made me feel like - - the one

PLATFORMS

PC · XBOX 360 · X · DS · GAME BOY ADVANCE · Wii

SPEC

Developer:
Sony (London Studio)
Publisher:
Sony
Initial release:
SingStar (2004),
PlayStation 2

GAMEPLAY

Music videos and lyrics are displayed on screen and players sing along into special microphones. Performances are analyzed and compared to the original recording, and points are scored according to how closely they match the original in pitch and tone. SingStar PS3 works with the PlayStation Eye camera and allows players to share videos online.

◤ Most successful singing game series

The first *SingStar* game ❶ was published in May 2004 and went straight to the top of the charts in most countries. Since then, more than 25 instalments have been released for PS2 including *SingStar Pop Hits* ❿, *SingStar Rocks* ❹ and *SingStar R'n'B*. *SingStar PS3* launched in December 2007 and a sequel followed in June 2008. More than 12 million *SingStar* titles have now been sold and the games are available in over 67 countries worldwide.

◤ Most viewed SingStar player

SingStar fan "Netcasty" ❷, who lives in Germany, has uploaded more than 70 videos of himself performing tracks from the game. His YouTube channel has been viewed more than 28,000 times. His performances proved so popular that he was spotted by Sony Germany and in June 2008 he appeared in a television advert for *SingStar* itself.

◤ Best-selling SingStar track

In December 2007 Sony launched the SingStore, a new service that lets *SingStar PS3* ❸ players buy downloadable tracks. In the first four months after it opened, 1 million songs were downloaded. The most popular track across PAL regions was "Total Eclipse of the Heart" by Bonnie Tyler ❺.

◤ First music game to let users share performances online

SingStar PS3 was the first music game to let players record their singing performances and upload videos to the internet. Since December 2007, more than 140,000 people have registered to use the game's networking feature, *My SingStar Online*. Together with visitors to the official website, SingStarGame.com, they have shared over 20,000 performances and watched more than 2.5 million videos.

◤ Most country-specific instalments in a series

While most *SingStar* games are themed according to musical genre, there are 15 designed specifically for certain countries or regions. For example, *SingStar Latino* ❼ is only available in Spain and Portugal and *SingStar Deutsch Rock Pop* ❻ was only released in Germany, Austria and Switzerland. Localized *SingStar* games are now available with songs in French, German, Italian, Spanish, Portuguese, Dutch, Norwegian, Swedish, Danish, Finnish, Polish and Croatian.

◤ **NEW RECORD**

▽ **UPDATED RECORD**

140,000 – the number of people who have registered to use *SingStar PS3*'s networking feature, which allows players to share videos of their *SingStar* performances online.

> *MySpace is really the new MTV. Television is online, music is digital, products are tools and players are becoming creators... It's a new era.*
>
> **Paulina Bozek, series producer, SingStar**

◣ First game to let players choose the sequel

In May 2008, Sony ran a poll to let *SingStar* fans decide what the next PS2 instalment in the series would be. Those who took part were also allowed to vote on which tracks they'd like to see in the game. Votes were registered via MySpace, Facebook and the PlayStation forums and the winning title was *SingStar: Boy Bands versus Girl Power*.

◀◀▶ FACT

Songs from the 1980s and 1990s are equally popular with *SingStar* fans, each accounting for 45% of tracks in the top 40. A total of five songs from the 2000s have made it into the chart, compared to just two each from the 1960s and 1970s.

ⓘ TRIVIA

> The most-downloaded *SingStar* songs in selected countries:

Switzerland, Denmark, Sweden, Finland, Norway
Final Countdown
Europe **8**

UK, Ireland
Suspicious Minds
Elvis Presley **9**

Australia
Down Under
Men at Work

Spain
Muneca de trapo
La Oreja de Van Gogh

Germany, Austria
Ohne Dich (Schlaf Ich Heut Nacht Nicht Ein)
Munchener Freiheit

Italy
"Cleptomania"
Sugarfree

France
"Le Chemin"
Kyo featuring Sita

TOP 20 BEST-SELLERS

SingStar PS3 was the first instalment in the series to let players download extra tracks. Here are the top 20 best-selling songs across PAL territories as of June 2008.

RANK	SONG	ARTIST
1	Total Eclipse of the Heart	Bonnie Tyler
2	Final Countdown	Europe
3	Just Like a Pill	Pink
4	Suspicious Minds	Elvis Presley
5	Girls Just Wanna Have Fun	Cyndi Lauper
6	It's Raining Men	The Weather Girls
7	Down Under	Men At Work
8	Torn	Natalie Imbruglia
9	Bitch	Meredith Brooks
10	How to Save a Life	The Fray
11	Do You Really Want To Hurt Me	Culture Club
12	Take On Me	A-ha
13	Walking on Sunshine	Katrina And The Waves
14	Enjoy The Silence	Depeche Mode
15	Heaven Is A Place On Earth	Belinda Carlisle
16	Red Red Wine	UB40
17	American Pie	Don McLean
18	Baby One More Time	Britney Spears
19	U Can't Touch This	MC Hammer
20	Sing	Travis

LIGHT GUNS

▣▶ FACTS

> In 1976, Nintendo released an electro-mechanical toy called *Duck Hunt* eight years before it released the video game of the same name.

> Ralph Baer, considered to be the father of the modern video game, worked for US Military Intelligence in Europe during World War II. He has donated all of his hardware prototypes, including light guns, to the Smithsonian Museum in Washington, USA.

> *Time Crisis* was first released as an arcade game in 1995 and was followed by *Time Crisis II* in 1998 ⑨.

▧ NEW RECORD

▽ UPDATED RECORD

▧ Longest-serving light gun technology

The first digital light gun was developed in 1968 for Ralph Baer's Brown Box, and the "frame flashing" technology used remained essentially the same for 38 years. The technology has now been superseded by infrared sensors, such as those used in the Wii's sensor bar, that work better with flatscreen televisions.

> **GAMER'S BYTE**
> *House of the Dead: Overkill*, a prequel to the *House of the Dead* series, is currently being developed for the Wii by Headstrong Games.

▧ First combined light gun/FPS game controller

The Guncon 3 ④, supplied with the PlayStation 3 version of *Time Crisis 4* ②, features a unique two-handed control scheme, with a standard control pad held in the left hand. This is to enable the first-person shooter sections of the game, which require the player to move a character around the levels.

▧ Maximum achievable level on Duck Hunt (NES)

After beating level 99 on *Duck Hunt* ⑦, a glitch causes the game to restart at level 0, however, because the programmers never expected anyone to get this far, the ducks are impossible to hit, resulting in Game Over. This is an example of a video game "kill screen". In the USA, the NES version of *Duck Hunt* used the Nintendo Zapper ⑥.

▧ First light gun game

While not a video game as such, the first game to use a light gun was the *Ray-O-Lite*, released in 1936 by Seeburg ⑤. It featured a small, moving model duck with a light-sensing vacuum tube in it to detect when it was "shot" by the game's in-built rifle.

▧ Highest score on Link's Crossbow Training

The world record score on the first stage of *Link's Crossbow Training* is 83,930, achieved by Michael Estep (USA) and verified by Twin Galaxies on 2 August 2008.

200,869 – points scored at expert difficulty level by Hector Rodriguez (USA) on *Point Blank* in October 2006.

👍 **IF YOU LIKE THIS...**

... you should shoot off to p.168, where we take aim at shooters.

? GWR QUIZ

Q21. In what year did *Time Crisis* first appear in arcades?

▼ First live-action light gun game

The first game to combine digitized actor images with light gun play was Nintendo's electro-mechanical *Wild Gunman* in 1974. Laserdisc game *Mad Dog McCree* ③ developed the live-action gun game further, adding more of a narrative element. *McCree* also has the dubious honour of being the worst-reviewed game in the history of *PC Gamer US*, with a truly cringe-inducing 4%.

▼ Highest score on Point Blank (PlayStation)

The highest score ever achieved on *Point Blank* ① for PlayStation was set by Hector Rodriguez (USA), who scored 200,869 points at expert difficulty on 13 October 2006.

HIGHEST SCORE ON HOUSE OF THE DEAD (ARCADE)

The highest score on *House of the Dead* (Arcade) without using continues was achieved by Ottis Pittman at Sega Gameworks, Ontario, CA, USA, on 6 November 2004.

RANK	SCORE	GAMER	NATIONALITY
1	107,300	Ottis Pittman	USA
2	92,102	Brandon Trickey	USA
3	90,140	Tyrone Rodriguez	USA
4	81,020	Ben Caton	USA
5	77,160	-JC- Padilla	USA
6	57,704	Jason Gwynne	USA
7	55,585	Eugene Boac	USA
8	34,900	Stephen Krogman	USA
9	29,300	Jody Banks	USA
10	22,500	Danny Rodriguez	USA

HEALTHY GAMING

FROM WII FAT TO WII FIT? FROM COUCH POTATO TO CULTURE VULTURE IN JUST A MONTH? *GAMER'S* EDITOR-IN-CHIEF CRAIG GLENDAY ASKS: "CAN VIDEO-GAMING IMPROVE MY LIFESTYLE?"

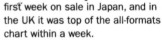

▐▐▶ FACTS

> In March 2008, Nintendo revealed that smoking could damage your Wii's health. Apparently, tar from tobacco smoke reduces the efficacy of Wii's disc reader. The solution? Don't smoke **4**.

> Get fit while strutting your stuff with *Dance Dance Revolution (DDR)*. The West Virginia Public Employees Insurance Agency (USA) placed *DDR* mats in the homes of 85 children to encourage more physical activity, as demonstrated by 11-year-old K.D. Jones **2**.

> ¿Habla Español? You soon will using *My Spanish Coach* for the DS **3**. It uses games to make language learning fun.

? GWR QUIZ

Q22. How many calories do you burn playing *Wii Sports – Boxing* for one hour?

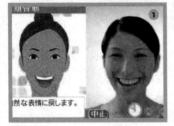

Is video-gaming bad for you? Is *Pokémon* the Devil's work, as claimed by the Christian Coalition? Should *Space Invaders* be banned, as one British politician suggested? Should *all* gaming be banned, as nearly happened in Greece a couple of years ago?

The answer to all of the above is, of course not. *Too much* gaming is bad for you, certainly, but then too much of *anything* is bad for you – that's what "too much" means. But there is increasing evidence that gaming isn't just not *bad* for your health… it's actually *good* for you, mentally and physically. (See the evidence opposite!)

Take the most obvious contender for healthy gaming: *Wii Fit*. Using a balance-board peripheral, you attempt various exhausting games such as step aerobics, hula hooping and ski jumping. The board measures your weight, centre of gravity and Body Mass Index (BMI), which is your weight divided by the square of your height. The "game" also logs your activities and calculates your Wii Fitness Age – in the same way that *Brain Training* tracks your Brain Age – so it means you keep wanting to go back to improve your score.

Wii Fit sold over 250,000 copies in its first week on sale in Japan, and in the UK it was top of the all-formats chart within a week.

But self-improvement isn't limited to fitness regimes. I learned years ago to touch-type playing a *Missile Command*-style video game on the BBC Micro – instead of shooting at nuclear missiles, you typed them out of existence. You can now learn to smile using *Facial Training* **1** and become not a Master Chief but a masterchef on your DS.

Even regular video-gaming can improve your life. A 2007 study at the University of Rochester proved that playing games such as *Halo* **5** improved eyesight, spatial awareness and hand-eye coordination. "These games push the human visual system to the limits and the brain adapts to it," the study concluded.

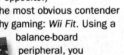

GUINNESS WORLD RECORDS

BRAIN AGE REACHED: 20

Please say the color of the words you are about to see.

...

Blue

Red!

Quit

Back

More

L

Answer: red.

WII SPORTS

The **best-selling Wii game** – and now the 5th best-selling game of all time (as of August 2008) – this classic compendium certainly burns the calories... well, if you really make the effort. In 15 minutes, you can work off about 125 calories boxing and 100 calories playing tennis – the two most energetic games.

COCKTAIL RECIPES IN BARTENDER DS: 850

CALORIES BURNED IN 15 MINS: 125

DR KAWASHIMA'S BRAIN TRAINING

First off was a cerebral workout with the **biggest-selling brain-training game**. Started off with the mental age of an 82-year-old; after a few days of maths and memory tests, reached the goal of 20! Easy, fun and engaging.

NEW RECORD

UPDATED RECORD

ROCK BAND

An hour of real drumming can burn off 400–500 calories, but what about playing the kit on *Rock Band*? It's challenging, especially on higher levels, but strenuous? Not really. However, it is incredibly addictive and kept me out of the fridge for an hour.

CONTROLS
T-Tomatoes
L-Lettuce
M-Meat
C-Cheese
Bun (LAST)

ss enter to
COOK
Press S to
SERVE

RECIEPT
- 1 sandwich
-melted, cooked
-just like cheese
bread and meat
$20

CALORIES BURNED IN 15 MINS: 50

WINE TASTING

Celebrate losing a few pounds by opening a bottle of wine. But which to choose? Luckily – if you're Japanese, at least – Square Enix and EA have both come to the rescue with wine-tasting guides for the DS. *Beginner's Wine* and *Bartender DS* offer tasting notes cocktail recipes and wine etiquette. Cheersh!

シチュエーションから

料理から

産地から

COOKERY

It's not all about losing calories – gaming can improve your lifestyle by teaching you how to cook. Forget the pure games such as *Cooking Mama*; instead, look out for real recipes and tips in titles such as *Cooking Navigator* for DS and *PSP Chef* for homebrew-enabled PSP.

RECIPES IN COOKING GUIDE: 250

DANCE DANCE REVOLUTION

The **first video game recognized as an official sport** (in Norway in 2003), *DDR* was certainly the most taxing of the physical games. The internet is choked with stories of how people have lost weight playing this game – and it's even being used by schools in the USA to encourage physical activity among students who don't like sports.

WII FIT

Basically gym for those who don't feel comfortable in a real gym, *Wii Fit* is also as boring as the real thing. Enormous sales would suggest otherwise, but for me the lack of fun is a real turn-off and it doesn't really get the heart pumping like other games.

CALORIES BURNED IN 15 MINS: 175

CALORIES BURNED IN 15 MINS: 200

GREAT!
14 combo

2nd

Party Lights

GADGETS & GIZMOS ROUND-UP

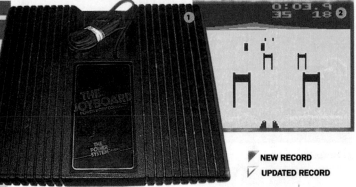

> The first rumbling controller for a console was the Nintendo Rumble Pak, which came packaged with *Star Fox 64* in 1997. It was used to give gamers physical feedback on in-game events and help players further immerse themselves in the game. Such devices have since become a standard feature in all the main console controllers.

> The Philips amBX (shorthand for "ambient experiences") add-on system ⑨ aims to give PC gamers an extra level of immersion by adding peripherals that create ambient light, as well as rumble-enabled pads, extra speakers and fans to simulate wind and movement.

▼ NEW RECORD
▽ UPDATED RECORD

First balance-board peripheral
The first balance board for a video game console was the Joyboard ①, which was released by Atari in 1982. The first game ever released for it was *Mogul Maniac* ②, which was sold with the board.

First universal exercise peripheral for consoles
The "GamerCize" stepper ⑤, released for PlayStation 2 in 2006, was the first peripheral that forced gamers to exercise in order to play games. The mini-stepper acts as a bridge between the controller and the console and only allows the controller to work when the player is moving.

First sonar-enabled game peripheral
Released in 1998, Gyogun Tanchiki: Pocket Sonar was an unusual console peripheral that allowed Game Boy owners who also enjoyed fishing to use their handheld console as a sonar device to detect fish under water.

First hand-cooling game controller
The Chillstream range of controllers ⑥ from Logitech has an integrated fan system that blows air through vents in the pad to keep gamers' hands cool. The Chillstream was designed for added comfort during extended gameplay sessions. It wasn't well received, however, and some gamers derrided the controller as an ineffective gimmick.

First light sensor built into a game cartridge
Many video games have featured a day/night cycle that affects the gameplay in some way – for example, recent *Pokémon* games have used an internal clock to tell whether it should be light or dark and changed the game's settings to match it. The Gameboy Advance title *Boktai* ④ took this idea one step further by including a light sensor on the cartridge that affected the strength of the game's vampire enemies. Many gamers were tempted to play only in bright sunlight ③.

standard analogue sticks and triggers

multiple vents facilitate air flow from internal fans

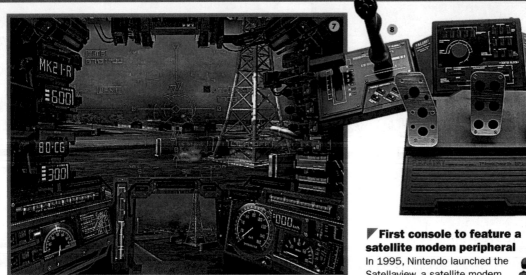

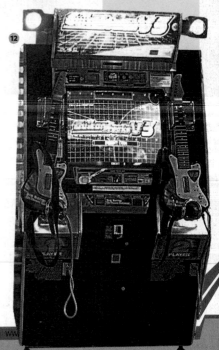

First voice-recognition peripheral for a console

Hey You, Pikachu! (or *Pikachu Genki Dechuu* as the game was known in Japan) was released for Nintendo 64 in 1998. It featured a microphone attachment that allowed gamers to talk directly to their very own pet Pikachu. Pikachu could recognize over 100 different phrases such as "come here", "stop that" and "eat it". The voice-recognition technology was later adapted for use in the Nintendo DS.

Most controls on a video-game peripheral

The controller ⑧ for *Steel Battalion* ⑦ features 49 different inputs, including foot pedals, a gear lever, two control sticks and a button that activates the in-game windscreen wipers. Designed to provide a simulation of piloting a walking tank, it is the most elaborate video-game controller to be commercially released.

First musical ensemble simulation

DrumMania and *GuitarFreaks*, both released in 1999, are able to link up to allow gamers to play along to the same song on different instrument peripherals, with a maximum of three players joining in at one time. A regular feature of Japanese arcades, *DrumMania* ⑪ and *GuitarFreaks* ⑫ predate *Rock Band* by eight years.

> **GAMER'S BYTE**
The only console of its generation to be launched without rumble controllers was the PlayStation 3. However, its original Sixaxis controller was soon superseded by the DualShock 3, with its rumble and motion-sensing abilities.

First console to feature a satellite modem peripheral

In 1995, Nintendo launched the Satellaview, a satellite modem add-on for the Super Famicom. Released in Japan, the gizmo enabled gamers who signed up with the relevant subscription services to download remixed versions of existing games that were "broadcast" over a satellite TV channel between 4.00 pm and 7.00 pm every day. While the Satellaview did have a number of exclusive titles, including the only two *Legend of Zelda* games to not feature Link, gamers needed to keep an eye on the broadcast schedules, as each game was only available for a short time during a specific time slot! Sadly, the service never launched worldwide.

ⓘ TRIVIA

> There have been many attempts at perfecting a glove-shaped controller, but the most successful is the Power Glove ⑩ for Famicom/NES. Despite reasonable sales in the early 1990s, its rudimentary motion-sensing and uncomfortable design mean it was of little use for actually playing games.

RECORDS AT A GLANCE

Even before its home console release, *Street Fighter IV* won awards for being the best fighting game at video games expo E3 2008 from gaming websites Gametrailers.com and IGN.com

CONTENTS

SPINNING BIRD KICKS, FATALITIES, BRUISES AND BROKEN BONES... IT'S ALL IN A DAY'S WORK FOR THE WORLD'S DEADLIEST FIGHTERS. WELCOME TO A WORLD OF PAIN.

▛ First fighting game

Game: *Heavyweight Champ*
Publisher: Sega
Although it bears very little resemblance to what we now consider to be modern fighting games, the first game to feature one-on-one brawling was Sega's *Heavyweight Champ* ①, a 1976 arcade game that boasted an impressive monochrome display and a boxing-glove controller allowing players to strike and block high or low punches.

▛ Most customization options in a fighting game

Game: *M.U.G.E.N.*
Publisher: Elecbyte
The freeware PC-based brawler *M.U.G.E.N.* ⑤ treads a fine line between game and development tool. It allows gamers to customize almost every aspect of its 2D fighting mechanics, and a continually active fan community has produced enormous amounts of user-generated content, including unique arenas and fighters as well as legally-dubious appearances by characters from TV, movies and other games.

▛ Largest character roster in a fighting game

Game: *Dragonball Z Budokai Tenkaichi 3*
Publisher: Namco
The largest number of playable characters in a fighting game is 161, held by

▛ NEW RECORD   ▽ UPDATED RECORD

Dragonball Z Budokai Tenkaichi 3 ②. The game features characters from throughout the extended *Dragonball* canon, including the manga, anime and spin-off movies.

First original dedicated online fighting game

Game: *Net Fighter*
Publisher: SEGA
Released in 1998, *Net Fighter* was the first dedicated online fighter. It was a cross between *Street Fighter II*, *Mortal Kombat* and *Virtua Fighter*.

▛ Most prolific fighting-game series

Game: *Street Fighter*
Publisher: Capcom
The fighting game franchise with the most versions is *Street Fighter* with a total of 124 games including the latest instalment, *Street Fighter IV* ④. Capcom Sales & Marketing Director for Europe, Michael Auer, accepted the series's record certificate at the Leipzig Games Convention in August 2008.

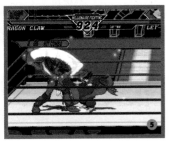

Console with the higest percentage of fighting games

A games machine that came in both arcade and console varieties, Neo Geo was widely regarded at the turn of the century as the top machine for fighting games, with more beat 'em ups released for it than any other genre. The system, renowned for its arcade-quality graphics, was supported by around 150 games, of which over 40% were 2D fighters, including fan-favourite franchises *King of Fighters*, *Fatal Fury* and *Samurai Spirits*.

First online fighting game for PlayStation 3

Game: *Tekken: Dark Resurrection*
Publisher: Namco

Tekken: Dark Resurrection 3 was released in Japan on 27 December 2006, with an update the following year that allowed gamers to take the fight online against opponents anywhere in the world. While this feature was available from launch on the Xbox 360 with *Dead or Alive 4* 8, this was the first time that gamers could get their online fighting fix on PS3. As of August 2008, *Tekken: Dark Resurrection* is one of the most popular online games on PlayStation Network.

INTERNET & MOBILE GAMES

> At the 11th Annual Interactive Achievement Awards held in Las Vegas, USA, on 7 February 2008, *Puzzle Quest: Challenge of the Warlords* **1** was chosen as Downloadable Game of the Year.

> iPhone gaming has already proved extremely popular, with Apple CEO Steve Jobs announcing in August 2008 that more than 60 million applications were downloaded from the App Store during its first month, and that games were the most popular type of application. The revenue from those applications was about $30 million (£17 million), of which 70% went to the developers, while Apple's cut was 30%. It was also announced that, at current rates, Apple will make around $360 million (£204 million) a year from app sales.

> *Hattrick* (www.hattrick.org) is not only the world's **largest online football manager game** but also the ▸ **first online game to be translated into Friulian**, a native language spoken by approximately 650,000 people in Friuli, an area in northeastern Italy.

THE POPULARITY OF CASUAL GAMES HAS EXPLODED IN RECENT YEARS, WITH INTERNET AND MOBILE PHONE DOWNLOADS DELIVERING BITE-SIZED CHUNKS OF GAMING JOY TO THE MASSES.

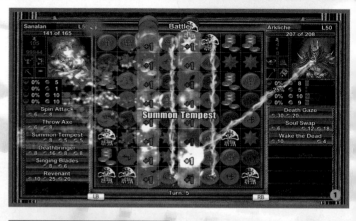

▸ Most popular non-bundled casual video game of the 21st century

Game: *Bejeweled*
Publisher: PopCap

Since its initial launch as an unassuming browser-based puzzle game back in May 2001, *Bejeweled* and its sequel *Bejeweled 2* have gone on to become the most popular casual games of the century so far, with 350 million downloads and sales across all formats (including desktop computers, consoles and mobile devices) standing at 25 million. PopCap says that, collectively, *Bejeweled* and *Bejeweled 2* have been played for an estimated 600 million hours – that's the equivalent of 60 people playing the game 24 hours a day since the last Ice Age, 11,400 years ago.

▸ Most addictive internet game

Game: *Peggle*
Publisher: PopCap

Peggle **2** was listed as the most addictive internet game ever in a feature on the "Top 5 most addictive games" by MSNBC.com, which said that PopCap's spin on pinball was "downright insidious".

If you've not yet experienced Apple's iPhone **3**, **5** then don't let the name fool you. This must-have device is much more than a mere mobile phone, and thanks to its touch-screen interface, built-in motion sensor and powerful multimedia capabilities, it's quickly becoming the perfect platform for gaming on the go.

Many industry pundits predict that the iPhone will revolutionize the mobile games market as it appeals to both gamers and developers. The former thanks to the touch and tilt controls, which are more intuitive to use than numeric keypads, and the latter as there is one single platform rather than lots of different models. To aid development of iPhone games and applications, Apple made a software kit available to third-party developers in March 2008, and 500 applications were available to download when the Apple App Store opened on 10 July 2008 – a number that has grown daily since.

$44 million (£22.5 million) – EA Mobile's revenue for the first fiscal quarter of 2008.

Pause
Hold   4949   Next
Items
3
2
2
3
3
Goal
53
level 5

◤ NEW RECORD ◸ UPDATED RECORD

◤ Best-selling mobile phone game
Game: *Tetris*
Publisher: EA Mobile
According to statistics from Nielsen Mobile, provider of consumer research to the mobile media markets, 19 million mobile phone games were downloaded in the US during the first three months of 2008, with the top-selling title being the perennial puzzle game favourite *Tetris* ④.

◤ Most advanced mobile phone game
Game: *Re-Volt*
Publisher: IUGO Mobile
In May 2008, Canadian developer IUGO Mobile demonstrated what has been described as the most advanced mobile phone game to date. *Re-Volt* ③ for iPhone is a first-person shooter in which the player tilts the device to move. *Re-Volt* is due to appear on iPhone and Ipod Touch in 2009.

◤ First ever iPod game
Game: *Brick*
Publisher: Apple
The original iPod model contained a version of the bat-n-ball game *Breakout* entitled *Brick*. It was included as an Easter egg and the only way to access the game was to visit the About menu and hold down Select for five seconds. In subsequent models, *Brick* was added to the Extras menu. It was fitting that *Brick* should be the first iPod game as Apple founders Steve Jobs and Steve Wozniak were involved with the design of the original *Breakout* arcade game in 1976.

> *EA Mobile is thrilled to be developing games for mobile products as truly revolutionary as the iPhone and iPod Touch.*
Travis Boatman, Vice President of Worldwide Studios, EA Mobile

PLATFORMERS

LEDGES, LADDERS AND LEAPING ARE ALL KEY INGREDIENTS FOR PLATFORM GAMES, A GENRE THAT HAS PROVED A STAPLE SOURCE OF FUN FROM CLASSIC CONSOLES TO THE LATEST MACHINES.

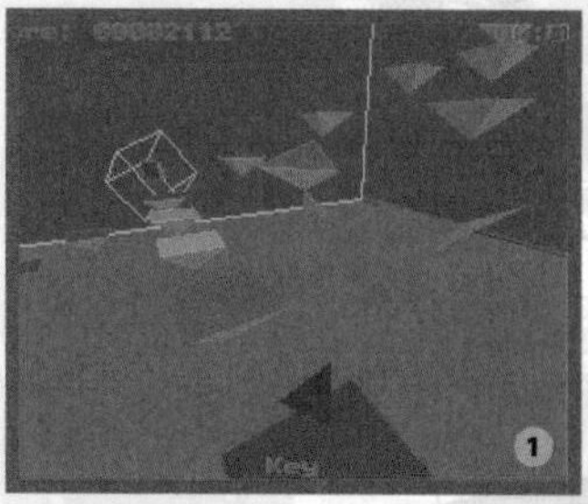

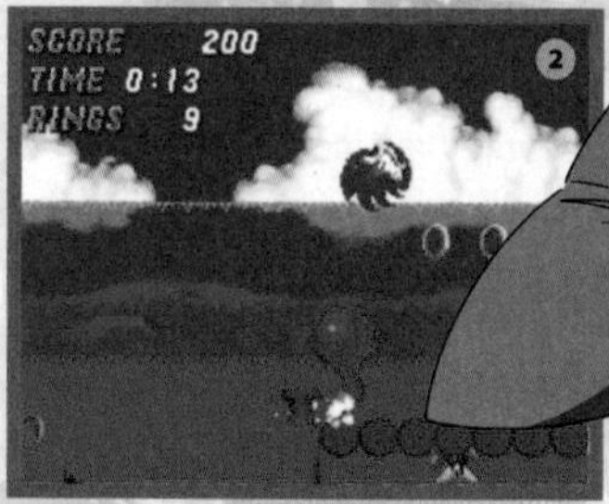

First retro revival on Wii-Ware

Game: *Mega Man 9*
Publisher: Capcom
The launch of *Mega Man 9* (3) in September 2008 was a significant milestone for retro gamers: it's a modern game using the exact same graphical style as its 1980s predecessors. The 8-bit stylings proved such a massive hit with fans, publishers Capcom even commissioned some ironic art work in the style of an NES game box.

Fastest speedrun in Sonic the Hedgehog 2 (Level 1)

Game: *Sonic the Hedgehog 2*
Publisher: Sega
The fastest completion of Emerald Hill, Zone 1 in *Sonic the Hedgehog 2* (2) on the Mega Drive/Genesis is 20 sec, achieved by Louis Tsiattalou (UK) at the Summer of Sonic event at Dragon Hall, Covent Garden, London, UK, on 8 August 2008.

First 3D platform game

Game: *Alpha Waves*
Publisher: Infogrames
Alpha Waves (1), published in 1990, is the first example of a true 3D platform game, albeit a very simple one by modern standards.

Best-selling platform game on PlayStation 3

Game: *Ratchet & Clank Future: Tools of Destruction*
Publisher: Sony
The best-selling platformer for PS3 is *Ratchet & Clank Future: Tools of Destruction* (4), which sold 1.25 million copies between its launch in October 2007 and August 2008.

Highest score for Rainbow Islands

Game: *Rainbow Islands*
Publisher: Taito
Using the multiple arcade machine emulator (MAME) version of *Rainbow Islands*, Jordi Schouteren (Netherlands) scored 3,815,710 points using the Twin Galaxies Tournament settings on 11 September 2006.

FACTS

> Unlike PCs, most consoles are not meant to be freely user-programmable. However, this has not stopped some industrious gamers from deploying various techniques to design new games for their consoles. The term used in the gaming industry to describe such efforts is "homebrew".

> The multiple arcade machine emulator, or MAME, is a popular method of ensuring that classic arcade games can still be played by new generations of gamers. Emulators such as MAME use modern software to mimic the arcade hardware that has become obsolete and is no longer commercially available. MAME is one of the platforms recognized by Twin Galaxies for record attempts.

> Mega Man, the hero of a popular series of Nintendo games of the same name, starred in his own animated TV series between 1994 and 1995. The show lasted two seasons and 28 episodes.

> When he made his first arcade appearence in *Mario Bros.*, Luigi looked exactly like his sibling Mario, only wearing a brown shirt and green overalls, as opposed to Mario's red shirt and blue overalls.

▼ NEW RECORD ▽ UPDATED RECORD

ⓘ TRIVIA

> While it's difficult to define the "hardest video game of all time" since there are so many different opinions on the matter, the freeware game *I Wanna Be The Guy: The Movie: The Game* is a strong contender. Its hardest difficulty level features no save points at all and every one of the game's many hazards (including giant cherries that fall upwards) results in instant death.

> The Japansese game *Doukutsu Monogatari* **5**, or *Cave Story* in English, is a free downloadable platform game for PC and homebrew-enabled PSP. It took over five years to produce by Japanese artist Daisuke Amaya (also known as Pixel) and has been praised for its engaging story, balanced gameplay and graphical style, which place it on a par with many commercial releases.

Most games in an action-adventure video game series

Game: *Castlevania*
Publisher: Konami

With 23 distinct and commercially released games, not including remakes or boxed compilations, there have been more titles in the *Castlevania* franchise, currently produced by Koji Igarashi **6**, than any other action-adventure series.

ROLE-PLAYING GAMES

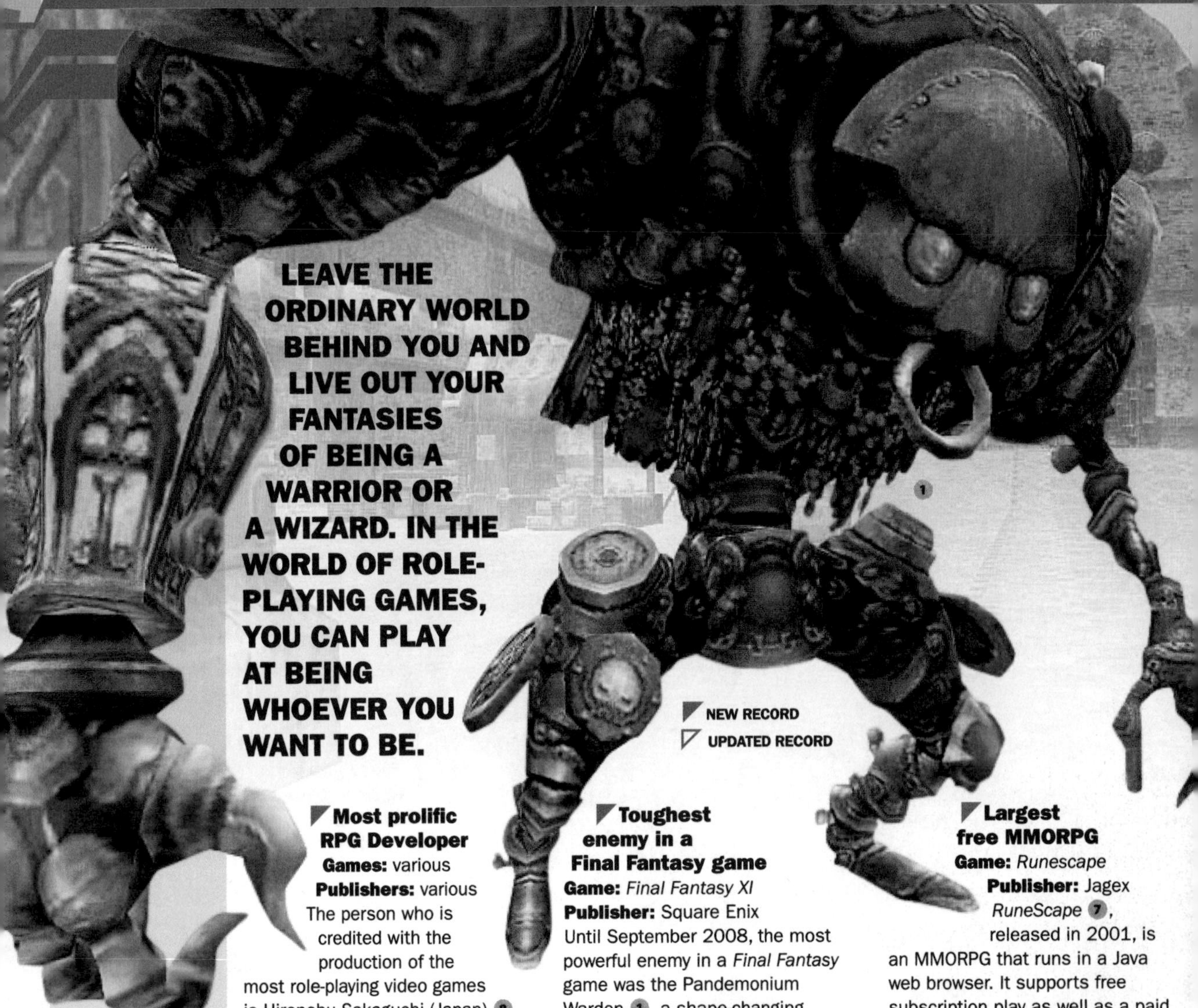

LEAVE THE ORDINARY WORLD BEHIND YOU AND LIVE OUT YOUR FANTASIES OF BEING A WARRIOR OR A WIZARD. IN THE WORLD OF ROLE-PLAYING GAMES, YOU CAN PLAY AT BEING WHOEVER YOU WANT TO BE.

◤ NEW RECORD
◸ UPDATED RECORD

◤ Most prolific RPG Developer

Games: various
Publishers: various

The person who is credited with the production of the most role-playing video games is Hironobu Sakaguchi (Japan) 8, creator of the *Final Fantasy* series, who had worked on 44 released titles as of June 2008.

◤ Best-selling Nintendo DS RPG

Game: *Pokemon Diamond/Pearl*
Publisher: Nintendo

The best-selling RPG on Nintendo DS is *Pokemon Diamond/Pearl* 2 with combined sales of 14.77 million units to March 2008.

◤ Toughest enemy in a Final Fantasy game

Game: *Final Fantasy XI*
Publisher: Square Enix

Until September 2008, the most powerful enemy in a *Final Fantasy* game was the Pandemonium Warden 1, a shape-changing villain in *Final Fantasy XI*. The monster proved too powerful for most players to defeat and Square Enix released a game update that significantly reduced the beast's abilities.

◤ Largest free MMORPG

Game: *Runescape*
Publisher: Jagex

RuneScape 7, released in 2001, is an MMORPG that runs in a Java web browser. It supports free subscription play as well as a paid membership option. At Leipzig this year, Jagex's Adam Tuckwell 3 was presented with a certificate for the record of attracting more than 10 million free accounts for the game.

FACTS

> *Runescape* was originally a game called *DeviousMUD*, created by Cambridge University student Andrew Gower back in 1998. It was retooled and revamped as *Runescape* a year later with the help of Gower's brother Paul.

108,000 units – estimated number of copies sold during the first week of Namco Bandai's game *Tales of Vesperia*.

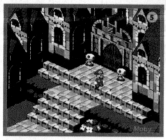

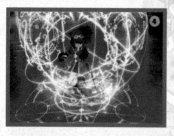

👍 **IF YOU LIKE THIS...**
... then why not check out CCP Games' *EVE Online*, available to play at www.eve-online.com

First RPG to feature Mario

Game: *Super Mario RPG: Legend of the Seven Stars*
Publisher: Nintendo

Surprisingly, Mario's last outing for the SNES was an RPG entitled *Super Mario RPG: Legend of the Seven Stars* ⑤. It was developed by Square, later known as Square Enix, who were same people behind the popular *Final Fantasy* series. The ▶ **fastest time to complete *Super Mario RPG: Legend of the Seven Stars*** is just 5 hr 31 min 21 sec, achieved by Stewart Seltz (USA), as verified on 9 August 2003 by Twin Galaxies.

First RPG released for Xbox Live Arcade

Game: *Penny Arcade: On the Rain-Slick Precipice of Darkness*
Publisher: Penny Arcade

The first episode of *Penny Arcade: On the Rain-Slick Precipice of Darkness* ⑥ went on sale on 21 May 2008. It was the first role-playing game to be released on the system in its history.

▶ Fastest-selling Xbox 360 game in Japan

Game: *Tales of Vesperia*
Publisher: Namco Bandai

With sales of 108,000 in its first week, *Tales of Vesperia* ④ had the best start for any Xbox 360 game in Japan. Released on the least popular console in the region, the game's launch was a huge success for the 360 – sales of the console leapt by 310% in one week, outselling the PS3 and PS2's combined sales over the same period. Two weeks after the game's launch, there were widespread reports of Japanese shops selling out of Xbox 360 consoles.

▶ First RPG to prompt a change in State law

Game: *Final Fantasy XI*
Publisher: Square Enix

When Alex Edwards of Illinois, USA, tried to cancel his *Final Fantasy XI* account, he soon found that there was nowhere online to allow him to do so. This prompted his parents, Frank and Cinda, to call on their friend State Representative Raymond Poe, who introduced a successful bill that forces all internet gaming services to provide a method of online cancellation for residents of the state of Illinois.

> *Of course, you cannot make a good game simply because of technology or its hardware. I am interested in dramatic presentation and visuals.*
> **Hironobu Sakaguchi, creator of the Final Fantasy series**

⑧

ℹ **TRIVIA**

> Frequently in MMORPGs, weapons, artifacts and sometimes even monsters are created that are so powerful that they can be exploited to disrupt gameplay. In such circumstances, the game's developers often created a patch, or addition, to the game code that will downgrade the power of the item. Such downgrading is called "nerfing".

> Starting life as a webcomic back in November 1998, written by Jerry Holkins and illustrated by Mike Krahulik, *Penny Arcade* took a look at the world of the video-game industry. Now, ironically, it is involved in making their own games.

SHOOTERS

MODERN SHOOTING GAMES ARE MOSTLY PLAYED IN FIRST-PERSON PERSPECTIVE. HOWEVER, TOP-DOWN, VERTICAL AND HORIZONTAL SHOOTERS ARE FINDING A NEW LEASE OF LIFE ON XBOX LIVE ARCADE OR PLAYSTATION NETWORK.

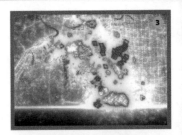

▶ First arcade game to be developed by a woman
Game: *Centipede*
Publisher: Atari
In 1981, Ed Logg and Dona Bailey created *Centipede* ① for Atari. At the time, Bailey was the only female software engineer employed by the company.

▶ Most protracted game development
Game: *Duke Nukem Forever*
Publisher: 2K Games
Originally announced on 28 April 1997 with a release date of mid-1998, *Duke Nukem Forever* has now famously been in development for over 11 years spanning two millennia and beating the previous longest production cycle held by *Prey*. During development, the world has witnessed Britney Spears' entire musical career, the filming and release of all three *Star Wars* prequel movies and the entire *Harry Potter* series of books and five movies. There is still no word on when the game will be finished.

▶ Fastest Portal completion
Game: *Portal*
Publisher: Valve/Electronic Arts
The fastest completion of the PC version of *Portal* ⑦ is an impressive 14 min 27 sec by Michael 'DemonStrate' Yanni on 26 February 2008. This includes a five-second penalty because the demo recording cuts out at the start of each level and the time was officially verified by speeddemosarchive.com.

First gaming clan to legally bind their players
Game: *Counter-Strike*
Publisher: Vivendi Universal
On 1 February 2003, the Swedish clan SK Gaming issued contracts to several of its *Counter-Strike* players, binding them to the clan and preventing them from going elsewhere. SK Gaming was also the first Western electronic sports club to receive a fee for a player transfer, when on 18 May 2004 rival clan – Team NoA – bought Ola "elemeNt" Moum out of his contract with SK Gaming for an undisclosed sum.

▶ Fastest creation of a musical score
Game: *Commando*
Publisher: Elite
Computer musician Rob Hubbard (UK) composed the Commodore 64 music for *Commando* ④ in 22 hours. "That's about the fastest, start to finish, that I've ever done," said Hubbard. "I'm still quite pleased with the main theme, but the Hi-Score tune, which I wrote at four in the morning, really sounds like the kind of thing you put on at a party at 4 o'clock in the morning!"

▶ Fastest completion of XIII
Game: *XIII*
Publisher: Ubisoft Paris
Based on Jean Van Hamme's comic book of the same name, *XIII* ⑥ is a FPS that uses cell-shading techniques to give the game's graphics the feel of a comic. Mika 'sp3ctum' Vilpas and Juha 'Muona' Vilpashas achieved the fastest ever completion of the game on 5 April 2007 in a time of 1 hr 38 min 20 sec. The time was verified by speeddemosarchive.com

Longest mass-participation LAN Party

Games: Various
Publishers: Various
The longest multiplayer LAN party lasted for 36 hours and was completed by 203 gamers at NVISION 2008, San Jose, California, USA, which took place from 23-25 August 2008 ⑤.

Highest score in deadline mode for Geometry Wars: Retro Evolved II

Game: *Geometry Wars: Retro Evolved II*
Publisher: Bizarre Creations
A player called Pva10x achieved the highest score in deadline mode of 69,107,480 points on *Geometry Wars: Retro Evolved II* ③.

Fastest completion of Area 51

Game: *Area 51*
Publisher: Atari
The quickest time to complete the game *Area 51* ⑧ is 1 hr 19 min 19 sec, achieved by Peter "Kibumbi" Knutsson on 10 August 2007. The run was completed on the PlayStation 2 version and the time was officially verified by speeddemosarchive.com

COUNTER-STRIKE LEADERBOARD 08

POS	TEAM	NATIONALITY	RANKING CHANGE	POINTS
1	Meet Your Makers	Poland	▲1	348
2	mTw	Denmark	▲1	293
3	Fnatic	Sweden	▼2	291
4	SK Gaming	Sweden	▶0	211
5	Roccat	Finland	▶0	132
6	mousesports	Germany	▲2	93
7	Made in Brazil	Brazil	▶0	75
8	emuLate	France	▼2	52
9	Team Alternate	Germany	▶0	46
10	Evil Geniuses	United States	new	31
10	e-STRO	South Korea	▶0	31

source: Gotfrag.com (19 August 2008)

SPORTS GAMES

EVER SINCE THE SEMINAL PONG APPEARED IN ARCADES IN 1972, VIDEO-GAME DEVELOPERS HAVE STRIVEN TO RECREATE THE REALISM AND FUN OF COMPETITIVE SPORTS IN OUR VIRTUAL WORLDS.

Most successful Madden game

Game: *Madden NFL 07*
Publisher: Electronic Arts
Madden NFL 07 ② has sold 7.7 million units in the USA, according to market researchers the NPD Group, making it not just the most successful Madden game in the series but also the country's third best-selling non-bundled game ever behind *GTA: San Andreas* (9.4 million) and *Guitar Hero III* (8.2 million). There are three other Madden games in the USA's top 10 best-sellers list – the 2006 version in fifth position with 6.7 million, the 2008 version in seventh with 6.6 million and the 2005 version in tenth with 6.1 million.

Current FIFA Interactive World Cup holder

Game: *FIFA 08*
Publisher: Electronic Arts
At the FIFA Interactive World Cup 2008, held at the Sony Center in Berlin, Germany, on 24 May 2008, Alfonso Ramos (Spain) ③ was crowned FIFA Interactive World Player 2008 after beating Michael Reibero (USA) 3-1 in the final. Alfonso skilfully shot past 31 other players to earn the title – and bagged himself a prize cheque for $20,000 (£10,100).

Best-selling sports title

Game: *Wii Sports*
Publisher: Nintendo
Wii Sports, the five-game compendium title featuring tennis, bowling, golf, boxing and baseball, is easily the most popular sports title ever, with more than 28.8 million copies sold (as of September 2008). Approximately 23 million of these sales are thanks to the title being bundled with the Wii hardware in every territory except Japan. As Wii console sales continue to grow, it's predicted that *Wii Sports* will soon become the most popular single release of all time.

Biggest winning margin in Madden NFL 08

Game: *Madden NFL 08*
Publisher: Electronic Arts
By scoring 90 more points than the computer on 4 May 2008, Patrick Scott Patterson of the USA set the record for the biggest landslide victory in a Madden NFL 08 exhibition game.

Most consecutive football series releases on a single platform

Game: *FIFA series*
Publisher: Electronic Arts
The FIFA football series holds the record for the highest number of consecutive yearly releases on a single platform. A FIFA-branded game has been released every year for 10 years on the Sony PlayStation, from 1996 to 2005. Current Line Producer David Rutter ④ accepted the certificate for the record on behalf of EA.

FIFA Interactive World Cup 2008
USD 20,000
4000 1234 5678 9010 DEBIT
VISA
CHAMPION

IF YOU LIKE THIS...

... then why not grapple with Midway Studios' *Total Nonstop Action*, available on Xbox, PS2, PS3 and Wii.

◥ Most football games in a series on a single platform

Game: *Winning Eleven*
Publisher: *Konami*
Since 2001, there have been 23 versions of *Winning Eleven* released on PlayStation 2 in Japan, with the last version being released in 2008 despite the emergence of the more advanced PlayStation 3. The series is known as *Pro Evolution Soccer* in Europe and America but has seen fewer releases under that title.

◥ Biggest winning margin in Mario Strikers Charged Football

Game: *Mario Strikers Charged Football*
Publisher: Nintendo
Playing a three-minute game in Domination Mode on Skill Level 1, the USA's Lance

▶ TRIVIA

skate **7** has impressed many real-life professional skaters with its Flickit dual analog control system. The Flickit system uses one stick to control upper body movement and the other to control leg and foot position to provide a gaming experience that is closer to how real skaters control their boards.

Eustache managed to score 25 more goals than his computer-controlled opponent – that's an average of one goal scored every 7.2 seconds. He achieved this feat on 20 July 2008.

◥ Fastest Knockout in Wii Sports – Boxing

Game: *Wii Sports - Boxing*
Publisher: *Nintendo*
It took Troy Whelan of the USA just 14 seconds to knock out his computer-controlled opponent in round one of *Wii Sports – Boxing*. He achieved this record on 10 February 2008, shaving 35 seconds off the previous best time of 49 seconds, which was listed in last year's *Gamer's Edition*.

ⓘ TRIVIA

Over the years and through its many different titles, the hugely popular FIFA video-game series has featured tracks from such successful musical acts as Blur, Fatboy Slim, Robbie Williams, Moby and Gorillaz. The 2009 FIFA title is no exception, featuring music from current hot bands such as The Fratellis and The Script.

¹²₃ FIGURES

> **37 million** – worldwide sales of the *WWE Smackdown* games **5** since 1999.

> **$2 billion (£1.1 bilion)** – the value of EA's annually updated *Madden* **6** franchise which celebrated its 20th anniversary in 2008.

◤ NEW RECORD
▷ UPDATED RECORD

STRATEGY & SIMULATION GAMES

¹²₃ FIGURES

17 million – copies sold of the *SimCity* series since the original game launched in 1989.

16 million – copies sold of the original PC version of *The Sims* since launch in 2000.

250,000 – downloads of the *Football Manager 2008* demo during the first two days of its release.

FOR THOSE IN SEARCH OF CEREBRAL GAMING EXPERIENCES, STRATEGY AND SIMULATION GAMES OFFER THE PERFECT RESPITE FROM THE FRENZIED THRILLS OF ACTION AND SHOOTING TITLES.

> *The Sims ❻ has universal appeal like no other video game.*
> **Nancy Smith, head of EA's Sims division**

▽ Best-selling simulation series

Game: *The Sims*
Publisher: Electronic Arts
On 16 April 2008, EA announced that combined sales of all *The Sims* games had broken the 100 million mark, making it the best-selling simulation series ever. Executive Producer of *The Sims 3*, Ben Bell ❷ is pictured receiving a certificate marking the achievement.

▽ Best-selling Sims game on Nintendo consoles

Game: *MySims*
Publisher: Electronic Arts
Based on figures compiled by Edge Online, *MySims* ❻, the 2007 series spin-off specially designed for the Nintendo Wii and DS, sold 3.72 million copies in its first six months on sale.

Featuring cute cartoon-style graphics and full support for the Wii Remote, the game was aimed at younger gamers and proved that playing the game of life was appealing to all ages. In comparison, *Sims 2 Castaway*, which was released shortly afterwards on Wii, DS, PlayStation 2 and PlayStation Portable, sold just 1 million copies, despite appearing on two additional formats.

▽ Highest scores on PixelJunk Monsters

Game: *PixelJunk Monsters*
Publisher: Sony
Downloadable tower-defence game *PixelJunk Monsters* ❸ for the PS3 features localized online leaderboards for tracking high scores, so the ranking is always changing as the best players continually better each other. The table below shows a snapshot of the best single-player scores taken on 18 August 2008.

PIXELJUNK MONSTERS

RANK	USERNAME	SCORE
1	*Wooki94*	38,464
2	*DALTIS*	38,235
3	*CrimsonB*	37,328
4	*Ken111R*	36,883
5	*Magnias*	35,931

▶ FACT

Following an Xtreme Quest special event held across the USA between August and October 2007 – during which 128 registered contestants took part in almost 500 matches of *Supreme Commander* 4 – Eric Wright of Maryland, USA, was announced as the event champion. Eric won $1,000 (£495) and some PC hardware for his commanding performance.

▽ Longest-running Microsoft franchise
Game: *Flight Simulator*
Publisher: Microsoft
The first version of *Microsoft Flight Simulator* debuted on the IBM PC in November 1982, which makes it one year older than Microsoft Word and three years older than Microsoft Windows. There have been 11 updates since that original version, the most recent being *Flight Simulator X* 7, which was released in October 2006.

▽ Highest-rated current-gen console strategy game
Game: *Civilization Revolution*
Publisher: 2K Games
Based on reviews aggregated by MetaCritic.com, 2008 release *Civilization Revolution* 5 on Xbox 360 and PlayStation 3 earned an average rating of 84 out of 100, making it the best-scoring strategy game on current-generation home consoles as of September 2008.

▽ Most expensive current-gen strategy game
Game: *Eye of Judgment*
Publisher: Sony
Eye of Judgment, the trading-card strategy title for PlayStation 3, went on sale in October 2007 with a recommended retail price of £69.99 ($140). The reason for this inflated price was the inclusion of a playing board, a deck of trading cards and the PlayStation Eye camera 9 – all of which are required to play the game.

① TRIVIA

> *Command and Conquer 3: Tiberium Wars* 8 was named best Strategy/Simulation Game of the Year at the 11th Annual Interactive Achievement Awards held in Las Vegas, USA, on 7 February 2008.

> Europe's Team Dignitas are the champions of PC strategy game *World in Conflict* 1, having won the Cyberathlete Professional League (CPL) World Tour Finals in London, UK, on 27-28 February 2008. Team Dignitas defeated Don't Care (USA) in the final match to land a cash prize of $60,000 (£33,500). Shortly after the event, the CPL announced that it was to cease operations so Team Dignitas' victory cannot be contested.

▼ NEW RECORD   ▽ UPDATED RECORD

OVERVIEW

Some argue that games will one day replace movies as complete interactive entertainment, whereas others cite movies such as Alone in the Dark as a good reason to keep films and games separate! It's true that crossover movies are not always hits, but games will always provide ready-made stories for the film–makers.

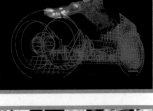

MOVIE DIRECTORS DIDN'T LEAP LOVINGLY INTO THE ARMS OF MARIO AND HIS FRIENDS; IN FACT, IT TOOK A WHILE FOR HOLLYWOOD TO WARM TO THE IDEA OF MOVIES BASED ON VIDEO GAMES, BUT IT'S REALLY STARTING TO CATCH ON.

Movies featuring video games have been around for about a quarter of a century. The first movie to feature video gaming as a central theme was the 1982 sci-fi classic *Tron* (USA/Taiwan) **2**. Directed by Steven Lisberger (USA) and starring Jeff Bridges (USA), the unique special effects generated a sense of gaming immersion few films have replicated. (Interestingly, the arcade game based on the movie

out-grossed the actual movie!) A year later, *WarGames* (USA, 1983) starred Matthew Broderick as a teenage hacker who saves the world from nuclear Armageddon by tricking US defence computer (WOPA) into playing tic-tac-toe.

Seemingly inspired by the success of these two movies, 1984 proved to be a boom year for vidoe-game-based films. The most notable of these was *The Last Starfighter* (USA) **1**, in which the lead character, a talented gamer, is recruited to fight along real aliens in a genuine space war.

But it wasn't until *The Wizard* (USA) **6** in 1989 that we saw a contemporary story about video games integrated fully into the plot; young Jimmy Woods discovers he has a natural talent for playing video games and runs away to Los Angeles to compete in the ultimate video-game championship. *Super Mario Bros. 3* for the NES featured heavily in the film.

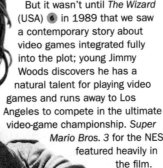

The **first movie to be based on a video game** was

not released until 1993 – *Super Mario Bros.* (USA) **3** may have had a dazzling cast list including Bob Hoskins, who was the **first Oscar-nominated actor to star in a game-licensed movie**, and John Leguizamo, but it lacked broad appeal. Worse still, Mario fans were upset by the film's worrying lurch away from the plot of the game.

In 1994, *Double Dragon* (USA) beat *Street Fighter* (USA/ Japan) to the record of **first movie based on a beat 'em up video game**. *Street Fighter* eventually won through in terms of box-office gross and went on to

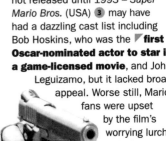

FRED SAVAGE
THE WIZARD
IT'S MORE THAN A GAME...
IT'S THE CHANCE OF A LIFETIME.

TIMELINE

1982	1983		1984	1987	1989
Tron movie released; suddenly everybody wants a light cycle.	Emilio Estevez gets stuck in a video game in a movie called *Nightmares* (USA) **12**.		*Cloak & Dagger*, *The Dungeon-master* and *The Last Starfighter* (all USA) movies released.	*Double Dragon* coin-op released. It goes on to inspire a 1994 movie of the same name, which in turn inspires a Neo Geo video game released in 1995 (see opposite).	*The Wizard* (USA), starring Luke Edwards, acts as a mini-advert for *Super Mario Bros. 3* and Nintendo's Powerglove.

rake in an impressive $99.4 million (£65 million), though not quite as impressive as the $122 million (£80 million) taken by *Mortal Kombat* (USA, 1996) **4**, which still holds the record for the ▷ **highest-grossing movie based on a beat 'em up video game**.

The natural fit of beat 'em up characters to the big screen buoyed Hollywood, and the idea of converting a space game to the big screen seemed ripe. In 1999, *Wing Commander* (USA/Luxembourg) became the ▷ **first PC game to become a movie**, although sadly the film-makers didn't seem to be as inspired as the creators of the original game and the movie was panned by critics.

When the first mainstream game-to-movie success story finally appeared, it was no surprise to find Lara Croft at the helm. *Lara Croft: Tomb Raider* (UK/Germany/USA/Japan) **7**, released in 2001, is still the **highest-grossing video game movie** with $274 million (£188.4 million) taken at the box office. At the time, it looked like movie producers had hit a rich vein when it came to video-game crossovers, but *Tomb Raider*'s success was quickly followed by another disappointment with *Final Fantasy: The Spirits Within,* (USA/Japan, 2001) failing to capture the public's imagination.

Proving the fickle nature of film critics and movie-goers alike, just

▷ **NEW RECORD**   ▷ **UPDATED RECORD**

as things looked bleak again for the video-game crossover genre, along came *Resident Evil* (UK/Germany/France, 2002) starring ex-supermodel Milla Jovovich, which received a positive reception. Other movies based on the series also garnered reasonable critical acclaim, and the release of *Resident Evil: Extinction* (France/Australia/Germany/UK/USA, 2007) **5** marked the completion of the ▷ **first live-action movie trilogy based on a video game**.

Certainly, from this point on, there was more willingness from major movie studios to jump aboard the gaming bandwagon.

In 2005, one of the most controversial games ever, *Doom* (UK/Czech Republic/Germany/USA) **8** finally made it on to the big screen. Even what some would consider as niche games received the celluloid treatment with *Alone in the Dark,* (Canada/Germany/USA, 2005) **9**, *Bloodrayne* (USA/Germany,

2005) **11**, *Silent Hill* (Canada/France, 2006), *Postal* (USA/Canada/Germany, 2007), *Hitman* (France/USA, 2007) **15** and In the *Name of the King: A Dungeon Siege Tale* (Germany/Canada/USA, 2007) **10**, starring Burt Reynolds, all making the transition with varying degrees of success.

Finally, it seems, movie games are no longer out of bounds for respected movie luminaries. The barriers have been broken down but how long will it be before we finally see an Oscar for "Best Adapted Gameplay"?

RISE AND FIGHT
IN THE NAME OF THE KING
A DUNGEON SIEGE TALE

IN THEATERS JANUARY 11, 2008

11

? GWR QUIZ

Q23. What is the only game series to have spawned a live-action movie trilogy?

1990
First *Wing Commander* game released.

1993
Super Mario Bros. (USA) **13**, the first video game-licensed movie, is released.

This Ain't No Game.
13
SUPER MARIO BROS.

1994
Double Dragon and *Street Fighter* (both USA) movies open.

1995
Double Dragon (Technos) becomes the ▷ **first game based on a film based on a game!**

1997
Tekken: The Motion Picture (Japan) **14** makes little impact.

2001
Lara Croft: Tomb Raider is released.

TEKKEN

14

2007
BloodRayne II: Deliverance (Canada/Germany) fails to get a cinema release, making the *BloodRayne* series the first to feature two loss-making films based on the same game licence.

15

MOVIES & GAMES ROUND-UP

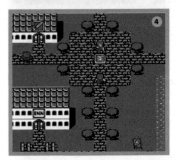

> In the auction scene during the movie *Lara Croft: Tomb Raider* (UK/Germany/USA/ Japan, 2001) **1**, the item being auctioned is the Dagger of Xian, the very artefact that Lara Croft is searching for in *Tomb Raider II.*

> Steven E. de Souza, the writer of action movie classics such as *Die Hard* (USA, 1988) and *The Running Man* (USA, 1987), directed and wrote the *Street Fighter* (USA/Japan, 1994) movie and also wrote the story for *Lara Croft Tomb Raider: The Cradle of Life* (USA/ Germany/Japan/ UK/Netherlands, 2003).

> In the movie *Doom* (UK/Czech Republic/ Germany/USA, 2005), two of the scientists are called Dr Willits and Dr Todd Carmack. These names pay homage to Tim Willits, John Carmack and Todd Hollenshead, three of the leading lights behind id Software's legendary *Doom* video game series.

> If you watch the 2007 movie *Hitman* (France/USA) carefully, you'll see that when Agent 47 jumps from the hotel to the room with the children playing a video game, *Hitman: Blood Money* is being played on the PlayStation 2.

First Hollywood movie based on a video game
Game: *Super Mario Bros.*
Publisher: Nintendo
Super Mario Bros. (UK/ USA, 1993), was inspired by the classic 1985 NES game of the same name **2** and was the first Hollywood movie to be based on a game.

First game based on an official movie licence
Game: *Raiders of the Lost Ark*
Publisher: Atari
Raiders of the Lost Ark **3** was the first game based on an official movie licence. The game was released on the Atari 2600 in 1982, narrowly beating *E.T. The Extra-Terrestrial,* the game inspired by Steven Spielberg's other blockbuster hit movie.

Longest wait for a movie based on a game franchise
Game: *Final Fantasy*
Publisher: Square/Nintendo
The movie *Final Fantasy: The Spirits Within* (USA/Japan, 2001) **5** was released 14 years after the 1987 release of *Final Fantasy* **4** on the NES – the longest time between the release of a game-licensed movie and the game on which it is based. The second-longest wait was the 12 years between the *Doom* game and movie (1993 and 2005).

Biggest budget for a game-licensed movie
Game: *Final Fantasy*
Publisher: Square/Nintendo
Final Fantasy: The Spirits Within was the first completely computer-

🏴 **NEW RECORD**   🏴 **UPDATED RECORD**

generated movie based on a video game and the most expensive game-licensed movie of all time with a budget of $137 million (£94.2 million). It is also estimated to have made a loss of around $105 million (£72.4 million), including marketing costs.

Longest wait for a game based on a movie franchise
Game: *Fantasia*
Publisher: Sega
The longest period between the release of a movie-licensed game and the film on which it is based is a staggering 51 years. In 1940, Disney released their classic animation *Fantasia* (USA); in 1991, over five decades later, Sega released *Fantasia* for their Mega Drive/Genesis platform.

Most prolific game-license franchise director

Game: Various
Publisher: Various

German director Uwe Boll holds the record for directing the most movies based on video games franchises. Boll's current total stands at five: *In the Name of the King: A Dungeon Siege Tale* (Germany/Canada/USA, 2007), *Postal* (USA/Canada/Germany, 2007), *BloodRayne* (USA/Germany, 2005), *House of the Dead* (Germany/Canada/USA, 2003) and *Alone In The Dark* (Canada/Germany/USA, 2005). This number is set to rise with Boll currently directing and scheduled to direct *Far Cry* and *Zombie Massacre*, which are due out in 2009 and 2010, as well as a further *BloodRayne* sequel.

Most video games voiced by an actor

Game: various
Publisher: various

Movie, TV, radio and video game actor Kerry Shale has voiced characters in more video games than any other person. His games tally currently stands at 38 and includes such classic titles as *Battalion Wars*, *Dragon Quest VIII* and *Killzone*.

Most named characters voiced in a game by a single actor

Game: *Dog's Life*
Publisher: Sony

Voice maestro Kerry Shale provided individual voices for 32 named characters in *Dog's Life* 6 on PlayStation 2. In achieving this vocal feat, Shale set the record for the most named characters voiced in a game by a single actor.

TOP 10 HIGHEST-GROSSING GAME-LICENSED MOVIES

RANK	GAME	YEAR	AMOUNT
1	Lara Croft: Tomb Raider (USA)	2001	$274 million
2	Pokémon: The First Movie (USA)	1998	$163 million
3	Lara Croft Tomb Raider: Cradle of Life	2003	$156 million
4	Resident Evil: Extinction (USA)	2007	$147 million
5	Pokémon the Movie 2000 (USA)	1999	$133 million
6	Resident Evil: Apocalypse (USA)	2004	$129 million
7	Mortal Kombat (USA)	1995	$122 million
8	Resident Evil (USA)	2002	$102 million
9	Hitman (France/USA)	2007	$99.9 million
10	Street Fighter (USA)	1994	$99.4 million

> *The hardest thing is the constant yelling. There have been games, generally war games, where I have literally shouted myself hoarse.*
> **Kerry Shale, record-holding video game voice actor reflecting on the downside of his job.**

Most successful live-action transfer

Game: *Tomb Raider*
Publisher: Eidos

Lara Croft: Tomb Raider already ranks as the **highest grossing video-game movie**, but together with its sequel, *Lara Croft Tomb Raider: The Cradle of Life* (USA, 2003), the franchise has grossed in excess of $431 million (£216 million) as of July 2008, making it the most successful live-action game-to-film transfer of all time.

TOP 50 CONSOLE GAMES

CONTENTS

TASKED WITH SELECTING THE BEST CONSOLE GAMES OF ALL TIME, THE GAMER'S EDITION CONTRIBUTORS HAVE POURED OVER HUNDREDS OF RELEASES AND THRASHED OUT A LIST OF THE TOP 50 TITLES RANKED ON THEIR INITIAL IMPACT AND LASTING LEGACY. THESE ARE NOT JUST IMPORTANT GAMES – THEY'RE ALSO GAMES THAT YOU SIMPLY MUST PLAY.

50 OUT RUN 2
Publisher: Sega **Released:** 2004

A tyre-squealing smash on the original Xbox – the perfect anecdote to stodgy racing sims.

49 CRASH BANDICOOT ①
Publisher: Sony **Released:** 1996

Crash delivered the goods in this super-smooth platform game that was a joy to play.

48 SATURN BOMBERMAN ②
Publisher: Hudson Soft **Released:** 1996

The only thing better than *Bomberman* was this extremely volatile Saturn version. Explosive stuff.

47 WARIOWARE, INC.
Publisher: Nintendo **Released:** 2003

A brilliant collection of mini-games. Possibly the most innovative title in the last 10 years.

46 ELDER SCROLLS IV: OBLIVION
Publisher: 2K Games **Released:** 2006

Building on the previous *Elder Scrolls* games, *Oblivion* presented the player with a vast and beautiful world to discover and savour.

45 STAR FOX 64
Publisher: Nintendo **Released:** 1997

This on-rails 3D shooter surpassed the original SNES game thanks to its intense gameplay and strong cinematic quality.

44 SEGA RALLY CHAMPIONSHIP
Publisher: Sega **Released:** 1995

A real showcase title for the Saturn that successfully transported the coin-op classic into the home, complete with its distinct handling style and superb track design.

43 GOD OF WAR ③
Publisher: Sony **Released:** 2005

This gorgeous-looking game showed that PlayStation 2 could still cut it amid all the next-gen hype. Worthy of inclusion for the amazing boss battles alone. Look out for the PS3 version coming soon.

42 THE LEGEND OF ZELDA: LINK'S AWAKENING
Publisher: Nintendo **Released:** 1993

While SNES owners enjoyed *A Link to the Past*, handheld fans were gifted this exclusive Link adventure that was comparable in size and scope. A sparkling Game Boy gem.

41 STAR WARS: KNIGHTS OF THE OLD REPUBLIC
Publisher: LucasArts **Released:** 2003

A vast RPG created by BioWare and set in the *Star Wars* universe. It couldn't really fail, and the awards and praise lauded on the game were all richly deserved. Worth playing even for non-*Star Wars* fans.

40 BIOSHOCK
Publisher: 2K Games **Released:** 2007

The setting, the story, the characters, the combat, the overall feel of the game… all perfect.

39 GTA: VICE CITY
Publisher: Rockstar **Released:** 2002

For many it's the coolest *GTA*, with its neon-lit city, 80s' soundtrack and dog-eat-dog storyline.

38 CASTLEVANIA: SYMPHONY OF THE NIGHT
Publisher: Konami **Released:** 1997

This sublime platformer updated the *Castlevania* series with non-linear gameplay and RPG elements, but retained its classic 2D styling to the delight of fans. Wonderful whip-cracking action.

ℹ TRIVIA

The first three *Crash Bandicoot* games have combined sales of over 20 million, making it the **best-selling character-based series on PlayStation**.

ℹ TRIVIA

Star Fox 64 came bundled with the "Rumble Pak", a peripheral that provided gamepad force-feedback. It was the first game on any Nintendo system to offer this now commonplace feature.

37 SUPER METROID 4
Publisher: Nintendo **Released:** 1994

▪▶ The excellent *Metroid* series hit its zenith with this stunning SNES entry, which refined the trademark open-ended gameplay until it was flawless.

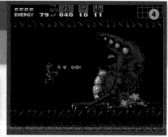

36 RIDGE RACER
Publisher: Namco **Released:** 1994

▪▶ It wasn't an arcade-perfect conversion, but the original *Ridge Racer* console game was vital to the development of the PlayStation brand.

35 ADVANCE WARS
Publisher: Nintendo **Released:** 2001

▪▶ *Advance Wars* was a cracking little title that proved there was still a valid place for turn-based strategy games. It was even better with four players linked up together.

34 SOUL CALIBUR
Publisher: Namco **Released:** 1999

▪▶ A striking 3D brawler. Edge Master Mode remains the best addition in a fighting game ever.

33 GUNSTAR HEROES
Publisher: Sega **Released:** 1993

▪▶ The greatest Mega Drive game not to star a spiky blue hedgehog. A run-and-gun classic.

32 CHRONO TRIGGER
Publisher: Square Soft **Released:** 1995

▪▶ Epic in scale and with a grand storyline that twisted and turned towards multiple conclusions, *Chrono Trigger* stands out as one of the best Japanese RPGs ever created.

31 ICO
Publisher: Sony **Released:** 2001

▪▶ This beautiful but sombre adventure has developed a cult following since its release and it's easy to understand why. A magical, unfogettable and haunting experience.

30 RESIDENT EVIL 5
Publisher: Capcom **Released:** 1996

▪▶ *Resident Evil* was the closest thing to an interactive horror movie and the first video game to actually make people jump. Sure, *Alone in the Dark* may have done it first - but *RE* did it better.

29 SUPER MARIO GALAXY
Publisher: Nintendo **Released:** 2007

▪▶ After the slight misfire that was *Super Mario Sunshine*, Mario's Wii debut represented a dizzying return to form. A worthy successor to the venerable *Mario 64*.

28 PROJECT GOTHAM RACING 2
Publisher: Microsoft **Released:** 2003

▪▶ Arguably the best racing game on the Xbox, this super-slick sequel managed to surpass the excellent original chiefly thanks to its online multiplayer support. Kudos indeed.

27 GUITAR HERO
Publisher: RedOctane **Released:** 2005

▪▶ This music rhythm game with a guitar-shaped controller quickly became a massive mainstream hit, spawning a series of successful sequels.

26 POKEMON RED/BLUE 6
Publisher: Nintendo **Released:** 1996

▪▶ The games that introduced monster hunting to the West and showed that there was still life in the Game Boy almost 10 years after its launch.

25 WII SPORTS
Publisher: Nintendo **Released:** 2006

▪▶ One of the most important bundled titles ever. This compendium perfectly showcased Wii functionality and ensnared gamers and non-gamers alike.

ⓘ TRIVIA

> The first *Metroid* game, which was released for the Famicom Disc System in 1986, featured a major surprise at the end. If you managed to complete the game in under three hours, bounty hunter Samus Aran was revealed as, shock, a woman!

ⓘ TRIVIA

> Since the release of the original game in 1996, *Resident Evil* has gone on to become Capcom's best-selling franchise of all time, with the 50 games in the series (across all formats) selling in excess of 34.5 million copies.

24 TEKKEN 2
Publisher: Namco **Released:** 1996

⫸ The pick of the PlayStation 1 *Tekken* trilogy, this hand-to-hand fighting-game sequel – based on the fictional King of the Iron Fist Tournaments ("Tekken" means "Iron Fist") – features a wide roster of characters and a multitude of modes. Unlike the first and third games, part two was superior to the arcade original.

22 THE ORANGE BOX
Publisher: Valve **Released:** 2007

⫸ Valve's gift to console owners – five games in one and no filler – is ridiculously generous, including *Half-Life 2*, its two episode packs, *Team Fortress 2* and *Portal*.

21 PRO EVOLUTION SOCCER 4
Publisher: Konami **Released:** 2004

⫸ It's difficult to pick one *Pro Evo* game, but general consensus says that the 2004 iteration is the finest. Perfectly balanced.

20 FINAL FANTASY VII
Publisher: Sony **Released:** 1997

⫸ The RPG masterpiece that saw the series – and the genre – explode in popularity in the West. (It also helped make the PlayStation a success in Japan.) The emotive storyline, the believable, beloved characters and the cinematic sensibilities still resonate with gamers today.

19 GRAN TURISMO
Publisher: Sony **Released:** 1997

⫸ With *Gran Turismo*, Polyphony Digital crafted a racing game where the sheer depth and attention to detail was without equal. The "Real Driving Simulator" subtitle could not be more apt.

18 ZELDA: A LINK TO THE PAST
Publisher: Nintendo **Released:** 1991

⫸ Released in Japan as *Zeruda no Densetsu Kamigami no Tofaifousu*, this game stands out as one of the greatest adventure games ever released, with the world of Hyrule providing the backdrop.

17 SUPER MARIO BROS.
Publisher: Nintendo **Released:** 1985

⫸ This was the game that made Mario a star and introduced the world to the first side-scrolling platform game of note. It remains the **best-selling video game of all time** with over 40 million units sold.

16 GRAND THEFT AUTO: SAN ANDREAS
Publisher: Rockstar **Released:** 2004

⫸ Without doubt, the most ambitious, most elaborate and most controversial GTA game to date. Opportunities for fun and profit in sprawling San Andreas seemed almost limitless.

15 SONIC THE HEDGEHOG 2
Publisher: Sega **Released:** 1992

⫸ The best of all the 2D Sonic games, thanks to more varied and interesting level design, the new Spin Dash move, the fantastic 3D bonus round and the split-screen races with sidekick Tails.

23 LEGO STAR WARS: THE COMPLETE SAGA
Publisher: LucasArts **Released:** 2007

⫸ Combining two great brands from everyone's childhood – *Star Wars* and LEGO – this brilliant "best of" for the PS3, Xbox 360 and Wii combines two *LEGO Star Wars* games and throws in a bunch of bonus extras. Affectionate, clever and irresistible to all ages. In a word: fantastic.

▶ Replay

GRAN TURISMO
THE REAL DRIVING SIMULATOR

PlaySt

ⓘ TRIVIA

> The two *LEGO Star Wars* games that make up *The Complete Saga* have sold nearly 7 million copies in the USA alone. *Star Wars II: The Original Trilogy* was the third best-selling title of 2006.

> *GTA: San Andreas* is the UK's fastest-selling single-format title. When released for the PS2 on 29 October 2004, the game sold 501,000 copies in its first 24 hours on sale.

> While under development at Sega, Sonic the Hedgehog was known by the codename Mr Needlemouse!

> Mario and Sonic were among the first four video-game characters inducted into the Walk of Game in San Francisco. The area is modelled on Hollywood's Walk of Fame, honouring video games and their creators.

> *LEGO Star Wars* developer, TT Games, also created *Guinness World Records: The Videogame*.

14 CALL OF DUTY 4
Publisher: Activision **Released:** 2007

▪▶ Set in a fictional war in the Middle East and Russia (not World War II for a change), this was easily the biggest surprise of its generation. *Call of Duty 4*'s plot-driven campaign mode is absolutely compelling and packed with spine-tingling set pieces. The multiplayer modes rock too.

13 METAL GEAR SOLID ⑤
Publisher: Konami **Released:** 1998

▪▶ Even though it's built on the earlier, simpler 8-bit games, *MGS*'s brand of cleverly structured, stealth-based gameplay was a revelation on release. Compared with the sequels, it's pleasingly restrained.

12 TOMB RAIDER ⑥
Publisher: Eidos **Released:** 1996

▪▶ The game that gave us Lara Croft and a breathtaking underwater world to explore. The original *Tomb Raider* set the bar so high that the many sequels could never quite match it. An all-time great.

11 SUPER MARIO 64
Publisher: Nintendo **Released:** 1996

▪▶ In terms of initial impact, no other Mario game (or maybe video game, period) has made such a groundbreaking impression on gamers. The first true 3D adventure with proper analogue controls. Simply essential.

10 GOLDENEYE
Publisher: Nintendo **Released:** 1997

▪▶ The first FPS games on a console to actually work. The superb single-player missions were bolstered by the riotous four-player modes, making this the best movie-licensed game ever made. Another all-time great that still holds up well today.

09 STREET FIGHTER II TURBO
Publisher: Capcom **Released:** 1993

▪▶ This update delivered a devastating dragon punch to the original SNES version by including the bosses as playable characters and cranking up the speed.

08 FINAL FANTASY XII ⑦
Publisher: Square Enix **Released:** 2006

▪▶ It was a long time coming, but worth the wait. Full of fresh ideas and gameplay updates, it satisfied newcomers and fans alike.

07 RESIDENT EVIL 4
Publisher: Activision **Released:** 2005

▪▶ *Resident Evil* redefined... and not before time! The fourth entry in the long-running series upped the ante in almost every single way: more devious enemies, amazing visuals, awesome set pieces and an intuitive control system. A bloody masterpiece.

06 HALO
Publisher: Microsoft **Released:** 2001

▪▶ With the Xbox sci-fi spectacular *Halo*, Bungie delivered the perfect console FPS and the first must-have Xbox game – the console's first "killer app" (application). Despite a few claims to the contrary, there hasn't been a "*Halo* killer" released on any console since.

05 ZELDA: OCARINA OF TIME
Publisher: Nintendo **Released:** 1998

▪▶ *Zelda* for the N64 was a stunning triumph, with the world of Hyrule depicted in beautiful and richly detailed 3D. Throw in some charming characters, challenging puzzles and the most devious dungeons yet seen and the end result is one of the finest adventure games ever and the most cherished episode of the longest-running action-adventure video game series of all time.

04 SUPER MARIO WORLD
Publisher: Nintendo **Released:** 1990

▪▶ First released in Japan on the Super Famicom, this is not just the best Mario platformer but the best platform game, period, as anyone who has reached all 96 exits knows! It's a side-scroller from the master – Shigeru Miyamoto – that's packed with moments of pure magic; it succeeds in getting every detail absolutely right and – forgive the cliché – set the standard for the entire genre.

ⓘ **TRIVIA**

> Although *Tomb Raider* is best known as a PlayStation brand, it actually made its debut on the Sega Saturn in November 1996. The PS1 version followed shortly afterwards and quickly became a best-seller, reversing the fortunes of Eidos.

ⓘ **TRIVIA**

> *Final Fantasy XII* became the first ever PS2 game to receive a perfect review score of 40 out of 40 in the Japanese gaming magazine *Famitsu*. In 2006, readers of the magazine voted *Final Fantasy X* the best video game ever.

TOP 3

> **ALEXEY PAJITNOV LIKES...**
> ...simplicity and accessibility: "I try to eliminate the complexity and just give the pure joy."

ⓘ TRIVIA

> None of our judging panel awarded *Tetris* top marks, but the game "which takes a minute to learn and a lifetime to master" hoovered up enough high-ranking scores to secure a place on the runner's-up podium!

> Alexey Pajitnov, creator of *Tetris*, received the first ever Penguin Award for "diving into unknown territory" and "pioneering the casual games market" at the 2007 Game Developers Choice Awards. At the same awards ceremony, Mario's creator, Shigeru Miyamoto (Japan), won the Lifetime Achievement Award.

❓ GWR QUIZ

Q24. What are the two highest-ranking games in this chart designed or produced by Shigeru Miyamoto?

Q25. What was Mario's original name?

⌐ TETRIS

The world's **most ported video game** – available on at least 59 different gaming platforms – slots neatly into second place thanks to its simplicity and devilish addictiveness. Based on an ancient Roman puzzle and first released as a video game in 1985, it continues to engage and frustrate each new generation of gamers... and will no doubt do so for years to come!

> *Tetris gave birth to the casual game industry and set the bar which every puzzle game to follow would aim to match.*
> **Game Developers Choice Awards advisory board**

350 – the number of "Pandora's Box"-style puzzles created by *Tetris* creator Alexey Pajitnov before settling on his record-breaking game.

SUPER MARIO KART

Skidding into first place – not even Nico Bellic could car-jack the plucky Italian – is the world's **most prolific video game character** in his greatest outing yet. Originally called Jumpman, Mario has starred in more than 116 titles.

In this game he joins his buddies go-karting in the ultimate racing game, enhanced with an array of crazy weapons and hazards. Not only is it the **best-selling racing game on the N64** (it shifted more than 9 million units), it's the **best-selling racer on the SNES** (8 million units), the **GameCube** (nearly 7 million) and the **DS** (10 million units). It is everything a game should be: fun, surprising, addictive, sticky and a joy to play in eithier single- or multi-player modes. Weeeee!

GRAND THEFT AUTO IV

The latest offering from the world's **most controversial series of games** has received near-perfect scores in virtually every review. In fact, most experts agree that Rockstar Games' *GTA IV* is the perfect example of a next-gen game, boasting incredible graphics, a top-quality script, brilliant voice acting and great gameplay. No wonder, then, that *GTA IV* is the **fastest-selling video game ever**.

ⓘ TRIVIA

> At the Super Nintendo launch at The Ark in London, UK, in 1992, SEGA projected a huge image of *Sonic the Hedgehog* on to the side of the building from a projector hidden in a bush.

> Shigeru Miyamoto produced the top game in our poll: *Super Mario Kart* (and designed the No.4 game, *Legend of Zelda*). Miyamoto has worked for Nintendo throughout his career; in 1977, having completed a degree in industrial design, Miyamoto arranged a meeting with Hiroshi Yamauchi, head of Nintendo of Japan and also a friend of his father. Yamauchi hired Shigeru as a "staff artist" and assigned him to the planning department. Miyamoto is now Nintendo's Senior Managing Director.

> Electronic Arts has tried repeatedly to buy TakeTwo Interactive Software, Inc., the parent company of Rockstar Games and distributor of *GTA IV*. EA's last reported offer of $2 billion (£1.1 billion) was declined for being too low!

The **most successful video-game documentary** is *The King of Kong: A Fistful of Quarters* (USA, 2007), which grossed $775,682 in the USA alone in a single year since its release on 17 August 2007.

HIGH SCORES & FASTEST TIMES

DID YOUR FASTEST TIME OR HIGHEST SCORE MAKE IT INTO THE 2009 CHARTS? FIND OUT HERE, AS TWIN GALAXIES PRESENT THEIR PICK OF RECORD-BREAKING ACHIEVEMENTS...

GAME	PLATFORM	RECORD	PLAYER (NAT.)	DATE	NOTES
3D Deathchase	ZX Spectrum ☺	16,342	Carsten Hirche (Germany)	29 Mar 2008	TGTS
APB	Lynx	709,680	Ed Hershey (USA)	12 Aug 2005	
Area 51	PlayStation	46,875	Andrew Gallagher (USA)	11 Jun 2004	Medium difficulty points
Asteroids ①	Arcade	41,336,440	Scott Safran (USA)	13 Nov 1982	
Astrosmash	Intellivision	4,201,875	Rick D. Fothergill (Canada)	9 May 2001	
Atic Atac	ZX Spectrum ☺	8 min 9 sec	Carsten Hirche (Germany)	27 Mar 2008	
Attack of the Killer Tomatoes	NES	13 min 26 sec	Andrew D. Furrer (USA)	7 Jul 2008	
Attack of the Mutant Camels	C64	56,868	Terence O'Neill (USA)	19 Dec 2007	
ATV Simulator	ZX Spectrum	17,420	Andrew Pete Mee (UK)	16 Mar 2008	
Axelay	SNES	1,271,480	Scott Kessler (USA)	22 Aug 2006	Normal; No codes or continues
Baku Baku Animal	Saturn	30,397	Nik Meeks (USA)	16 Apr 2007	Expert
Balloon Fight	NES	507,070	Kyle M. Orland (USA)	25 Nov 2005	Game C: Balloon Trip
Banjo-Kazooie	Nintendo 64	3 hr 32 min 45 sec	Alex Penev (Australia)	11 Jun 2004	
Barbarian	C64 ☺	99,950	Clay W. Karczewski (Canada)	29 Dec 2007	
Batman	Arcade	178,000	Kelly R. Flewin (Canada)	2 Jun 2008	3 lives
Batman Returns	NES	24 min 32 sec	Daniel C. Teixeira (Canada)	11 Aug 2005	No continues
Batman: The Movie	Amiga	511,550	Graham Hawkins (NZ)	26 Oct 2005	
Beach Head	C64 ☺	114,400	Duane Briley (USA)	7 Jun 2008	
Berzerk	Arcade	325,270	Chris Ayra (USA)	29 May 2005	Fast bullets
Bionic Commando	NES	18 min 23 sec	Scott Kessler (USA)	28 Apr 2004	TGTS
Blast Corps	Nintendo 64	26.9 sec	Rodrigo Lopes (Brazil)	25 Nov 2003	Twilight Foundry
Blaster Master	NES	52 min 52 sec	William Armstrong (UK)	18 Apr 2004	
Blitz	Vectrex	14	William Grablauskas Jr. (USA) /Alan Hewston (USA)	6 Jul 2001/ 1 Sep 2001	Game 1
Blue Lightning	Jaguar	1,364,150	Wes Powell (USA)	11 Jun 2004	
Boing	Atari 2600	28,605	Rodrigo Lopes (Brazil)	3 Sep 2006	Game 1; Difficulty B
Bomb Jack	Arcade	20,010,960	Giauco Bondavalli (Italy)	3 Nov 1984	TGTS
Bomberman ②	NES	1,000,093,700	Kristina Sakundiak (Canada)	18 Jun 2005	Marathon
Bomberman 93	Wii Virtual Console	103,700	William Willemstyn III (USA)	7 Jul 2008	One player; No continues
Bonanza Bros.	Genesis/MD	946,100	David J. Stuart (USA)	18 Apr 2008	
Booty	ZX Spectrum ☺	89	Andrew Pete Mee (UK)	5 Jun 2008	Booty collected
Borg	Apple II	18,960	Matt Sesow (USA)	30 Sep 1983	
Boulder Dash	Atari 400/800/XL	2,579	Tom Duncan (USA)	6 Mar 2006	
Breakout	Arcade	896	Zachary B. Hample (USA)	25 Jun 2002	TGTS

100 – the number of TV appearances made by Walter Day in the early 1980s as an official video-game high-scores referee.

GAME	PLATFORM	RECORD	PLAYER (NAT.)	DATE	NOTES
Bruce Lee	ZX Spectrum ☺	811,925	Peter Gatland (UK)	25 Jun 2008	
Bubble Bobble	Arcade	5,823,600	Tom Gault (USA)	4 Mar 1988	Normal mode; TGTS
Buck Rogers	Atari 2600	909,826	Tom Duncan (USA)	17 Aug 2005	Game 1; Difficulty B
Buggy Boy	Arcade	103,200	Peter Huesken (Holland)	4 Oct 1986	
Burnout ③	PlayStation 2	7 min 18 sec	Troy Whelan (USA)	19 Jul 2005	Time Attack: Interstate
Burnout 2: Point of Impact	PlayStation 2	$32,671,092	Tom Duncan (USA)	2 May 2008	Crash: Sandstorm Shredder
Burnout 3: Takedown	PlayStation 2	$624,860	Tom Duncan (USA)	5 Nov 2006	Crash: Grapes of Wrath
Burnout Legends	PSP	5.84 sec	Tom Duncan (USA)	4 Sep 2007	Pursuit: Europe – Alpine Forward
Burnout Revenge	Xbox 360	$18,723,100	Troy Whelan (USA)	14 Aug 2007	Crash: Forest Bump
Bust-A-Move	3DO	147,420	Wing Yau (USA)	11 Jun 2004	Challenge Points
Bust-A-Move 2	PlayStation	84,612,710	Si Janna (USA)	26 Mar 2000	Arcade Puzzle
Buster Bros.	Arcade	2,228,150	Greg F. Mott (UK)	4 Jun 2006	
California Games	C64 ☺	157,790	Marc Cohen (USA)	3 Dec 2007	Footbag
Capcom Vs SNK	PlayStation	41,455	Bruno Augusto (Brazil)	15 Dec 2006	Arcade Mode
Captain Skyhawk	NES	539,860	John Matthews (USA)	23 Jul 2008	
Castle of Illusion	Genesis/MD	297,700	Terence O'Neill (USA)	2 Feb 2006	
Castlevania ④	NES	14 min 10 sec	Eric Cummings (USA)	27 Jul 2006	
Castlevania Adventure	GB/GBC	31,060	Rudy J. Ferretti (USA)	2 Apr 2007	
Castlevania Bloodlines	Genesis/MD	10,158,440	Mike K. Morrow (USA)	13 Aug 2002	
Castlevania Chronicles	PlayStation	179,630	Ryan Sullivan (USA)	25 Apr 2008	
Castlevania II: Belmont's Revenge	GB/GBC	192,280	Rudy J. Ferretti (USA)	4 Feb 2008	
Castlevania II: Simon's Quest	NES	47 min 7 sec	Mike K. Morrow (USA)	13 Mar 2005	
Castlevania III: Dracula's Curse	NES	999,999	Tom Votava (USA)	6 Mar 2007	
Castlevania: Dracula X	SNES	29 min 53 sec	Rudy J. Ferretti (USA)	1 Feb 2008	
Championship Sprint	C64 ☺	13,023	Terence O'Neill (USA)	20 Feb 2007	
Championship Sprint II	C64 ☺	6,282	Terence O'Neill (USA)	19 Jan 2007	
Chaos Engine ⑤	Amiga	46,590	Graham Hawkins (NZ)	27 Apr 2005	
Choplifter	C64	51	John Sato (USA)	3 Aug 2008	
ChuChu Rocket!	Dreamcast	4 secs	Tom Duncan (USA)	10 May 2008	Stage Challenge A1; Time
Chuckie Egg	ZX Spectrum	254,790	Andrew Pete Mee (UK)	29 Sep 2007	Marathon
Chuckie Egg 2	ZX Spectrum	46,374	Andrew Pete Mee (UK)	5 Oct 2007	
Cliffhanger	SNES	895,500	Scott Kessler (USA)	2 Nov 2006	
Commando	Arcade	10,051,200	Tim Balderramos (USA)	11 Jun 2004	Normal; TGTS
Contra	Arcade	443,400	Isaiah TriForce Johnson (USA)	1 Jun 2008	Single Player
Contra III: The Alien Wars	Wii Virtual Console	1,931,276	Isaiah TriForce Johnson (USA)	29 Apr 2008	No continues
Cooking Mama	Nintendo DS	8	William Willemstyn III (USA)	12 Jan 2007	Stuff Cabbages

HIGH SCORES & FASTEST TIMES

FACTS

> Twin Galaxies holds pinball statistics dating from the 1930s and video-game statistics from the early 1970s.

> The so-called video-game "Golden Age" ran from January 1982 to January 1986, during which video-game high scores were featured on TV and in countless magazines.

> According to the Killer List of Video Games website, the arcade version of *Defender* shares the record with *Pac-Man* for the **highest-grossing arcade game**, raking in over $1 billion since its launch in 1980.

> *Donkey Kong: Jungle Beat* has a unique peripheral for a platform game: a pair of bongos! Hit the left to go left, the right to go right and both together to jump!

GAME	PLATFORM	RECORD	PLAYER (NAT.)	DATE	NOTES
Cool Boarders	PlayStation	10,140	Aaron Marsh (NZ)	11 Jun 2004	
Crash Bandicoot: Warped	PlayStation	43.76 sec	Victor H. de Souza (Brazil)	2 May 2006	Toad Village
Crash Nitro Kart	PlayStation 2	40.470	Hector T. Rodriguez (USA)	1 Nov 2006	Jungle Boogie Fastest Lap
Crash Team Racing	PlayStation	1 min 16.08 sec	Hector T. Rodriguez (USA)	5 Jan 2006	Oxide Station Fastest Lap
Darius Twin	Saturn	5,365,200	Stephen Krogman (USA)	11 Jun 2004	
Dark Star	C64	26,640	Fred Bugmann (Brazil)	12 Jul 2008	ACE version
Darkstalkers 3	PlayStation	862,700	Aaron M. Price (USA)	12 May 2006	Arcade Mode
Darkstalkers: The Night Warriors	Arcade	687,800	Justin M. Wong (USA)	5 Jun 2008	Difficulty 8; Damage 5; No continues
Darkwing Duck	NES	25,600	David R. Archey (USA)	19 Apr 2008	TGTS; Limited Leeching Allowed
Daytona USA	Saturn	3 min 11.88 sec	Jesse Mills (Australia)	11 Jun 2004	NTSC; Total/ Expert
Dead or Alive	Arcade	1 min 58.38 sec	Steve O'Donnell (USA)	11 Jun 2004	Very Hard
Dead or Alive 3 ①	Xbox	7 min 14.39 sec	Patrick Scott Patterson (USA)	8 Jul 2008	Time Attack Mode
Death Race	Colecovision	130	Tom Duncan (USA)	4 Jul 2008	Skill 1
Decathlon	C64 ☺	10,605	Fred Bugmann (Brazil)	25 Aug 2008	
Defender	Atari 2600	5,443,150	Frankie Cardulla (USA)	3 Feb 2007	Game 1; Difficulty B
Defender 2	NES	139,400	Andrew D. Furrer (USA)	25 Jul 2008	Difficulty A
Defender 2000	Jaguar	4,395,156	Wes Powell (USA)	11 Jun 2004	
Defender of the Crown	NES	19 min 52 sec	Eric Cummings (USA)	17 Apr 2008	
Deja Vu	NES	17 min 26 sec	Kelly R. Flewin (Canada)	6 Apr 2005	
Delta	C64	28,570	Stig Remnes (Norway)	26 May 2003	
Destruction Derby ②	PlayStation	426	Terence O'Neill (USA)	25 Jan 2008	Division 1 Championship
Destruction Derby	PSP	406	Terence O'Neill (USA)	3 Jan 2008	Division 1 Championship
Destruction Derby 2 ②	PlayStation	1,020	Terence O'Neill (USA)	22 Apr 2006	Division 1; Hardest Difficulty; TGTS
Die Hard	PlayStation	4,314,927	Mike McKenzie (USA)	16 May 1999	
Die Hard Trilogy	Saturn	67,141,200	Elijah Parker (USA)	10 Dec 1997	
Dogs of War	Amiga	400,500	Graham Hawkins (NZ)	26 Oct 2005	
Donkey Kong	Wii Virtual Console	243,500	Jason D. Doi (USA)	10 Apr 2008	Difficulty A
Donkey Kong Country	SNES	54 min	Harry J. Hong (USA)	30 Oct 2005	Fastest 101% Completion; No Saves
Donkey Kong Country: Competition Pak	SNES	3,297	Nik Meeks (USA)	30 Jan 2006	TGTS
Donkey Kong Jr.	Wii Virtual Console	159,300	Andrew D. Furrer (USA)	5 Jun 2008	Difficulty A
Donkey Kong: Jungle Beat ③	GameCube	1 hr 21 min 48 sec	Niccolo C. Mundell (USA)	22 Feb 2008	Minimalist Completion
DOOM	PlayStation	12 sec	Mike K. Morrow (USA)	29 Jun 2005	Stage 01: Hangar

GAME	PLATFORM	RECORD	PLAYER (NAT.)	DATE	NOTES
Double Dribble	Wii Virtual Console	163	Andrew D. Furrer (USA)	31 Jul 2008	NES Biggest Blowout; 10 minutes
Dragonfire	Atari 2600 ☉	16,440	Rodrigo Lopes (Brazil)	15 Sep 2005	Game 1; Difficulty B
Dragon's Lair II: Time Warp	Arcade	1,006	Greg R. Sakundiak (Canada)	27 Feb 2007	3 Lives; Medium Difficulty
Drop Zone	Atari 400/800/XL	1,728,780	Graham Hawkins (NZ)	28 Nov 2005	
E.T.	Atari 2600	1,011,657	Todd Rogers (USA)	10 May 2001	Game 1, Difficulty BB
Electro Cop	Lynx	12,975	Terence O'Neill (USA)	20 May 2007	
Elevator Action	Wii Virtual Console	36,150	Andrew D. Furrer (USA)	18 Jul 2008	3 Lives
Enduro Racer	Arcade	40,973,617	Jack Gale (USA)	20 May 1987	TGTS
Eternal Champions	Genesis/MD	18 min 17 sec	Daniel C. Teixeira (Canada)	16 Aug 2005	
Evander Holyfield's "Real Deal" Boxing	Genesis/MD	8 min 2 sec	Daniel C. Teixeira (Canada)	16 Aug 2005	
Evil Dead: A Fistful of Boomstick ④	Xbox	37,822	Mike K. Morrow (USA)	10 Apr 2005	Arcade; Dearborn Outskirts 1
Excitebike	NES	44.04 sec	Hector T. Rodriguez (USA)	18 Nov 2007	Track 1
EyeToy Play	PlayStation 2	77,600	William Willemstyn III (USA)	1 Feb 2008	Kung Foo; Medium
EyeToy Play	PlayStation 2	65,926	William Willemstyn III (USA)	1 Feb 2008	Beat Freak; Freaky Beats; Medium
EyeToy Play	PlayStation 2	78,164	William Willemstyn III (USA)	28 Feb 2008	Beat Freak; Bangin'; Medium
EyeToy Play	PlayStation 2	72,308	William Willemstyn III (USA)	12 May 2008	Beat Freak; Sing it Back; Medium
EyeToy Play	PlayStation 2	77,782	William Willemstyn III (USA)	12 May 2008	Kung Foo; UFO Juggler; Medium
F-15 Strike Eagle	Arcade	399,000	Blaine Locklair (USA)	30 Jul 2007	3 Planes; Medium Difficulty
Fantastic Voyage	Atari 2600 ☉	258,510	Robert Macauley (Australia)	10 May 2001	Game 1; Difficulty B
FIFA Street	Xbox	222,774	Andrew Pete Mee (UK)	11 Sep 2007	Easy; 12 Minutes
Fighting Wings	Arcade	101,400	Braedon Bird (UK)	18 Jan 1985	
Final Fantasy III	SNES	8 hr 24 min 50 sec	Rodrigo Lopes (Brazil)	11 Oct 2004	
Final Fantasy VII ⑤	PlayStation	16,700	Bruno Augusto (Brazil)	15 Dec 2006	Gold Saucer; Motorcycle game; TGTS
Final Lap	Arcade	38.98 sec	Brian Kuh (USA)	31 May 2007	Fastest Lap; Medium
Final Lap	Arcade	2 min 35.68 sec	Jim Killy (USA)	27 Jul 1988	Fastest Race; Medium
Firefly	ZX Spectrum	66,180	Riccardo Moretti (Italy)	12 Nov 2007	
Flak	Atari 400/800/XL	1,777,000	Graham Hawkins (NZ)	28 Nov 2005	
Formula 1	PlayStation	1 min 11.9 sec	Bruno Pascuzzi (Australia)	11 Jun 2004	Australia; Fastest Lap

❶ TRIVIA

> Through tracking high scores, Twin Galaxies referee Walter Day determined that his home town of Ottumwa, Iowa, had the highest concentration of record-breaking video gamers of any town in the USA – 35 champions. And, on 30 November 1982, a proclamation was issued by the city of Ottumwa laying claim to the title of "Video Game Capital of the Universe".

> Rumours have been circulating around the internet for two years that *Final Fantasy VII* will be remade for the PS3. Square Enix has yet to confirm or deny such rumours.

> *EyeToy: Play* was the **first game developed for the EyeToy peripheral** – a USB camera that uses motion detection to allow players to interact with elements on screen. It won Best Puzzle/Trivia/Parlour Game at E3 in 2003.

HIGH SCORES & FASTEST TIMES

GAME	PLATFORM	RECORD	PLAYER (NAT.)	DATE	NOTES
Frequency	PlayStation 2	961	Ryan Sullivan (USA)	13 Jan 2007	Freezepop – Science Genius Girl; Hard Difficulty
Frequency	PlayStation 2	535	Ryan Sullivan (USA)	13 Jan 2007	Crystal Method – The Winner; Normal Difficulty
Ghost Squad ❶	Wii	8,000	Patrick Scott Patterson (USA)	19 Jul 2008	Training Mode; Shooting Match
Ghost Squad	Wii	472,461	William Willemstyn III (USA)	10 Aug 2008	Arcade; Continues Allowed
Ghosts 'N' Goblins	Arcade	277,900	Chris Whiteside (USA)	30 May 2008	TGTS
Goldeneye 007	Nintendo 64	1 min 6 sec	Wouter Jansen (Netherlands)	7 May 2004	Agent; Silo
Gradius	NES	10,102,000	Tom Votava (USA)	6 Oct 2007	
Gradius III	SNES	2,569,100	Scott Kessler (USA)	28 Aug 2007	Normal Difficulty
Gran Turismo	PlayStation	44.886 sec	Mike Burt (USA)	16 Apr 2007	Arcade; High Speed Ring; Fastest Lap
Gran Turismo 3 A-Spec	PlayStation 2	1 min 26.754 sec	Frankie Cardulla (USA)	29 Apr 2007	Arcade; Mid-Field Raceway II; Fastest Lap
Gran Turismo 4	PlayStation 2	30.624 sec	Andrew Pete Mee (UK)	16 Mar 2008	License Center; Test B-03
Great Giana Sisters	Amiga	56,796	Graham Hawkins (NZ)	29 Sep 2006	
Green Beret	ZX Spectrum ☉	17,500	Andrew Pete Mee (UK)	27 Jun 2008	
Gremlins	Atari 2600 ☉	54,640	Robert Macauley (Australia)	10 May 2001	Game 1; Difficulty B
Gridrunner	C64 ☉	72,640	John Eden (Australia)	19 May 2008	
Guardian Heroes ❷	Saturn	54 min 45 sec	Adam R. Wood (USA)	4 Jun 2005	Hard Difficulty
Gumball	Atari 400/800/XL	49,370	Stephen Knox (USA)	11 Jun 2004	
Gun Smoke	Arcade	2,134,300	Dwayne Richard (Canada)	31 Dec 2002	TGTS
Gunstar Heroes	Wii Virtual Console	5,325,564	Andrew D. Furrer (USA)	5 Jun 2008	Genesis; Default
Gyromite	NES	1,091,830	Tom Duncan (USA)	18 Sep 2005	1 Player; Game A
Gyruss	Arcade	1,306,100	Richard W. Marsh (USA)	2 Jun 2004	TGTS
Hang-On	Master System	1,314,960	Nik Meeks (USA)	24 Aug 2006	Level 1
Hang-On (Cabinet)	Arcade	7,385,200	Ashton Harden (USA)	23 Sep 2005	
Hang-On (Simulator) ❸	Arcade	40,715,030	Don Novak (USA)	11 Jun 2004	
Hard Drivin'	Arcade	219,758	David Nelson (USA)	23 Jun 2006	Medium Difficulty
Hatris	GB/GBC	74,259	Gary A. Hatt (USA)	26 Feb 2007	
Hatris	NES	129,605	Gary A. Hatt (USA)	3 Dec 2005	
Haunted House	Atari 2600	11 sec	Douglas A. Loyd (USA)	14 Aug 2004	Level 1; Difficulty B
Heist	Colecovision	38,534	Tom Duncan (USA)	30 Dec 2004	Skill 1
Helicopter Rescue	Odyssey²	11	Jared Jordan (USA)	23 Jun 1983	
Hot Rod	Arcade	272,380	Brian Kuh (USA)	1 Jun 2006	TGTS
Hyper Sports	Arcade	538,340	Kelly Kobashigawa (USA)	30 Jun 1985	Normal Difficulty

GAME	PLATFORM	RECORD	PLAYER (NAT.)	DATE	NOTES
Ikari Warriors	Arcade	1,414,500	Walt Price (USA)	24 Mar 1987	Normal; TGTS
In the Groove	PlayStation 2	3.31	Kelly R. Flewin (Canada)	5 Jun 2007	Breaking Point; Intense; TGTS; Singles Marathon; TGTS
In the Groove	PlayStation 2	2.61	Kelly R. Flewin (Canada)	30 Jun 2007	Caddywhompus; Intense; Singles Marathon; TGTS
In the Groove	PlayStation 2	14.51	Kelly R. Flewin (Canada)	1 Jun 2007	Charlene; Expert; Singles Mode
In the Groove	PlayStation 2	90.26	Kelly R. Flewin (Canada)	1 Jun 2007	Da Roots; Expert; Singles Mode
In the Groove	PlayStation 2	6.59	Kelly R. Flewin (Canada)	5 Jun 2007	Delirium; Expert; Singles Mode
Indy 4	Arcade	166	David Nelson (USA)	19 Nov 2006	Single Player
Indy 500	Atari 2600	12 laps	Frankie Cardulla (USA)	24 Feb 2007	Game 2; Difficulty B
International Karate Plus	Amiga	202,600	Graham Hawkins (NZ)	29 Sep 2006	
Jail Break	Arcade	265,450	Martin Deem (UK)	21 Feb 1985	TGTS; Difficult
Jaws	NES	4 min 4 sec	Daniel Brown (USA)	23 Apr 2007	TGTS
Jet Moto	PSP	2 min 13.5 sec	Terence O'Neill (USA)	5 May 2008	Blackwater Falls; Fastest Time
Jet Moto	PSP	2 min 32 sec	Terence O'Neill (USA)	5 May 2008	Joyride; Fastest Time
Jet Moto	PSP	1 min 31 sec	Terence O'Neill (USA)	5 May 2008	Suicide Swamp; Fastest Time
Jetman	Atari 400/800/XL	16,650	Tom Duncan (USA)	28 May 2006	Level 1
Jetpac 4	ZX Spectrum ⊕	500,525	Peter Gatland (UK)	4 Jul 2008	Marathon
Jetpac	ZX Spectrum ⊕	134,460	Peter Gatland (UK)	4 Jul 2008	Tournament; TGTS
John Madden Football	Genesis/MD	56	Nik Meeks (USA)	15 Jan 2007	Biggest Blowout
John Madden Football '92	Genesis/MD	60	Nik Meeks (USA)	15 Jan 2007	Biggest Blowout
John Madden Football '93	Genesis/MD	59	Nik Meeks (USA)	15 Jan 2007	Biggest Blowout
Jordan vs Bird: One on One	GB/GBC	370	Rudy J. Ferretti (USA)	4 Feb 2008	Biggest Blowout
Juiced 5	Xbox	2 min 54.72 sec	Fabiano G. Souza (Brazil)	15 Jul 2006	Arcade; Prototype; W. Anderson; Route 4 reverse; Fastest Race
Jurassic Park Lost World DX	Arcade	53,780	John Q. Nguyen (USA)	29 Aug 1998	
Kamikazi Saucers	Atari 2600 ⊕	32,850	Kelly R. Flewin (Canada)	14 Jul 2003	Game 1; Difficulty B
Karate Champ	Arcade	259,800	Jack Gale (USA)	28 Jun 1987	Difficulty Hard
Karate Champ 2	Arcade	224,400	Fabio Bertazzoli (Italy)	26 Mar 1985	
Karnov	Arcade	855,540	R. Hastings (UK)	24 Apr 1987	
Katamari Damacy	PlayStation 2	22 sec	Tom Batchelor (USA)	18 Sep 2006	Make a Star 1; Fastest Time

i TRIVIA

> *Hatris* is a puzzle game creator by *Tetris* inventor Alexey Pajitnov. Instead of falling blocks, pairs of hats cascade down the screen, and to keep the playing area clutter-free, five identical hats must be stacked together, causing them to vanish. Funnily enough, it didn't go down quite so well as *Tetris* did...

⬤▶ NOTE

> Got a high score or fastest time you want recognized by Twin Galaxies? The procedure for registering your claim is the same as logging a Guinness World Record. Visit the Gamer's Edition website at www.guinnessworldrecords.com/gamers and select "SET A RECORD". Your claim will be forwarded to the relevant researcher.

HIGH SCORES & FASTEST TIMES

SUMMER PROMOTION '83
KRULL
Gottlieb

THE MOVIE

THE VIDEO GAME

THE PROMOTION

⊪▶ FACTS

> *Jetpac* (1983) was the very first release for Ultimate Play the Game (aka just Ultimate). It sold over 300,000 copies on the Spectrum alone – a phenomenal achievement, given that there were only 1 million Spectrum owners at the time.

> Twin Galaxies Founder Walter Day was working as a travelling salesman in the early 1980s, which allowed him to pursue his interest in arcade gaming. Covering the length and breadth of the USA for his work, Walter took time out to visit as many video-game arcades as possible to record the high scores he found.

> *Link's Crossbow Challenge* came bundled with the Wii Zapper peripheral in most territories. The Zapper is a shell that houses the Wii remote and nunchuck together in one unit.

GAME	PLATFORM	RECORD	PLAYER (NAT.)	DATE	NOTES
Katamari Damacy	PlayStation 2	0.2 metres	Tom Batchelor (USA)	18 Sep 2006	Make a Star 1; Largest Diameter
Katamari Damacy	PlayStation 2	883.77 metres	Tom Batchelor (USA)	18 Sep 2006	Make the Moon; Largest Diameter
Kickle Cubicle	NES	6,415,500	Nik Meeks (USA)	10 Mar 2005	No continues
Kid Icarus	Wii Virtual Console	57 min 29 sec	Andrew D. Furrer (USA)	3 Jul 2008	No continues
Kid Icarus	Wii Virtual Console	1,062,700	Andrew D. Furrer (USA)	3 Jul 2008	No continues
Killer Instinct	Arcade	477,250	Brad Russell (USA)	11 Jun 2004	Very Hard Difficulty
King Kong	Atari 2600 ⊙	2,855	Jeffrey D. Lowe, Jr. (USA)	6 Jun 2001	Game 1; Difficulty B
Kirby's Dream Land	GB/GBC	391,750	Jeff Sumerlin (USA)	8 Sep 2008	
Kirby's Star Stacker	GB/GBC	239	Tom Duncan (USA)	5 Nov 2005	Challenge; Very Hard
Kiss	PC	579,103,170	Kiril Statev (Belgium)	5 May 2005	Netherworld; Arcade
Kiss	PC	877,290,250	XMeTaL XMeTaL (UK)	5 May 2005	Oblivion; Arcade
KISS Pinball	PlayStation	72,862,040	Terence O'Neill (USA)	4 Apr 2006	Last Stop; Oblivion Arcade Mode
Klax	NES	2,021,025	Tom Votava (USA)	8 Jun 2008	Drop Meter On; Medium; Ramping On
Knights of the Round	Arcade	431,450	Len Hanley (USA)	15 Jan 1999	TGTS
Knuckles Chaotix	Sega 32X	356,000	Sam Hartmann (USA)	11 Jun 2004	
Krull ①	Arcade	441,780	Jason Cram (USA)	30 May 2007	No Hiding in the Alcove Allowed
Kung Fu Master	Arcade	1,349,040	Mike Sullivan (USA)	30 Jun 1985	
Leaderboard Golf	C64	76	Marc Cohen (USA)	21 Sep 2007	Strokes
Legend of Mana	PlayStation	2 hr 1 min 53 sec	Rodrigo Lopes (Brazil)	2 Dec 2007	
The Legend of Zelda	Wii Virtual Console	100	Andrew D. Furrer (USA)	18 Jul 2008	NES; Extreme Challenge; 1st Quest
Legendary Axe II	TurboGrafx-16	879,950	Rudy J. Ferretti (USA)	17 Feb 2008	3 Lives; No continues
Legendary Wings	Arcade	612,500	Quentin E. Bolduc (USA)	11 Jun 2004	1 Player Only; No continues; TGTS
LeMans	Arcade	100	Martin Bedard (Canada)	19 Nov 2006	TGTS
Lilo & Stitch	PC	3,664,000	Albert Daubee (Belgium)	5 May 2005	Adults
Lilo & Stitch	PC	5,451,000	Albert Daubee (Belgium)	5 May 2005	Kids
Lilo & Stitch	PC	2,072,500	Albert Daubee (Belgium)	5 May 2005	Wizards
Link's Crossbow Training	Wii	83,930	Michael E. Estep (USA)	2 Aug 2008	Stage 1-1
LocoRoco ②	PSP	15,401	Andrew Mee (UK)	29 Aug 2008	World 1; Stage 1
Lode Runner	Wii Virtual Console	83,100	Patrick Scott Patterson (USA)	10 May 2008	5 Lives Only; TGTS Scoring
Lode Runner	Apple II	117,875	Ryan Gavigan (USA)	19 Jul 2005	
Lode Runner's Rescue	Atari 400/800/XL	2,950	Stephen Knox (USA)	11 May 2003	
Lotus Esprit Turbo Challenge	Amiga	295	Graham Hawkins (NZ)	27 Apr 2005	League Points; Hard

GAME	PLATFORM	RECORD	PLAYER (NAT.)	DATE	NOTES
Lotus Turbo Challenge 2	Amiga	131,505,760	Graham Hawkins (NZ)	13 Jan 2005	
Lumines II	PSP	562,101	Samantha R. Lopez (USA)	20 Sep 2007	Challenge Mode; Class S
Madden NFL '04	Genesis/MD	31	Nik Meeks (USA)	15 Jan 2007	Biggest Blowout
Madden NFL '08 ③	Xbox	100	Patrick Scott Patterson (USA)	23 Aug 2008	Biggest Blowout
Madden NFL '95	SNES	46	Thomas J. Myers (USA)	10 Apr 2008	Biggest Blowout
Madden NFL '96	SNES	48	Nik Meeks (USA)	30 Jan 2006	Biggest Blowout
Madden NFL '97	Genesis/MD	25	Nik Meeks (USA)	15 Jan 2007	Biggest Blowout
Manic Miner	ZX Spectrum	27,147	Andrew Pete Mee (UK)	16 Mar 2008	TGTS; 5 Lives
Marble Madness [Romset 1]	Arcade	187,880	Stan Szczepanski (USA)	11 Jun 2004	Difficulty Normal; 1 Player Only
Marble Madness 2: Marble Man	Arcade	671,050	Scott Evans (USA)	8 Sep 2002	
Mario Adventure	C64 ☉	38,037	Terence O'Neill (USA)	19 Aug 2006	
Mario Bros	Arcade	3,481,550	Perry Rodgers (USA)	2 Jul 1985	TGTS
Mario Kart 64	Nintendo 64	1 min 25.9 sec	Daniel Mescon (USA)	11 Jun 2004	Wario Stadium
Mario Kart 64	Nintendo 64	1 min 52.49 sec	Japanese National Record (USA)	11 Jun 2004	Banshee Boardwalk
Mario Kart 64	Nintendo 64	2 min 3.85 sec	Japanese National Record (USA)	11 Jun 2004	Bowser's Castle
Mario Kart 64	Nintendo 64	1 min 28.27 sec	Japanese National Record (USA)	11 Jun 2004	Koopa Troopa Beach
Mario Kart 64	Nintendo 64	1 min 42.61 sec	Japanese National Record (USA)	11 Jun 2004	Luigi Raceway
Mario Kart 64	Nintendo 64	4 min 5.88 sec	Japanese National Record (USA)	11 Jun 2004	Rainbow Road
Mario Kart DS	DS	2 min 3.626 sec	Alex L. Shepherd (UK)	10 Dec 2007	Airship Fortress
Mario Kart DS	DS	1 min 48.975 sec	Alex L. Shepherd (UK)	10 Dec 2007	Delphino Square
Mario Kart DS	DS	2 min 7.371 sec	Alex L. Shepherd (UK)	10 Dec 2007	DK Pass
Mario Kart DS	DS	2 min 20.738 sec	Alex L. Shepherd (UK)	10 Dec 2007	Waluigi Pinball
Mario Kart DS	DS	58.263 sec	Alex L. Shepherd (UK)	10 Dec 2007	Yoshi Falls
Mario Party 2	Nintendo 64	27.3 sec	Matthews S. Leto (USA)	23 Mar 2001	Handcar Havoc
Mario Party 2	Nintendo 64	1 min 11.13 sec	Rocky L. Rose (USA)	23 Apr 2008	Bobsled Run
Mario Party 2	Nintendo 64	49.5 sec	Rocky L. Rose (USA)	20 Feb 2008	Sky Pilots
Mario Party 4	GameCube	331	April P. Simmonds (Canada)	7 Jan 2006	Barrel Baron
Mario Party 4	GameCube	37.96 sec	Hector T. Rodriguez (USA)	10 Feb 2006	Jigsaw Jitters; 20 Piece Puzzle Completion
Mario Party 4	GameCube	13.4 sec	Jennifer B. Carmichael (Canada)	7 Jan 2006	Take a Breather; Longest Breath
Mario Party 5	GameCube	19	April P. Simmonds (Canada)	6 Apr 2007	Dinger Derby
Mario Party 8	Wii	53	Ginger Stowe (USA)	18 Apr 2008	Saucer Swarm
Mario Party 8 ④	Wii	32.03 sec	William Willemstyn III (USA)	18 Apr 2008	Alpine Assault
Mario Party Advance	GBA	10,510	Tee Jester (USA)	26 May 2008	Bill Bounce
Mario Strikers Charged	Wii	25	Lance Eustache (USA)	25 Jul 2008	Domination Mode; Biggest Blowout
Mario Tennis	Nintendo 64	569	Jason M. Whalls (USA)	13 Aug 2002	Ring Mode; Most Points Within Time Limit

ⓘ TRIVIA

> On 9 February 1982, Walter Day's growing database of high-score statistics was made available to the public as the Twin Galaxies National Scoreboard. The release received immediate recognition from the major game manufacturers of the day – Atari, Midway, Williams Electronics, Universal, Stern, Nintendo and Exidy – in addition to support from RePlay and Playmeter magazines, the two premier coin-op publications of the era.

> LIFE magazine visited Twin Galaxies on 8 November 1982 to capture 16 of North America's best players in a group photograph.

HIGH SCORES & FASTEST TIMES

GAME	PLATFORM	RECORD	PLAYER (NAT.)	DATE	NOTES
Marvel Super Heroes	Arcade	1,682,500	Virgilio Villasenor (USA)	20 Apr 1997	Hardest Difficulty
Marvel Super Heroes Vs Street Fighter	PlayStation	1,448,500	Paul Luu (USA)	11 Apr 1999	
Marvel Vs Capcom	PlayStation	1,489,700	Bruno Augusto (Brazil)	3 Jan 2007	Arcade Mode; TGTS
Marvel Vs Capcom	Arcade	3,435,016	Robert Weber (USA)	4 Oct 1999	Expert Difficulty
Marvel Vs Capcom 2	Arcade	2,017,730,000	Zach Robinson (USA)	6 Feb 2008	Easy Difficulty
Masters of the Universe	Atari 2600	48,700	David B. Yancey (USA)	30 May 2005	Game 1; Difficulty B
Mega Force	Atari 2600	23,673	Greg Troutman (USA)	6 Nov 2004	
Mega Man	NES	5,111,100	Dominick Festagallo (USA)	19 Aug 2008	TGTS; 3 Lives to Start; 5 Lives Max
Mega Man Anniversary Collection	PlayStation 2	3 min 31.01 sec	Ryan Sullivan (USA)	29 Jan 2007	Power Battle; Course 1-2
Mega Man II	NES	30 min 42 sec	Richard Ureta (USA)	24 Aug 2004	TGTS
Mega Man III	NES	49 min 10 sec	Daryl Kiddey (USA)	22 Jun 2008	TGTS
Mega Man IV	NES	55 min 54 sec	Kevin Tukey (USA)	1 Mar 2007	TGTS
Mega Man V	NES	48 min 17 sec	Ben J. Zaugg (USA)	8 Jul 2008	TGTS
Mega Man X ❶	SNES	46 min 27 sec	Adam Sweeney (USA)	8 Sep 2004	
Mega Turrican	Genesis/MD	51,780	Greg Troutman (USA)	11 Jun 2004	
Mercury Meltdown	PSP	70,766	Terence O'Neill (USA)	29 Jul 2007	Astro Lab 1
Metal Gear Solid	PlayStation	1 hr 55 min 31 sec	Rodrigo Lopes (Brazil)	30 Jun 2000	
Metal Slug Anthology	Wii	108,140	Lance Eustache (USA)	11 Apr 2008	Metal Slug; Super Vehicle 001
Metal Slug Anthology	Wii	544,840	Lance Eustache (USA)	11 Apr 2008	Metal Slug X; Super Vehicle 001
Metro Cross	Arcade	793,940	Gavin Davies (UK)	12 Aug 1985	TGTS
Metroid	NES	17 min 22 sec	Cristopher Knight (USA)	30 Oct 2005	Minimalist Speed Run
Midtown Madness 3	Xbox	45.340 sec	Andrew Pete Mee (UK)	16 Mar 2008	Blitz; Washington DC; Alleycat
Mike Tyson's Punch Out!!/ Punch Out!!	NES	155,540	Nik Meeks (USA)	21 Jul 2007	Completion Points; TGTS
Mikie	C64 ☺	12,500	Jordi Schouteren (Netherlands)	19 Jul 2008	
Missile Command 3D	Jaguar	267,725	Wes Powell (USA)	11 Jun 2004	3D
Monster Truck Madness	Nintendo 64	3 min 32.9 sec	Matthew S. Leto (USA)	23 Mar 2001	Graveyard
Moon Cresta	Arcade	152,100	Bill Awalin (USA)	29 Feb 1984	
Mortal Kombat II	SNES	13 min 54 sec	Dustin Dionizio (USA)	10 Apr 2008	
Moto GP 2 ❷	Xbox	1 min 46.82 sec	Fabiano G. Souza (Brazil)	21 May 2006	Time Trial; Best Lap; Cataluyna
Motocross	Atari 2600	104	David B. Yancey (USA)	30 May 2005	
Namco Museum Remix	Wii	122,020	Patrick Scott Patterson (USA)	27 Jun 2008	Super Pac-Man; Tournament; TGTS
Narc	Arcade	609,025	Kelly R. Flewin (Canada)	19 Nov 2005	No continues
NBA Jam	Genesis/MD	19	Brandan J. Lumzy	10 Apr 2008	Biggest Blowout

GAME	PLATFORM	RECORD	PLAYER (NAT.)	DATE	NOTES
Need For Speed Underground	Xbox	1 min 48.23 sec	Fabiano G. Souza (Brazil)	26 Jun 2006	Olympic Square; Forward Track; Fastest Race
Need For Speed Underground 2	PlayStation 2	56.51 sec	Tee Jester (USA)	31 May 2007	City Hall; Forward Track; Fastest Lap
Nemesis ③	Arcade	1,195,500	Paul Ashworth (UK)	12 Jul 1985	3 Lives; Easy
New Super Mario Bros.	DS	161	Ginger Stowe (USA)	16 Dec 2006	Wanted!
New Super Mario Bros.	DS	14.9 sec	William Willemstyn III (USA)	6 Oct 2006	Snowball Slalom
Ninja Gaiden	Arcade	19,100	Jason Wilson (USA)	2 Jun 1999	TGTS
Ninja Gaiden III: The Ancient Ship of Doom	Lynx	36,400	Ron Corcoran (USA)	17 Mar 2002	
Ninja Golf	Atari 7800	136,860	Aaron D. Sanders (USA)	10 Jul 2001	
Novastorm	PlayStation	89,995	Eric Dahl (USA)	11 Jun 2004	
Off Road Challenge	Arcade	1 min 49.68 sec	Scott Evans (USA)	10 Jun 2000	Baja
Operation Wolf	Arcade	212,350	Mark Twitty (USA)	19 Sep 1987	No continues; TGTS
P.O.W.: Prisoners of War	NES	23 min 1 sec	Daniel C. Teixeira (Canada)	13 Nov 2006	
PAC 'N Roll ④	DS	30.4 sec	William Willemstyn III (USA)	6 Oct 2006	Time Attack: Level 1-1
PAC-Land	Arcade	4,150,400	Mark Mendes (UK)	14 May 1986	TGTS
Paper Boy 2	SNES	117,600	Rudy J. Ferretti (USA)	3 Feb 2008	
Paper Boy 64	Nintendo 64	8,230	Nick Ortakales (USA)	11 Jun 2004	Easy Street
Perfect Dark	Nintendo 64	4 sec	Scott R. Jones (UK)	8 Aug 2008	Duel: Agent
Phalanx	SNES	1,342,890	Scott Kessler (USA)	22 Aug 2006	5 Lives; Easy; No continues
Phantasy Star	Master System	4 hr 22 min 18 sec	Rodrigo Lopes (Brazil)	9 Oct 2005	
Pharoah's Curse	C64	1,740	Jeremy W. Gregory (USA)	30 Oct 2007	
Pin Bot	NES	99,999,999	Tom Votava (USA)/ Todd Rogers (USA)	17 Sept 2002 1 Oct 2004	
Pinball Dreams	PC	80,521,447	Egbert Matthé (Germany)	5 May 2005	Ignition
Pinball Dreams	PC	71,521,360	Mike Sobioch (Germany)	5 May 2005	Beat Box
Pinball Dreams	PC	700,594,403	Mike Sobioch (Germany)	5 May 2005	Nightmare
Pinball Dreams	PC	158,879,254	Rick Maultra (USA)	5 May 2005	Steel Wheels
Pinball Hall of Fame: The Gottlieb Collection ⑤	PSP	5,060,000	Tom Duncan (USA)	9 Aug 2008	Ace High
Pinball Hall of Fame: The Gottlieb Collection	Xbox	198	Tom Duncan (USA)	15 Dec 2006	Tournament Mode
Pinball Hall of Fame: The Williams Collection	Wii	1,207,390	Marc Cohen (USA)	28 Aug 2008	Firepower
Pinball Hall of Fame: The Williams Collection	PlayStation 2	96	Nik Meeks (USA)	10 Aug 2008	Tournament; 5 Tables
Ping Pong	Arcade	27,970	Marco Maltese (Italy)	9 Sep 1985	
Pipe Dream	NES	15,409,450	Tom Votava (USA)	25 Nov 2003	Game A
Pitfall II	Atari 2600	14 min 8 sec	Marc Cohen (USA)	27 Feb 2008	Game 1; Difficulty B; Fastest Perfect Game
Pitfall!	Atari 400/ 800/XL	114,000	Todd Rogers (USA)	6 May 2001	
Platoon	NES	1,719,300	Tom Votava (USA)	21 Nov 2002	

ⓘ TRIVIA

> *Mercury Meltdown* is a PSP puzzler in which the player has to tilt the playing surface in order to guide a blob of mercury through a series of finishing posts. The original game – simply *Mercury* – was developed for the PSP's motion sensor, which never saw the light of day. A new Wii version, however, allows players to tilt the environment in 3D space using the Wiimote.

> When Nintendo's licence to use boxer Mike Tyson's name for *Mike Tyson's Punch-Out* expired, they chose not to renew it. Tyson had just lost the Heavyweight Championship to James "Buster" Douglas so the game was restyled as *Punch Out!! Featuring Mr Dream*.

HIGH SCORES & FASTEST TIMES

FACTS

> *Project X* was parodied in one level of Team 17's own *Superfrog* as *Project-F* (with the F presumably standing for "Frog"), even going as far as using a remixed version of the original game's theme tune.

> Following television exposure on ABC-TV's *That's Incredible* in 1983, the first US video-game team was formed, made up of the very best talent. With Walter Day as the founding captain, the US National Video Game Team issued international video-game challenges to Japan, Italy and the UK, even hand-delivering proclamations to their respective embassies in Washington, DC! Eventually, the team toured the USA, Europe and Asia. during the 1980s.

GAME	PLATFORM	RECORD	PLAYER (NAT.)	DATE	NOTES
Pokémon Puzzle League	Nintendo 64	58	Christopher McMullen (USA)	8 May 2003	Biggest 3D Chain
Pong!	Odyssey²	100% hits	Terence O'Neill (USA)	25 Jun 2007	3 Minute Game; Least Misses
Porsche Challenge	PlayStation	42.8 sec	Stuart Morrison (UK)	11 Jun 2004	Japan; Short
Project Gotham Racing	Xbox	40.016 sec	Tom Duncan (USA)	14 Aug 2006	Time Trial Lap; Trafalgar; Leicester Sq.
Project Gotham Racing	Xbox	45.314 sec	Tom Duncan (USA)	14 Aug 2006	Time Trial Lap; Westminster; Bankside
Project Gotham Racing 2	Xbox	52.863 sec	Tom Duncan (USA)	14 Aug 2006	Edinburgh; Terrace Sprint
Project Gotham Racing 2	Xbox	23.233 sec	Tom Duncan (USA)	14 Aug 2006	Yokohama; Honcho Dori
Project X ①	Amiga	650,861	Graham Hawkins (NZ)	26 Oct 2005	
Pssst	ZX Spectrum ☉	44,305	Peter Gatland (UK)	4 Jul 2008	Single Player Only; TGTS
Puzznic	NES	11,505,900	Tom Votava (USA)	15 Jun 2006	Puzznic Mode; No Continues
Quake	PC	100%	Ron Corcoran (USA)	13 May 2001	Nightmare completion
Quake II	PC	100%	Ron Corcoran (USA)	13 May 2001	Hard completion
Quantum	Arcade	2,116,240	Edward Carpenter (Canada)	2 Dec 1983	TGTS
R.C. Pro-Am	NES	562,772	Junior Tetreault (Canada)	2 Mar 2007	1 Life Only; No continues
R.C. Pro-Am II	NES	180	Nik Meeks (USA)	24 Aug 2006	1 Life Only; No continues
Race Drivin'	Arcade	152,642	David Nelson (USA)	23 Oct 2005	
Raiden III	PlayStation 2	2,494,700	Kelly R. Flewin (Canada)	13 Jun 2008	No continues
Raiders of the Lost Ark	Atari 2600	82	Todd Rogers (USA) Scott Stilphen (USA) Troy Whelan (USA)	30 Oct 2002 11 Nov 2004 11 April 2005	Game 1; Difficulty A or B
Rainbow Islands: The Story of Bubble Bobble 2	NES	854,800	Kelly R. Flewin (Canada)	10 Jul 2006	No continues
Rampart	Lynx	11,105	Ron Corcoran (USA)	14 Mar 2002	
Rayman ②	PlayStation	4 min 3.21 sec	Paul McCallon (USA)	14 Oct 2005	No continues; No saves
Rayman Raving Rabids	Wii	1,834	William Willemstyn III (USA)	8 Oct 2007	Bunnies are Fantastic Dancers
Renegade	Wii Virtual Console	6 min 39 sec	Andrew D. Furrer (USA)	5 Jun 2008	Difficulty 1
Resident Evil (Director's Cut)	PlayStation 2	1 hr 11 min 43 sec	Tyson R. Pelz (Australia)	2 Apr 2003	Chris; Normal; All Weapons
Resident Evil 2	PlayStation	1 hr 27 min 29 sec	Ben Greenman (USA)	21 Mar 2008	Claire A; Normal; All Weapons
Return of the Jedi	Arcade	1,938,010	Mike Sullivan (USA)	11 Jun 2004	No continues
Revenge of Shinobi	Genesis/MD	887,800	Daniel C. Teixeira (Canada)	13 Nov 2006	3 Lives; Normal
Ridge Racer	PlayStation	50.197 sec	Hector T. Rodriguez (USA)	28 Oct 2006	Beginner; Fastest Lap; Any Vehicle
Ridge Racer Revolution	PlayStation	36.543 sec	Cristiano T. Assumpcao (Brazil)	2 Sep 2002	Free Run Mode

175 million – cumulative sales of *Pokémon* games as of 23 April 2008, making the brand the second most successful video-game franchise after *Mario*.

GAME	PLATFORM	RECORD	PLAYER (NAT.)	DATE	NOTES
R-Type Leo (World Rev. C)	MAME	670,000	Didier Sénéchal (France)	20 May 2006	Difficulty Normal; No continues
S.T.U.N. Runner	Arcade	792,865	Blaine Locklair (USA)	25 Nov 2007	TGTS
Salamander	Arcade	1,700,650	Keith Bradley (UK)	28 Apr 1986	
Sanxion	C64 ☉	154,730	Riccardo Moretti (Italy)	1 Dec 2007	
Scramble	C64 ☉	1,840	Carsten Hirche (Germany)	31 Mar 2008	
Section Z	Arcade	1,694,630	Stephan Wimmer (USA)	30 Sep 1986	TGTS; No continues
Sega Genesis Collection	PlayStation 2	305,400	Ryan Sullivan (USA)	29 Apr 2007	Altered Beast; Single Player
Sega Rally Championship	Saturn	2 min 30.8 sec	Cristiano T. Assumpcao (Brazil)	14 Aug 2002	Desert; 3 Lap Race
Sewer Shark	Sega CD	4,088,394	Jon Piornack (USA)	26 Nov 2007	
Shadow of the Beast	Amiga	100%	Graham Hawkins (NZ)	6 Mar 2006	Percentage Complete
Shadowgate	NES	16 min 6 sec	Jim Hanson (USA)	15 Jul 2008	
Shikigami no Shiro II	Dreamcast	743,757,640	Rodrigo Lopes (Brazil)	5 May 2008	Arcade Mode; No continues; Easy
Silent Hill	PlayStation	35 min 52 sec	Tyson R. Pelz (Australian)	9 Feb 2005	
Simpson's Road Rage ③	Xbox	$104,343	Rodrigo Lopes (Brazil)	31 Aug 2007	Downtown
Skate or Die	NES	10,229	Robert L. Garner Jr (USA)	17 Apr 2007	Practice Mode; Downhill Race
Snake Rattle N Roll	NES	171,850	Patrick Scott Patterson (USA)	11 Aug 2008	No continues
Sonic & Knuckles	Genesis/MD	100,350	Mike Condon (USA)	11 Jun 2004	TGTS
Sonic 3D Blast	Saturn	109,500	Matthieu Tourenne (USA)	11 Jun 2004	
Sonic Rush	DS	2 min 37 sec	Ben W. Townsend (UK)	17 Jul 2008	Time Attack; Alt. Limit; Act 2
Sonic Spinball	Wii Virtual Console	13,129,700	William Willemstyn III (USA)	3 Jun 2007	Genesis; Points
Sonic the Hedgehog	Genesis/MD	280,780	William H. Smith (USA)	2 Sep 2006	TGTS; Points
Sonic the Hedgehog 2 ④	Genesis/MD	488,250	Timothy J. Keister (USA)	27 Jun 2008	TGTS; Points
Sonic the Hedgehog 3	Genesis/MD	188,700	Jon Taber (USA)	27 Aug 2006	TGTS; Points
Space Harrier	Arcade	35,774,740	Nick Hutt (UK)	13 Aug 2005	Medium Difficulty
Spider-Man	Atari 2600 ☉	1,600	Giovanni Flamand (Belgium)	12 May 2001	Game 1; Difficulty B
Spider-Man 2	Xbox	48 sec	Mike K. Morrow (USA)	10 Apr 2005	Defeat of Rhino
Spider-Man: Return of the Sinister Six	NES	10 min 38 sec	Andrew D. Furrer (USA)	25 Jul 2008	
Splatterhouse	Wii Virtual Console	52,700	Andrew D. Furrer (USA)	31 Jul 2008	No continues; Only Kill Final Boss Once
SSX	PlayStation 2	3 min 36.69 sec	Wolff K. Morrow (USA)	31 Aug 2001	Elysium Alps; Race Mode
SSX Tricky ⑤	PlayStation 2	411,290	Jon Taber (USA)	19 Sep 2006	Alaska; Showoff Mode
Star Fox	SNES	60,000	Scott Kessler (USA)	2 Oct 2007	Course 1
Star Trek	Arcade	123,467,525	Darren Harris (USA)	8 Jul 1985	TGTS; Marathon
Star Trek	Atari 2600	737,400	Tom Swingle (USA)	11 Jun 2004	Game 1; Difficulty B

❶ TRIVIA

> *The Simpsons: Road Rage*, launched in 2001, was so similar to *Crazy Taxi* that, in 2003, Sega filed a patent infringement lawsuit against Fox Interactive, Electronic Arts and Radical Entertainment. The case, Sega of America, Inc. vs Fox Interactive, et al., was eventually settled in private for an unknown amount.

> *SSX Tricky* has an impressive list of voice talent for its characters including David Arquette, singer Macy Gray, Lucy Liu (*Charlie's Angels*) and Oliver Platt.

HIGH SCORES & FASTEST TIMES

▶▶ FACTS

> A gaming oddity was *Star Wars: Episode I Racer*, which was only released on the Dreamcast, despite the fact it was part of one of the most recognizable franchises in gaming history.

> *Tetris* has even been played on the side of buildings. The record holder for the world's **largest fully functional game of Tetris** was an effort by Dutch students in 1995 that lit up all 15 floors of the Electrical Engineering department at the Delft University of Technology in Holland.

> Isaiah Triforce Johnson **2** achieved a score of 99,999,999 points, the maximum possible score, on *Tetris DS* using endless settings on 18 June 2008.

GAME	PLATFORM	RECORD	PLAYER (NAT.)	DATE	NOTES
Star Wars	Arcade	31,660,614	David Palmer (USA)	4 Aug 2004	TGTS; Tournament
Star Wars: Dark Forces	PlayStation	100%	Simon Wilmer (UK)	11 Jun 2004	Hard Difficulty; Percentage Complete; TGTS
Star Wars: Episode I Racer **1**	Dreamcast	1 min 49.12 sec	Tom Duncan (USA)	25 May 2006	Zugga Challenge; Time Trial; Fastest Lap
Star Wars: Rogue Squadron	Nintendo 64	42 sec	Matthew S. Leto (USA)	23 Mar 2001	Ambush at Mos Eisley
Star Wars: The Empire Strikes Back	Arcade	1,556,836	David Palmer (USA)	17 Jun 1985	Hard; TGTS
Street Fighter II: Hyper Fighting	SNES	474,100	Kelly R. Flewin (Canada)	1 Oct 2005	Normal Mode; Timer on
Summer Games	C64	25	Ilias G. Florakis (Greece)	8 Jun 2006	Skeet Shooting
Summer Games II	C64 ☺	40.68 sec	Marc Cohen (USA)	8 Sep 2007	Equestrian
Super Bomberman	SNES	337,090	Sheldon J. Marsh (UK)	26 Sep 2004	
Super Empire Strikes Back	SNES	59,945	Joseph D. Smith (USA)	1 Jul 2008	
Super Mario 64	Nintendo 64	1 hr 43 min 25 sec	Michael B. Damiani (USA)	4 May 2007	Fastest Minimalist Completion; 70–119 Stars Required
Super Mario All-Stars	SNES	883,660	Kevin M. Lalonde (USA)	21 Oct 2006	Super Mario Bros. 3; Points
Super Mario Bros.	NES	20 min 2 sec	Andrew J. Gardikis (USA)	4 Apr 2007	Fastest Full Completion
Super Mario Bros.: The Lost Levels	Wii Virtual Console	1,309,300	Alan J. Bootier (USA)	4 Jul 2008	NES
Super Mario Galaxy	Wii	54.46 sec	Jeffrey D. Lowe, Jr. (USA)	31 Mar 2008	A Very Spooky Sprint
Super Mario Kart	SNES	19.34 sec	Scott Simpson (USA)	15 Aug 2008	Bowser's Castle
Super Return of the Jedi	SNES	55,750	Joseph D. Smith (USA)	1 Jul 2008	
Super Star Wars	SNES	2,211,200	Ron Corcoran (USA)	13 May 2001	
Tecmo Bowl	Wii Virtual Console	105	Shaun B. Baker (USA)	29 May 2008	
Teenage Mutant Ninja Turtles IV: Turtles in Time	SNES	1,549	James Sorge (USA)	4 Aug 2008	No continues
Tempest 2000	Jaguar	5,116,818	Tomas Berndtsson (Sweden)	11 Jun 2004	
Tetris DS	DS	1,202,000	Isaiah TriForce Johnson (USA)	4 May 2008	Game Ends at 200 Lines; Marathon
The Way of the Exploding Fist	ZX Spectrum	31,300	Gazz Halliwell (UK)	26 Jun 2008	
Tom Clancy's Ghost Recon **6**	Xbox	15 min 17 sec	Patrick Scott Patterson (USA)	8 Jul 2008	TGTS; Airbase "Firefight"
Tomb Raider	PlayStation	9 min 22 sec	Mike K. Morrow (USA)	8 May 2003	Stage 10
Tomb Raider 2 **3**	PlayStation	1 min 3.9 sec	Wolff K. Morrow (USA) Shin Sato (Japan) Niral Shah (USA) Nobuyuki Takebe (Japan) Matthias De Scheerder (Begium)	13 Aug 2002 1 Apr 2004 5 Mar 2005 5 Mar 2005 5 Mar 2005	Lara's Obstacle Course; TGTS

GAME	PLATFORM	RECORD	PLAYER (NAT.)	DATE	NOTES
Tony Hawks Pro Skater 2	PlayStation	3,356,122	Hector T. Rodriguez (USA)	28 Oct 2006	Bull Ring Mexico; Best Combo
Tony Hawks Underground 2	Xbox	4,833,375	Michael P. Waks (USA)	27 Jul 2006	Airport; High Combo
U.N. Squadron	Arcade	1,960,400	Dwayne Richard (Canada)	11 Jun 2004	TGTS
Uncle Fester's Quest	NES	26 min 55 sec	Rodrigo Lopes (Brazil)	18 Oct 2004	1 Life; No continues
Uridium	C64 ☉	49,270	John Eden (Australia)	14 Apr 2008	
Virtua Cop	Saturn	14,266,500	Valter A Treib "TRB" (Brazil)	30 Jun 2000	Arcade Mode; Difficulty Normal; No continues
Virtua Tennis	Dreamcast	$3,821,367	Javier Bustamante (USA)	19 Nov 2004	3 Game Sets; Dollars; TGTS
WarioWare Smooth Moves	Wii	3,470 metres	William Willemstyn III (USA)	26 Jul 2007	Balloon Trip; High Score
WarioWare Smooth Moves ④	Wii	282	William Willemstyn III (USA)	1 Feb 2008	Tower Tennis; High Score
WarioWare Touched!	DS	53	William Willemstyn III (USA)	6 Oct 2006	Wario; High Score
Wave Race 64 ⑤	Nintendo 64	19,854	Cristiano T. Assumpcao (Brazil)	12 Aug 2002	Dolphin Park
We Love Katamari	PlayStation 2	30 sec	Tom Batchelor (USA)	12 Jan 2006	As Fast as Possible; Racetrack
Wii Fit	Wii	462	Christopher C. Tirpak (USA)	27 Jul 2008	Aerobics; Advanced Step
Wii Play	Wii	637	Troy Whelan (USA)	29 Feb 2008	Shooting Range
Wii Sports	Wii	14 sec	Troy Whelan (USA)	14 Feb 2008	Boxing; Fastest KO
Winter Games	C64 ☉	212	Marc Cohen (USA)	26 Nov 2007	Ski Jump; Points
WWF No Mercy	Nintendo 64	57 sec	Jesse Kreger (USA)	1 Jun 2001	Fastest Victory; TGTS
X-Men	Arcade	830	Bill Toups (USA)	11 Jun 2004	Difficulty 8; Mutant Power 3
X-Men Vs Street Fighter	PlayStation	6,954,600	Hector T. Rodriguez (USA)	31 Jan 2008	Maximum Difficulty; No continues
Yie Ar Kung Fu	Arcade	534,340	Antonio Colangelo (Italy)	9 Sep 1985	TGTS
Zzyzzyxx	Arcade	1,068,010	Kris MacLillivray (Canada)	11 Jun 2004	

④

ⓘ TRIVIA

> *Smooth Moves* is the first WarioWare game to feature almost completely 3D graphics that are rendered to appear 2D.

> Red Storm, who produced *Tom Clancy's Rainbow Six*, were also responsible for another Tom Clancy video game series: *Ghost Recon*.

5

> The Wii Virtual Console is an area within the Wii Shop Channel that allows you to download classic games from older systems such as the NES, SNES, Nintendo 64, Sega Mega Drive/Genesis and Commodore 64. The games use a software emulator to convert from their original form on to the Wii.

> 2009 will see the 25th anniversary of Teenage Mutant Ninja Turtles, stars of game, film and comic.

6

Page	Photo Credit		
6	Andy Paradise/GWR	43	Thomas Kienzle/AP/PA	117	PA
7	Joe McGorty/GWR	48	Getty Images	120	Alamy
7	Paul Hughes/GWR	51	Johnny Greig	124	Albert L. Ortega/
8	Jakobsen Pictures	51	Joe McGorty/GWR		Getty Images
9	Quinn Rooney/Getty Images	60	Michael Bezjian/	125	Lucas Jackson/Reuters
9	Ranald Mackechnie/GWR		Getty Images	128	Ethan Miller/Getty Images
9	Ranald Mackechnie/GWR	60	MJ Kim/Getty Images	130	PA
9	David Anderson/GWR	60	Nils Jorgensen/Rex Features	136	Universal/
9	Drew Gardner/GWR	60	Dave Hogan/Getty Images		Ronald Grant Archive
10	Frazer Harrison/Getty Images	60	Rex Features	150	Reuters
10	Frazer Harrison/Getty Images	60	Rex Features	150	Scott Barbour/Getty Images
11	Richard Kendal/BAFTA	60	Tim Whitby/Getty Images	151	AP/PA
12	Spencer Platt/Getty Images	61	Dave Hogan/Getty Images	151	Arcade Flyer Archive
14	Chung Sung-Jun/	66	Reed Saxon/AP/PA	152	Serge Thomann/
	Getty Images	67	New Line Cinema		Getty Images
15	Chung Sung-Jun/	68	Mark Lennihan/AP/PA	154	Paul Michael Hughes/GWR
	Getty Images	79	Vince Bucci/Getty Images	155	Paul Michael Hughes/GWR
15	Chung Sung-Jun/	81	Getty Images	156	Tammie Arroyo/AP/PA
	Getty Images	85	Gregg DeGuire/Getty Images	157	Paul Michael Hughes/GWR
16	Justin Sullivan/Getty Images	88	Graham Harrison/	158	Rex Features
18	John Pratt/Getty Images		Rex Features	159	Getty Images
18	Computer History Museum	88	Arcade Flyer Archive	161	Arcade Flyer Archive
18	Alamy	97	20th Century Fox/Kobal	161	Peter M. Wilson/Alamy
18	Wendy White/Alamy	98	Arcade Flyer Archive	162	Paul Michael Hughes/GWR
18	Roger Ressmeyer/Corbis	99	Alamy	162	AP
19	Computer History Museum	99	Sergei Remezov / Reuters	182	Moviestore Collection
19	The Advertising Archives	99	NASA	182	Sony
19	Paul Sakuma/AP/PA	102	Arcade Flyer Archive	182	Moviestore Collection
20	Arcade Flyer Archive	102	Arcade Flyer Archive	182	Ronald Grant Archive
20	David J. Green/Alamy	102	Arcade Flyer Archive	182	New Line Cinema
22	The Advertising Archives	103	George Nikitin/AP/PA	183	Paramount Pictures
22	Yuriko Nakao/Reuters	104	Jennifer Jacquemart/	183	Universal Pictures
23	Miwa Suzuki/Getty Images		Rex Features	183	Lions Gate Films
28	Yoshikazu Tsuno/	108	David Fisher/Rex Features	183	Brightlight Pictures
	Getty Images	108	Ronald Grant Archive	183	Twentieth Century Fox
34	Peter J. Carroll/AP/PA	109	Lucas Jackson/Reuters	184	Paramount/Rex Features
34	James Merithew/Wired.com	110	Arcade Flyer Archive	184	Columbia Pictures
35	Rex Features	110	Getty Images	185	New Line/Rex Features
35	Pablo M. Monsivais/AP/PA	111	Brian Ach/Getty Images	196	Arcade Flyer Archive
40	Arcade Flyer Archive	111	Khaled Al-Sayyed/	200	Arcade Flyer Archive
43	Mike Nelson/Getty Images		Getty Images	202	Arcade Flyer Archive
		112	PA	205	Arcade Flyer Archive

ACKNOWLEDGEMENTS

Guinness World Records would like to thank the following individuals, groups and websites for their help in the creation of Guinness World Records: Gamer's Edition 2009: Adam Mersky, Aki Sato, Alana Jane, Alejandro, Andrew, Boris, Stan and Tom at Club SLI, Amber Fechko at Penny Arcade, Andy Reif, Anita, Cari, Martin and Suzie at The Clan, Anita-Lynne Henderson, Annabel at Fleece Road Sanctuary, Asam Ahmad, Aurli Bokovza,

Benj Edwards, Brian Rubin at Fortyseven, Cathy Campos at Panache PR, Cedric Lagarrigue, Ceri Davies and Charlotte O'Brien from Davies Media, Chris Glover, Chris Sheedy, Christian Slater, Claudia Knowlton, Col. Casey Wardynski, Major Michael Marty and all at America's Army, Danielle Woodyatt and Mark Robins at Lunch PR, David Blundell, David Walsh, Davinder Jalaf, Derek Cave, Ed Rolf, Emily Morganti, gamerankings.com,

Gareth Ramsay, George Williams, Grant Will, Leon and David at Call Print, Gwil, Louis, Matt and Stew at FiveAges, Iain Simons, Jason Katz Jim Carless and Dean Johnson from Brandwidth, Joanna Waitzmann, Jon Cave and all the team at Exient, Jon Rooke, Jonnie Bryant, Julie Skinner, Maria Deevoy and Hestor Woodliffe from Warner Bros Interactive Entertainment, Kate White, Katy McNeil, Linda Cave, Lori Mezhoff, Madalyn

Byfield, Marc Denton and all at NeoEmpire, Mark Baer, Markus Häberlein, Martyn Richards at Martyn Richards Research, Matt Atwood, Melanie Johnson, metacritic. com, Michael O'Dell, Michael Pass, Mike Jones, Mark Karges, Shannon Swaggerty, Brian Reinert at Bender Helper Impact, Nadia Thevenot, Nick and Rich at TT Games, Nikki Brin, Oli Welsh, Peter Bouvier, Phil Brannely, Res Kahraman, Richard Coshott, Richard Eddy,

Rob Rutter, Rowan Evans, Sam Tehrani, Sheryl and Michael at Nvidia, Simon Byron, Simon Smith-Wright, speeddemosarchive. com, Steve Hill, Steve Merrett, Stuart Taylor, Stuart Whyte, Svend Joscelyne, Thea Smith, Tim Hirschmann, Tommy Talarico, Tomy Boulding and Rob O'Farrell at Pulse.TV, Tony Hinds, vgchartz. com, Walter Day, Wolfgang Ebert, Zeno Colaco and Zizou & Mike at SonicCageDome.com. **Thank you.**